About this Book

"The highest praise that I ca̲ⁿ ... ͨ Frithjof Schuon is that they are worth̲ ...͟chings of the great spiritual traditions. W̲ ...͟pported or challenged by these writings, any se̲ⁱ ...͟eel grateful to be confronted by such a generously d̲. ͟ ͜intellect and to witness the emergence of authentic contemplative thought in this darkening time."

> **—Jacob Needleman**, San Francisco State University, author of *Lost Christianity*

"Professor Cutsinger has gathered a florilegium of Schuon's illuminating insights into Christianity; his editor's notes will be unobtrusively helpful to many readers. *The Fullness of God* is a must-read for any person who senses that something essential is lacking in most of what is routinely considered as Christianity today."

> **—Patrick Laude**, Georgetown University, author of *The Way of Poetry: Essays on Poetics and Contemplative Transformation*

"Frithjof Schuon's work has meant so much to me, and he has influenced my music perhaps more than anyone in recent years. Anyone, indeed, who is an artist concerned with the sacred should read him."

> **—Sir John Tavener**, composer, and author of *The Music of Silence: A Composer's Testament*

"*The Fullness of God: Frithjof Schuon on Christianity* is both a compelling and a stimulating book for students (at any level) of theology and philosophy, and a source of quiet insights and ascetic discipline for those seeking spiritual guidance. That one book can offer such diversity is a witness to the skill not only of Schuon, whose work has inspired generations of seekers after truth in all cultures, but also of the editor, James Cutsinger. His editorial additions and explanations provide an essential gloss on this challenging author's writings, and the upshot is an accessible yet scholarly read."

> **—Hannah Hunt**, independent scholar in Patristics and Early Church History

"In *The Fullness of God,* Professor Cutsinger does a masterful job of presenting us with Frithjof Schuon's profound insights into the nature of Christianity. Schuon starts from a metaphysical understanding of Christ's theandric reality and through this Christic prism leads the reader through a wide array of Christian themes. It seems no stone has gone unturned for Schuon; his insights and approach cannot but be refreshing, challenging, and inspiring for all serious seekers. I personally have been deeply moved by his work and newly reminded that the goal of the Christian life is to live in 'all the fullness of God.'"

—**Rev. Fr. Mark T. Mancuso**, a priest of the Orthodox Church

"Frithjof Schuon is undoubtedly one of the most penetrating exponents of the relationship between religion and metaphysics. Cutsinger has done us a great service in bringing together Schuon's widely scattered comments on Christianity. The insights of this wonderful book are essential for anyone who wishes to penetrate to the depths of the Christian tradition."

—**Rama Coomaraswamy**, author of *The Invocation of the Name of Jesus: As Practiced in the Western Church*

World Wisdom
The Library of Perennial Philosophy

The Library of Perennial Philosophy is dedicated to the exposition of the timeless Truth underlying the diverse religions. This Truth, often referred to as the *Sophia Perennis*—or Perennial Wisdom—finds its expression in the revealed Scriptures as well as in the writings of the great sages and the artistic creations of the traditional worlds.

The Perennial Philosophy provides the intellectual principles capable of explaining both the formal contradictions and the transcendent unity of the great religions.

Ranging from the writings of the great sages of the past to the perennialist authors of our time, each series of our Library has a different focus. As a whole, they express the inner unanimity, transforming radiance, and irreplaceable values of the great spiritual traditions.

The Fullness of God: Frithjof Schuon on Christianity appears as one of our selections in the Writings of Frithjof Schuon series.

The Writings of Frithjof Schuon

The Writings of Frithjof Schuon form the foundation of our library because he is the pre-eminent exponent of the Perennial Philosophy. His work illuminates this perspective in both an essential and comprehensive manner like none other.

English Language Writings of Frithjof Schuon

Original Books
The Transcendent Unity of Religions
Spiritual Perspectives and Human Facts
Gnosis: Divine Wisdom
Language of the Self
Stations of Wisdom
Understanding Islam
Light on the Ancient Worlds
Treasures of Buddhism (In the Tracks of Buddhism)
Logic and Transcendence
Esoterism as Principle and as Way
Castes and Races
Sufism: Veil and Quintessence
From the Divine to the Human
Christianity/Islam: Essays on Esoteric Ecumenicism
Survey of Metaphysics and Esoterism
In the Face of the Absolute
The Feathered Sun: Plains Indians in Art and Philosophy
To Have a Center
Roots of the Human Condition
Images of Primordial and Mystic Beauty: Paintings by Frithjof Schuon
Echoes of Perennial Wisdom
The Play of Masks
Road to the Heart: Poems
The Transfiguration of Man
The Eye of the Heart
Form and Substance in the Religions
Adastra & Stella Maris: Poems by Frithjof Schuon (bilingual edition)
Autumn Leaves & The Ring: Poems by Frithjof Schuon (bilingual edition)
Songs without Names, Volumes I-VI: Poems by Frithjof Schuon
Songs without Names, Volumes VII-XII: Poems by Frithjof Schuon
World Wheel, Volumes I-III: Poems by Frithjof Schuon
World Wheel, Volumes IV-VII: Poems by Frithjof Schuon
Primordial Meditation: Contemplating the Real

Edited Writings
The Essential Frithjof Schuon, ed. Seyyed Hossein Nasr
Songs for a Spiritual Traveler: Selected Poems (bilingual edition)
René Guénon: Some Observations, ed. William Stoddart
The Fullness of God: Frithjof Schuon on Christianity, ed. James S. Cutsinger
Prayer Fashions Man: Frithjof Schuon on the Spiritual Life, ed. James S. Cutsinger
Art from the Sacred to the Profane: East and West, ed. Catherine Schuon
Splendor of the True: A Frithjof Schuon Reader, ed. James S. Cutsinger

The Fullness of God
Frithjof Schuon on Christianity

Selected and edited by
James S. Cutsinger

Foreword by
Antoine Faivre

World Wisdom

The Fullness of God: Frithjof Schuon on Christianity
© 2004 World Wisdom, Inc.

Translated from the French by Mark Perry in collaboration
with Jean-Pierre Lafouge, Deborah Casey,
and James S. Cutsinger.

For the French editions upon which the present translation is based,
see the listing of Sources, pages 221-23.

Most recent printing indicated by last digit below:
10 9 8 7 6 5 4 3 2

Library of Congress Cataloging-in-Publication Data
Schuon, Frithjof, 1907-1998
The Fullness of God : Frithjof Schuon on Christianity / selected and edited
by James S. Cutsinger ; foreword by Antoine Faivre.
p. cm. – (The library of perennial philosophy) (The writings of Frithjof
Schuon) Includes bibliographical references and index.
ISBN 0-941532-58-5 (pbk. : alk. paper)
1. Christianity. I. Cutsinger, James S., 1953- II. Title. III.
Series.
BR121.3.S38 2004
230–dc22
2003026499

Cover Art: Painting by Frithjof Schuon

Printed on acid-free paper in the United States of America

For information address World Wisdom, Inc.
P.O. Box 2682, Bloomington, Indiana 47402-2682
www.worldwisdom.com

I bow my knees unto the Father of our Lord Jesus Christ, of whom the whole family in Heaven and on earth is named, that He would grant you, according to the riches of His great glory, to be strengthened with might by His Spirit in the inner man; that Christ may dwell in your hearts by faith; that ye, being rooted and grounded in love, may be able to comprehend with all the saints what is the breadth, and length, and depth, and height; and to know the love of Christ, which passeth knowledge, that ye might be filled with all the fullness of God.

Ephesians 3:14-19

CONTENTS

Frithjof Schuon in 1965

FOREWORD

Indisputably, Frithjof Schuon ranks among the foremost represen-
tatives of the perennialist current. He is certainly the major
spokesman for this school in the United States, whereas his main
predecessor, who heralded the movement and brought it to a head,
is René Guénon (1886-1951), the best known perennialist writer in
Europe, especially in France. Common to the proponents of the
perennialist point of view, also sometimes called the "traditionalist
school", is a belief in the existence of a "primordial tradition",
which runs throughout the apparent diversity of religions, and in a
"transcendent unity of religions", which is understood to overarch
the various spiritual traditions of the world. Derived from the Latin
phrase *philosophia perennis*, or "perennial philosophy", perennialism
may be traced back to the Renaissance, but it was not until the nineteenth century, and mostly and mainly in the twentieth, that it
developed to the point of becoming a widespread approach to the
history and essence of "religion(s)". Over the last several decades it
has been the object of debate among various religiously oriented
people, as well as among philosophers and historians of religions,
both secular and non-secular.

In the late 1980s, I had the privilege of participating in a series
of such debates with James S. Cutsinger and other scholars,
including Seyyed Hossein Nasr and Huston Smith. These discus-
sions, which were held within the framework of the American
Academy of Religion, gave me the occasion to familiarize myself
with the works of these writers and to develop a long-standing
friendship with Professor Cutsinger. In asking me to write a Foreword for the present anthology, he honors me all the more since he
knows that, as a historian with a secular approach to the study of
religions, I am not myself a proponent of perennialism. I have
accepted his invitation as a token of his intellectual honesty, and I
see in it an opportunity to state the reasons why I welcome this pub-
lication.

This is not the first anthology of Schuon's work—Professor
Nasr's collection of *The Essential Writings of Frithjof Schuon* is a must

for any library claiming to hold the major perennialist publications—but it is the first to focus on a specific religion. This choice is felicitous, particularly since the religion in question is one which is historically and theologically laden with dogmatic elements. This fact enables us to inquire more conveniently whether, and if so how far, Schuon's view of a transcendent unity of religions is compatible with the specificity of Christianity—and, by extension, with that of any other monotheistic religion. This issue has a wide bearing, not least in view of Schuon's privileged position within the traditionalist school.

That perennialist "unity" honors diversity is a generally admitted fact, but "honoring" could be a merely passive form of tolerance. In fact, however, a careful reading of the texts here assembled has had the effect, I confess, of helping me to realize that Schuon is interested in more than just "honoring"—that he is not content with simply exhibiting a tolerant attitude toward various traditions or with finding similarities or commonalities between Christianity and other religions. For him it is more a matter of understanding and experiencing, out of his own soul and in his intellect, the inner core of what is Christianity-specific. Interestingly enough, despite the presence of certain observations that lie outside the scope of Christianity proper—such as his belief in "the cyclical decadence of the human race"—some pages in this collection give the impression of having been written by a Christian who was desirous of putting forward arguments in favor of the truth of his faith. A comparative study of Guénon's and Schuon's approaches in this regard would prove rewarding and would lead, no doubt, to a clearer appreciation of their differences.

A reliable assessment of the place that Christianity actually occupies in Schuon's work would admittedly require going beyond the pages presented by Professor Cutsinger, and putting them into the context of that work taken in its entirety. In so doing, and in view of the fact that Schuon deals similarly with other religions, it is possible that we would discover a slightly different picture of his understanding of Christianity from the one that seems to spring from these pages. Be that as it may, and however interesting the nature of that larger picture might be, what is clear is that Schuon stands out as a remarkable "contextualizer", and in this respect he differs from many other perennialists insofar as he is keen to bring out and compare the various orientations that a given religion has followed over the sweep of centuries. Readers interested in the comparative study of Christian churches and denominations cannot but appreciate his ability to deal with the various branches of this religion. Although some historians might dispute certain of his interpretations, as unavoidably happens when a writer sets out to encompass a field so wide and variegated, these interpretations are always cogently documented.

Schuon focuses on what makes these churches and denominations so different from one another and pays tribute to most of them, and he does so in a way that does not seem to be biased by— or subservient to—the idea of a transcendent principle uniting them invisibly behind the veil of their multifarious differences. The same is true when he compares, not just branches within one religion, but "great" religions with one another, whether they are those of the "Book" or of the Far-East, and in this he proves to be—at least in the present anthology, and perhaps more so than Guénon—a comparativist who must be taken seriously by academe. Within the history of the History of Religions, Schuon appears to belong to the phenomenological school, exemplified by such scholars as Rudolf Otto and Mircea Eliade. Like them, he is committed to defending an essentialist idea of what "religion" *per se* is all about, as for example in the present volume when he writes that "the essence of all religions is the truth of the Absolute". Of course, the phenomenological approach comes in for its share of criticism by researchers involved in other orientations—the proponents of the various historicist schools, for example. But this should not prevent a scholar with an open mind from admitting that such an approach, within the general field of religious studies, has been and still is a fruit-bearing one, were it only in view of the illuminating, though often risky, parallels which are sometimes drawn, and in which Schuon's work abounds.

In some measure, it is because of my research in the history of "esoteric currents in modern and contemporary Europe" (fifteenth to twentieth centuries) that Professor Cutsinger has asked me to contribute this Foreword, and it may therefore be opportune to offer a few remarks relevant to these currents, which include perennialism.

Except for a brief reference to the "Cabalists", the absence of Jewish and Christian Cabala in this volume is conspicuous, and one notes as well that Schuon's speculations on numbers are strictly limited—notably, to 2, 3, and 6—serving only to illustrate metaphysical concepts. "Alchemy" remains a purely metaphorical term for him—as when he uses the phrase "alchemically speaking"—and while he says that he is employing the word "theosophy" in the "ancient and true sense of the word", the theosophical current typified by Jacob Böhme and his successors is obviously not the object of his interests. Meanwhile, the passages that Schuon devotes to Sophia, who is for him an equivalent of "absolute Truth" and whom he tellingly connects to the *sophia perennis*, remain deliberately outside the scope of the Böhmian tradition. These differences, of course, are not unique to Schuon, but are typical of perennialists in general. Whereas other esotericists—alchemists, Christian Cabalists, Rosicrucians, Hermeticists, theosophers, and so forth—have been borrowing from each other for centuries, thus accumulating a quasi-mandatory referential corpus, the perennialists, in the wake of Guénon, have preferred to remain aloof from these currents. Significantly, in order to differentiate themselves, they have preferred to use the term "esoterism" instead of "esotericism". Keen as they are to separate the wheat from the chaff, they consistently evince a marked tendency to deal with "metaphysical principles" rather than with what otherwise constitutes the essentials of Western esotericism. Reflective of this position is the fact that, as Schuon tells us here, "esoterism" is for him synonymous with *gnosis*.

At least two reasons account for this perspective: a negative attitude toward modernity, on the one hand, and the relatively minor place granted to Nature, on the other. In the first place, since modernity is understood by the perennialists to be a "dark age", the esoteric currents that appeared within it as early as the Renaissance often come in for their share of suspicion. We cannot help thinking that the quizzical thunderbolts that Schuon hurls at the baroque in these pages hit by the same token certain esoteric currents—including most alchemical and theosophical productions—which are part and parcel of this same baroque. Second, for those of a perennialist persuasion, nature is more or less an illusion. Indeed for Guénon it has "even less reality than the shadow of our body on a wall". Schuon grants here that, contrary to Calvin's view, "transcendence can tolerate immanence", but he also informs us—in Chapter 10, "Evidence and Mystery"—that "our world is but a furtive and almost accidental coagulation of an immense beyond, which one day will burst forth and into which the terrestrial world will be reabsorbed when it has completed its cycle of material coagulation". Hardly any statement could be further from the aforementioned esoteric currents, in which Nature plays a primary role within the economy of a holistic conception of the relationship between God, Man, and Nature. There are doubtless other sides to Schuon's teaching, which come to the fore when he is discussing, for example, the spirituality of the Native Americans, but what we can say, with respect to this volume at least, is that the interests of Schuon are a far cry from those of the Paracelsians. Hence his marked preference for theologians, who are generally more germane to his purpose. The pages of this book are thus replete with quotations from Augustine, Tertullian, Thomas Aquinas, and others, and of course from Far-Eastern metaphysicians.

Needless to say, these comments are not meant to be judgmental. They are simply intended to situate Schuon's worldview within its Western cultural and historical context. Nor are they meant to take anything away from his writing itself, which is such a pleasant respite from that of so many esoteric, theological, or metaphysical treatises. The clarity of his style, devoid of jargon, cannot be divorced from the clarity of his thought. Besides, he delights us with original metaphors well-fitted to spur on our reflections, as when, for example, he presents Catholicism as a "star" and Protestantism as a "circle", or when he imagines the Catholic Mass as a "sun", and the Lutheran Communion as a "ray" of the sun.

One closing remark. Our pleasure in reading and contributing to this collection is enhanced by the editorial work of Professor Cutsinger, which is evident throughout. The scholarly apparatus he has presented spares us the task of searching for a number of references, while inciting us in turn to venture further into the philosophy of Frithjof Schuon.

Antoine Faivre

Professor Emeritus at the
École Pratique des Hautes Études, Sorbonne

INTRODUCTION

It is a curious fact in the history of religions that Christianity, which took the form of a spiritual "way" (Acts 24:22) from its very beginning, and which continues to offer its initiates the means of seeing "the glory of God" (John 11:40) and of becoming "partakers of the divine nature" (2 Peter 1:4), should have become so adept at concealing the significance of its deepest and most transformative truths, "kept secret since the world began" (Romans 16:25), that serious Christian seekers in our day often forsake their religion in favor of such traditions as Yoga and Zen, where the promises of realization can be more easily discerned and where methods of spiritual development are often more accessible. Writing in the seventh century, Saint Maximos the Confessor explained that "the followers and servants of Christ were initiated directly by him into the *gnosis* of existent things, they in turn imparting this knowledge to those who came after them",[1] and a Greek Orthodox bishop has recently testified to meeting one of the latest links in this chain on the Holy Mountain of Athos, whom he describes as appearing to his wondering eyes "like lightning in the night" and as having "everything that God has".[2] Most Christians, however, seem altogether unaware of the fact that such things are still possible and that the attainment of so exalted a station of knowledge and union is precisely the purpose of their tradition.

This is a matter, in part, of sheer familiarity—though no doubt aggravated by the fideism and sentimentalism that have come to dominate in certain sectors of this ancient religion. Centuries of repetition have meant that Christians can now recite the creeds of the Church and take part in its sacramental mysteries without the freshness and wonder of the first Christian catechumens, who had

---

1. *Ambigua*, 91.
2. Hierotheos Vlachos, *A Night in the Desert of the Holy Mountain*, trans. Effie Mavromichali (Levadia, Greece: Birth of the Theotokos Monastery, 1991), p. 31.

been taught in secrecy and with great solemnity, and then only after lengthy periods of spiritual examination and discipline, that God was born as a man, died on a cross, and rose from the dead, and that through a conscious assimilation of the body and blood of this God-Man—the "medicine of immortality", in the words of Saint Ignatius of Antioch—men might be drawn into the inward life of Divinity, having acquired the "power to become sons of God" (John 1:12). No spiritual teaching is more esoteric than this, nor is there an initiatic or mystagogical path that offers any more lofty a goal or any greater promise of fulfillment, however neglectful many Christians may be of their tradition's innermost treasures and however difficult it may have therefore become for them to recover the awe and anticipation with which the earliest Christians entered upon their new way.

This collection of writings, selected from the works of one of the greatest spiritual teachers of our time, Frithjof Schuon, is intended to aid in this recovery; by removing the veils of familiarity, indifference, and forgetfulness, our aim is to assist the reader in gaining a fresh perception of Christianity and a keener sense of the underlying meaning and transformational power of its doctrines, symbols, and spiritual methods. The author is uniquely suited to guide us in this endeavor. Widely acknowledged as one of the twentieth century's foremost authorities on the world's religions, and the leading spokesman for the traditionalist or perennialist school of comparative religious philosophy,[3] Schuon was the author of over twenty books, as well as numerous articles, letters, texts of spiritual instruction, and other unpublished documents; the depth of his insights and the masterful quality of his early writing had brought him international recognition while he was still in his twenties, and by the time of his death in 1998 at the age of ninety, his reputation among many scholars of mysticism, esoterism, and contemplative traditions was unsurpassed.

Frithjof Schuon was much more than a scholar, however. An accomplished artist and poet,[4] he was above all a man of prayer,

3. René Guénon, Ananda Coomaraswamy, and Titus Burckhardt were also important figures in this school.
4. The painting on the cover of the present volume is by Schuon. A number of his other works have been collected in *Images of Primordial and Mystic Beauty: Paintings by Frithjof Schuon*, ed. Michael Pollack (Bloomington, Indiana: Abodes, 1992).

whose fundamental message, whatever its particular thrust in any given article or chapter, was always linked to the importance of faith and spiritual practice. "Even if our writings had on average no other result than the restitution for some of the saving barque that is prayer," he once wrote, "we would owe it to God to consider ourselves profoundly satisfied."[5] In the years since his death, a number of his close associates have begun to publish biographical memoirs, and as a result it is now widely known that Schuon's own practice was undertaken within the context of Sufism and that he was himself a master of the traditional Shadhiliyyah-Darqawiyyah lineage.[6]

Schuon did not himself speak of this role in his published writings, however, for he wished to distinguish very carefully between his function as a spiritual master, on the one hand, and his teaching as a metaphysician and philosopher, on the other—a teaching that is universalist in its scope and intention and worlds apart from any proselytizing or authoritarian aim. Born in Switzerland in 1907, where he was brought up as a Protestant before becoming a Roman Catholic, he knew that those who were aware of his background might falsely conclude that he had renounced Christianity and had "converted" to Islam. In fact, however, his Sufi affiliation was simply a matter of opportunity and vocation, the result of his quest, as a young man, for spirituality of a kind that he had been unable to find in the Western Church, and it did not conflict with his remaining, throughout his long life, an adamant defender of traditional Christological doctrine and other essential Christian truths, nor with his having a special affinity for the Christian East and the Hesychast method of prayer. "Being *a priori* a metaphysician," he wrote, "I have had since my youth a particular interest in *Advaita Vedânta,* but also in the method of realization of which *Advaita Vedânta* approves. Since I could not find this method—in its strict and esoteric form—

During the last three years of his life, Schuon composed nearly thirty-five hundred lyric poems in German; four volumes of these poems have been published to date: *Glück, Leben, Sinn,* and *Liebe* (Freiburg-im-Breisgau, Basel, Vienna: Herder, 1997). Bi-lingual editions of the poetry—German with an English translation—include *Songs for a Spiritual Traveler: Selected Poems* (Bloomington, Indiana: World Wisdom, 2002) and *Adastra and Stella Maris: Poems by Frithjof Schuon* (Bloomington, Indiana: World Wisdom, 2003).
5. *The Play of Masks* (Bloomington, Indiana: World Wisdom, 1992), p. vii.
6. This is an unbroken succession of traditional Sufi teachers which traces its beginnings to the thirteenth century master Abu al-Hasan al-Shadhili (1196-1258) and which includes among its subsequent branches an order founded in the early nineteenth century by Mawlay al-Arabi al-Darqawi (1760-1823).

in Europe, and since it was impossible for me to turn to a Hindu guru because of the laws of the castes, I had to look elsewhere; and since Islam *de facto* contains this method, in Sufism, I finally decided to look for a Sufi master; the outer form did not matter to me."[7] Although Schuon made a home for himself within this spiritual framework, he was in no sense an apologist for the Sufi tradition, but maintained close ties throughout his long life with authorities and wayfarers in a wide variety of orthodox religions, each of which, he insisted, is a saving expression of a single Truth, which he variously referred to as the *sophia perennis* or *philosophia perennis*, that is, the "perennial wisdom" or "perennial philosophy". Until his later years he traveled widely, from India to North Africa to America, and his personal friendships ranged from Hindu swamis to Native American chiefs and shamans, while thousands of correspondents and visitors, from nearly every religious background, looked to him for advice.

For obvious reasons, he was especially interested in Christianity, and as with every religion about which he wrote, his grasp of its inward and essential message was profound; steeped in the Scriptures and in the lives of the saints, and well acquainted with the works of Church Fathers and other Christian authorities, Schuon speaks with full knowledge of the Church's artistic and liturgical traditions, as well as its historic controversies and denominational divergences, and he exhibits again and again in his writing an extraordinary ability to bring to light the underlying meaning and validity of what might otherwise seem conflicting and mutually exclusive theological claims. Nor did his knowledge come simply from books; his own brother was a Trappist monk, and his numerous other contacts included the Athonite *starets* Sophrony, who was a noted disciple of Saint Silouan of the Holy Mountain; Metropolitan Anthony Bloom, a popular and much published Russian Orthodox writer on prayer; and the well-known Roman Catholic monk and contemplative author Thomas Merton, who near the end of his life wrote to Schuon in hopes of establishing a private spiritual correspondence.

7. From a letter dated January 1996.

There is no need to describe the author's perspective in any detail in this context; the following pages will provide a clear and ample picture of his views, and it makes better sense to let him speak for himself. On the other hand, it will perhaps be useful if we say just a word about how Schuon envisioned the relationship between the Christian religion and the *sophia perennis*. Christianity is well known, after all, for its widespread exclusivism—for the conviction that there can be no salvation apart from a conscious, explicit, and active faith in Jesus Christ and membership in his visible body, the Church—and some readers may therefore be hesitant, however extensive this author's knowledge and however numerous his friendships with serious Christian believers, to trust his insights and to benefit fully from his observations, given his universalist doctrine. If Christ is truly God incarnate, they will say, then it is surely impossible for a Christian to condone those religions which ignore or dismiss his Divinity, and it is therefore unacceptable for a Christian to subscribe to the perennial philosophy.

It is beyond the scope of the present introduction to undertake a full response to this criticism; what can be said, however, is that a number of unimpeachably orthodox Christians, including canonized saints, have themselves been "perennialists". According to Saint Augustine, for example, "That which today is called the Christian religion existed among the ancients and has never ceased to exist from the origin of the human race until the time when Christ himself came and men began to call 'Christian' the true religion which already existed beforehand."[8] Saint Justin the Martyr fully concurs with this dictum: "We have been taught that Christ is the First-begotten of God and have testified that he is the *Logos* of which every race of man partakes. Those who lived in accordance with the *Logos* are Christians, even though they were called godless, such as, among the Greeks, Socrates and Heraclitus and others like them. Those who lived by this *Logos*, and those who so live now, are Christians, fearless and unperturbed."[9] These ancient testimonies have been echoed in our own day by Saint Nikolai Velimirovich, a Ser-

---

8. *Reconsiderations*, I.13.3; see Chapter 2, "The Particular Nature and Universality of the Christian Tradition", note 4.
9. *First Apology*, 46.

bian Orthodox bishop and a survivor of Dachau, who teaches that the *Logos* or Word of God, manifest in every authentic religion, is the true and saving source of "precious gifts in the East": "Glory to the memory of Lao Tzu," he can therefore exclaim, "the teacher and prophet of his people! Glory to the memory of Krishna, the teacher and prophet of his people! Blessed be the memory of Buddha, the royal son and inexorable teacher of his people!"[10]

As will be evident from the following pages, these articulations of the *sophia perennis* provide a useful synopsis of Schuon's fundamental point of view. We do not mean to suggest that he thought deliberately or self-consciously in patristic, or other Christian, categories; the author of these pages was a metaphysician and esoterist, not a theologian or historian of religions, and it would therefore be a mistake to suppose that his aim was to provide a hermeneutic for interpreting religious texts or phenomena, or that his doctrine flowed from empirical considerations. On the contrary, his point of departure was always the underlying nature of things, as perceived by the Intellect, not the exoteric doctrines of any given religion or the pious opinions of its traditional authorities. Nevertheless, what we can say is that he was in full agreement, beginning from his own metaphysical starting-point, with the essential idea expressed by these saints; like them he taught that the incarnation of the Word as Jesus Christ (John 1:14) bestowed a particular form upon a pre-existing and eternal Truth, and that the substance of this form—the living heart of the Christic message[11]—is thus perennial and universal in its inward or essential meaning. This is a key to Schuon's entire approach to Christianity, and it helps to explain what he meant in writing that "all genuine religions are Christian",[12] that "every truth is necessarily manifested in terms of Christ and on his model",[13] and that "there is no truth or wisdom that does not come from Christ".[14]

10. *Prayers by the Lake* (Grayslake, Illinois: Free Serbian Orthodox Diocese of the United States, n.d.), Chapter 48.
11. See Chapter 1, "Outline of the Christic Message".
12. *Gnosis: Divine Wisdom*, trans. G. E. H. Palmer (London: Perennial Books, 1959), p. 67.
13. *Stations of Wisdom* (Bloomington, Indiana: World Wisdom, 1995), p. 49.
14. See Chapter 4, "Some Observations", p. 39.

The following chapters have been chosen from Schuon's published corpus of twenty-three books. Written originally in French, these selections are here presented in a fully revised English translation; bibliographical details, including information about previous English editions, may be found at the end of this volume. As it happens, most of Schuon's books are themselves anthologies, which he periodically assembled from articles that had been initially published, beginning in 1933 and continuing through 1997, in a variety of European, Persian, and American journals, including *Le Voile d'Isis, Études Traditionnelles, Studies in Comparative Religion, Sophia Perennis, Connaissance des Religions,* and *Sophia: A Journal of Traditional Studies.* Many of these articles were "occasional" in nature, having been composed in response to a broad spectrum of questions and problems, often put to Schuon by those who sought his spiritual counsel. As a result, his writings are often more meditative and maieutic than discursive in character, with any given essay ranging across a number of fascinating topics and including illustrations drawn from an astonishing variety of sources. The selections included in this present volume are intended to highlight this variety and to convey both the scope and the depth of Schuon's insights into the Christian tradition. We have certainly not meant to be exhaustive; a number of pertinent chapters, several of them focused on more "specialized" issues, such as the significance of the *epiclesis* in the Byzantine liturgy and the mysticism of Theresa of Avila and John of the Cross, have not been included. It has been said that Schuon's editor is like an artist cutting figures from gold leaf: the shapes that one keeps are all gold, but so is what remains.

Because of the wide-ranging nature of Schuon's work and its poetic—one might say "musical"—quality, a firm categorization of his writings is impossible; he himself spoke of the "discontinuous and sporadic manner" of his expositions, acknowledging that while "there is no great doctrine that is not a system", there is equally none that "expresses itself in an exclusively systematic fashion".[15] Nevertheless, there is an order, if not a system, to the arrangement of this book; in broad strokes, the chapters have been organized in a way that will guide the reader from matters of metaphysical prin-

15. *Survey of Metaphysics and Esoterism,* trans. Gustavo Polit (Bloomington, Indiana: World Wisdom, 1986), p. 1.

ciple, through various theological and hermeneutical issues, to somewhat more "operative" questions of spiritual practice and method. Specific topics include the relationship between Christianity and other religions; the distinction or divergence within Christianity between its main branches, Orthodox, Catholic, and Protestant; the place of reason and faith and their connection to spiritual knowledge or *gnosis*; the principles, and applications, of an anagogical or mystical exegesis of the Scriptures; the central dogmas of the Trinity and Incarnation, as well as Eucharistic and Marian doctrine; and Christian initiation, contemplative practice, and "prayer of the heart", especially the Jesus Prayer. The book concludes with a short Appendix of previously unpublished writings, including samples from Schuon's correspondence with Christian seekers.

The breadth of the author's erudition can be somewhat daunting, especially for those not accustomed to reading philosophical and religious works; his pages frequently contain allusions to ideas, historical figures or events, and sacred texts that illumine or amplify his meaning, but a citation or other reference is not usually provided. With this fact in mind and as an aid to the interested reader, we have added a series of Editor's Notes to this volume; in order to be as unobtrusive as possible, we have chosen not to interrupt Schuon's prose with asterisks or other symbols, leaving it to the reader to consult the notes when in need. It should be understood that this editorial apparatus does not presume to offer an interpretation of Schuon's own teaching; as remarked above, we prefer to allow his writings to speak for themselves. Organized by chapter and tagged to the relevant page numbers, the notes are designed simply to provide a few helpful supports for those who may be unacquainted with the details of Christian dogma and intellectual history or with other traditional teachings. Chapter and verse citations are given for quotations from the Bible and other sacred texts; dates and brief biographical summaries are provided for historical figures; explanations are offered concerning the fine points of theological controversies and the principal doctrines of various schools of thought.

One final point should be mentioned. It is customary for Schuon to use a number of "technical" terms in his writings, drawn from a multitude of traditions and involving several classical languages, including Sanskrit, Arabic, Latin, and Greek, and a Glossary has therefore been provided as well; here one will find, in transliteration, foreign words and phrases appearing both in Schuon's text and in our editorial notes, together with brief translations and definitions.

James S. Cutsinger

1

Outline of the Christic Message

If we start from the incontestable idea that the essence of all religions is the truth of the Absolute with its human consequences, mystical as well as social, the question may be asked how the Christian religion satisfies this definition; for its central content seems to be not God as such, but Christ—that is, not so much the nature of the divine Being as its human manifestation. Thus a Patristic voice aptly proclaimed: "God became man that man might become God"; this is the Christian way of saying that "*Brahma* is real; the world is appearance". Christianity, instead of simply juxtaposing the Absolute and the contingent, the Real and the illusory, proposes from the outset a reciprocity between the one and the other: it sees the Absolute *a priori* in relation to man, and man—correlatively—is defined in conformity with this reciprocity, which is not only metaphysical, but also dynamic, voluntary, eschatological. It is true that Judaism proceeds in an analogous fashion, but to a lesser degree: it does not define God in relation to the human drama, hence starting from contingency, but it does establish a quasi-absolute relationship between God and His people: God is "the God of Israel"; the symbiosis is immutable; however, God remains God, and man remains man; there is no "human God" or "divine man".

Be that as it may, the reciprocity posited by Christianity is metaphysically transparent, and it is necessarily so, on pain of being an error. Unquestionably, once we are aware of the existence of contingency or relativity, we must know that the Absolute is interested in it in one way or another, and this means first of all that contingency must be prefigured in the Absolute, and then that the Absolute must be reflected in contingency; this is the ontological foundation of the mysteries of Incarnation and Redemption. The rest is a matter of modality: Christianity proposes on the one hand an abrupt opposition between the "flesh" and the "spirit", and on the other hand—and this is its esoteric side—its option for "inward-

1

ness" as against the outwardness of legal prescriptions and as against
the "letter that killeth". In addition, it operates with that central and
profoundly characteristic sacrament which is the Eucharist: God
does not limit Himself to promulgating a Law; He descends to earth
and makes Himself Bread of life and Drink of immortality.

In relation to Judaism, Christianity comprises an aspect of esoterism through three elements: inwardness, quasi-unconditional
charity, the sacraments. The first element consists in more or less
disregarding outward practices and accentuating the inward attitude: what matters is to worship God "in spirit and in truth"; the second element corresponds to the Hindu *ahimsa*, "non-harming",
which can go so far as to renounce our legitimate rights, hence
deliberately to step out of the mesh of human interests and social
justice; it is to offer the left cheek to him who has struck the right
and always to give more than one has to. Islam marks a return to
Mosaic "realism", while integrating Jesus into its perspective as a
prophet of Sufic "poverty"; be that as it may, Christianity itself, in
order to be able to assume the function of a world religion, had to
attenuate its original rigor and present itself as a socially realistic
legalism, at least to a certain degree.

*　　*　　*

If "God became man", or if the Absolute became contingency, or if
Necessary Being became possible being—if such is the case, one can
understand the meaning of a God who became bread and wine and
who made communion a condition *sine qua non* of salvation; not, to
be sure, the sole condition, for communion demands the quasi-permanent practice of prayer, which Christ commands in his parable of
the unjust judge and the importance of which is stressed by Saint
Paul when he enjoins the faithful to "pray without ceasing". One
can conceive of a man who, prevented from taking communion, is
saved by prayer alone, but one cannot conceive of a man who would
be prevented from praying and who would be saved through communion alone; indeed, some of the greatest saints, at the beginning
of Christianity, lived in solitude without being able to take communion, at least for several years. This is explained by the fact that
prayer takes precedence over everything, consequently that it contains communion in its own way and does so necessarily, since in

principle we bear within ourselves all that we can obtain from without; "the kingdom of God is within you". Means are relative; not so
our fundamental relationship with the Absolute.

As regards the Eucharistic rite, the following specification
appears permissible: the bread seems to signify that "God enters
into us", and the wine that "we enter into God"; presence of grace
on the one hand and unitive extinction on the other. God is the
absolute and perfect Subject, who either enters into the contingent
and imperfect subject or else assimilates that subject by delivering it
from the shackles of objectified subjectivity, this subjectivity having
become exteriorized and thereby paradoxically multiple. It could
also be said that the bread refers more particularly to salvation and
the wine to union, which evokes the ancient distinction between the
lesser and the greater mysteries.[1]

In the Eucharist, the Absolute—or the divine Self[2]—became
Nourishment; in other cases, It became Image or Icon; in still others, Word or Formula: therein lies the entire mystery of concrete
assimilation of the Divinity by means of a properly sacramental symbol: visual, auditive, or some other. One of these symbols, and even
the most central one, is the very Name of God, quintessence of all
prayer, whether a Name of God as such or a Name of God become
man.[3] The intention of the Hesychasts is that "the heart drink the
Name so that the Name might drink the heart": thus the liquefied
heart, which, owing to the effect of the "fall", was "hardened",
whence the frequent comparison of the profane heart with a stone.
"For the hardness of your heart he (Moses) wrote you this precept";

---

1. In a more general sense, we would say that the Christian sacraments are exoteric
for exoterists, and esoteric or initiatic for esoterists; in the first case their end is salvation pure and simple, and in the second it is mystical union.

2. Once the Supreme Principle makes Itself man's interlocutor, It enters into cosmic relativity by the very fact of Its personification; It nonetheless remains the
Absolute with respect to man, except from the standpoint of the pure Intellect.

3. Let us quote Saint Bernardino of Siena, the great promoter—today forgotten—
of the invocation of the Name of Jesus: "Place the Name of Jesus in your homes, in
your chambers, and keep it in your hearts." "The best inscription of the Name of
Jesus is that in the heart, then that in the word, and finally that in the painted or
sculpted symbol." "All that God hath created for the salvation of the world is hidden in the Name of Jesus: all the Bible, from Genesis to the last Book. The reason
for this is that the Name is origin without origin. The Name of Jesus is as worthy of
praise as God Himself."

Christ intended to create a new man through his sacrificial body as God-Man and starting from a particular moral anthropology. Let us specify that a possibility of salvation manifests itself, not because it is necessarily better than another, but because, being possible, precisely, it cannot but manifest itself; as Plato said, and after him Saint Augustine, it is in the nature of the Good to wish to communicate Itself.

Not without relationship to the mystery of the Eucharist is that of the Icon; here too it is a question of a materialization of the heavenly and thus of a sensible assimilation of the spiritual. Quintessentially, Christianity comprises two Icons, the Holy Face and the Virgin with the Child, the prototype of the first icon being the Holy Shroud and that of the second, the portrait of Mary painted by Saint Luke. It is from these two sources that spring, symbolically speaking, all the other sacred images, ending with such liturgical crystallizations as the Byzantine iconostasis and the Gothic retable; it is also necessary to mention the crucifix—painted or sculpted—in which a primordial symbol is combined with a later image. Let us add that statuary—foreign to the Eastern Church—is closer to architecture than to iconography properly so called.[4]

* * *

"God become man": this is the mystery of Jesus, but it is also, and thereby, that of Mary; for humanly, Jesus had nothing that he did not inherit from his Mother, who has rightly been called "Co-Redemptress" and "divine Mary". Thus the Name of Mary is like a prolongation of that of Jesus; to be sure, the spiritual reality of Mary is contained in Jesus—the converse is also true—but the distinction between the two aspects has its reason for being; synthesis does not preclude analysis. If Christ is "the Way, the Truth and the Life", the Blessed Virgin, who is made of the same substance, holds graces which facilitate access to these mysteries, and it is to

---

4. Judaism and Islam, which proscribe images, replace them in a certain way with calligraphy, a visual expression of the divine discourse. An illuminated page of the Koran, a prayer-niche decorated with arabesques, are "abstract Icons".

her that this saying of Christ applies in the first place: "My yoke is easy, and my burden is light."

It could be said that Christianity is not *a priori* such and such a metaphysical truth, it is Christ, and it is participation in Christ through the sacraments and through sanctity. This being so, there is no escaping the quintessential divine Reality: in Christianity, as in every other religion, there are fundamentally two things to consider, abstractly and concretely: the Absolute, or the absolutely Real, which is the Sovereign Good and which gives meaning to everything, and our consciousness of the Absolute, which must become second nature for us and which frees us from the meanderings, impasses, and abysses of contingency. The rest is a matter of adaptation to the needs of given souls and societies; but the forms also have their intrinsic worth, for the Truth wills beauty, in its veilings as well as in ultimate Beatitude.

* * *

Intrinsically Christian, non-Hellenized, metaphysics is expressed by the initial statements of the Gospel of Saint John. "In the beginning was the Word": obviously what is meant is not a temporal origin, but a principial priority, that of the divine Order, to which the universal Intellect—the Word—pertains, while nonetheless being linked to cosmic Manifestation, of which it is the center both transcendent and immanent. "And the Word was with God": with respect to Manifestation precisely, the *Logos* is distinguished from the Principle, while being "with" it through its essence. "And the Word was God": with respect to the divine Order, the *Logos* is not distinct from the Principle; the distinction between the two natures of Christ reflects the inevitable ambiguity of the relationship *Âtmâ-Mâyâ*. "All things were made by him": there is nothing created that was not conceived and prefigured in the divine Intellect. "And the light shineth in darkness; and the darkness comprehended it not": it is in the nature of *Âtmâ* to penetrate into *Mâyâ*, and it is in the nature of a certain *Mâyâ* to resist it,[5] otherwise the world would

---

5. What is in question here is the negative dimension proper to sub-celestial *Mâyâ*, which is made of darkness inasmuch as it becomes distant from the Principle and

cease to be the world; and "it must needs be that offences come". Christ's victory over the world and over death retraces or anticipates the victory—as such timeless—of Good over Evil, or of Ohrmazd over Ahriman; a victory that is ontologically necessary because it results from the nature of Being itself, despite initial appearances to the contrary. Darkness, even in winning, loses; and light, even in losing, wins; Passion, Resurrection, Redemption.

of light inasmuch as it manifests aspects of the Principle. It is the domain of imperfection and impermanence, but also of potentially liberating theomorphism, whereas heavenly *Mâyâ* is the domain of archetypes and *hypostases.*

2

The Particular Nature and Universality of the Christian Tradition

What, for want of a better term, we are obliged to call "Christian exoterism" is not in its origin and structure strictly analogous to the Jewish and Islamic exoterisms; for whereas the exoteric side of the two latter traditions was instituted as such from the very beginning, in the sense that it formed part of the Revelation and was clearly distinguishable from its esoteric aspect, what we now know as Christian exoterism hardly figured as such in the Christian Revelation except in a purely incidental manner. It is true that in some of the oldest texts, particularly those of Saint Paul, there are suggestions of an exoterist or dogmatist mode. Such is the case, for example, when the principial, hierarchic connection existing between esoterism and exoterism is represented as a sort of historical relationship between the New Covenant and the Old, the former being identified with the "spirit that giveth life" and the latter with the "letter that killeth",[1] a comparison that leaves out of account the integral reality inherent in the Old Covenant itself, namely, that element in it which is identified principially with the New Covenant and of which the latter is simply a new form or adaptation. This is a good example of how the dogmatist or theological point of view,[2] instead of embracing a truth in its entirety, selects one aspect only as a matter

---

1. The interpretation of these words in an exoteric sense is really an act of suicide, for they are bound inevitably to turn against the exoterism that has annexed them. The truth of this was demonstrated by the Reformation, which eagerly seized upon the phrase in question (2 Cor. 3:6) in order to make of it its chief weapon, thus usurping the place that normally should belong to esoterism.

2. Christianity inherited this point of view from Judaism, whose form coincides with the very origin of this perspective; it is almost superfluous to stress the fact that its

of expediency and purports to give it an exclusive and absolute value; it should not be forgotten, however, that without this dogmatic character religious truth would be inefficacious with regard to the particular end imposed upon it by the motives of expediency already mentioned. There is thus a twofold restriction put upon pure truth: on the one hand an aspect of the truth is invested with the character of integral truth, and on the other hand an absolute character is attributed to the relative. Furthermore this standpoint of expediency carries with it the negation of all those things which, being neither accessible nor indispensable to everyone indiscriminately, lie for that reason beyond the purview of the theological perspective and must be left outside it—hence the simplifications and symbolical syntheses peculiar to every exoterism.[3] Lastly, we may also mention, as a particularly striking feature of these doctrines, the identification of historical facts with principial truths and the

---

presence in primitive Christianity in no wise invalidates the initiatic essence of the latter. "There exist," says Origen, "diverse forms of the Word under which It reveals Itself to Its disciples, conforming Itself to the degree of light of each one, according to the degree of their progress in saintliness" (*Contra Celsum* 4:16).

3. Thus Semitic exoterisms deny the transmigration of the soul and consequently the existence of an immortal soul in animals; and they also deny the total cyclic dissolution that the Hindus call *mahâpralaya*, a dissolution which implies the annihilation of the entire creation (*samsâra*). These truths are not at all indispensable for salvation and involve certain dangers even for the mentalities to which the religious doctrines are addressed; thus, an exoterism is always obliged to leave unmentioned any esoteric elements which are incompatible with its own dogmatic form, or even to deny them. However, in order to forestall possible objections to the examples just given, two reservations need to be made. In the first place, with regard to the immortality of the soul in the case of animals, it should be said that the theological denial is justified in the sense that a being cannot in fact attain immortality while bound to the animal state, since this state, like the vegetable and mineral states, is peripheral, and immortality and deliverance can be attained only from the starting point of a central state such as the human. It will be seen from this example that a religious negation which is dogmatic in character is never entirely senseless. In the second place, with regard to the refusal to admit the *mahâpralaya*, it should be added that this negation is not strictly dogmatic and that the total cyclic dissolution, which completes a "Life of *Brahmâ*", is clearly attested by such formulations as the following: "For verily I say unto you, till heaven and earth pass, one jot or one tittle shall in no wise pass from the law, till all be fulfilled" (Matt. 5:18). "They shall remain there (*khâlidîn*) for as long as the heavens and the earth endure, unless thy Lord willeth otherwise" (Koran, *Sûrah* "Hûd" [11]:107).

inevitable confusions resulting therefrom. For example, when it is said that all human souls, from that of Adam to the departed souls of Christ's own contemporaries, must await his descent into hell in order to be delivered, such a statement confuses the historical with the cosmic Christ and represents an eternal function of the Word as a temporal fact for the simple reason that Jesus was a manifestation of this Word, which is another way of saying that in the world where this manifestation took place, Jesus was truly the unique incarnation of the Word. Another example may be found in the divergent views of Christianity and Islam on the subject of the death of Christ: apart from the fact that the Koran, by its apparent denial of Christ's death, is simply affirming that Christ was not killed in reality—which is obvious not only as regards the divine nature of the God-Man, but also as regards his human nature, since it was resurrected—the refusal of Muslims to admit the historical Redemption, and consequently the facts that are the unique terrestrial expression of universal Redemption as far as Christian humanity is concerned, simply denotes that in the final analysis Christ did not die for those who are "whole", who in this case are the Muslims insofar as they benefit from another terrestrial form of the one and eternal Redemption. In other words, if it is true in principle that Christ died for all men—in the same way that the Islamic Revelation is principially addressed to everyone—in fact he died only for those who must and do benefit from the means of grace that perpetuate his work of Redemption;[4] hence the traditional distance separating Islam from the Christian Mystery is bound to appear exoterically in the form of a denial, exactly in the same way that Christian exoter-

---

4. In the same order of ideas, we may quote the following words of Saint Augustine: "That which today is called the Christian religion existed among the ancients and has never ceased to exist from the origin of the human race until the time when Christ himself came and men began to call Christian the true religion which already existed beforehand" (*Reconsiderations* I.13.3). This passage has been commented upon as follows by the Abbé P.-J. Jallabert in his book *Le Catholicisme avant Jésus-Christ:* "The Catholic religion is but a continuation of the primitive religion restored and generously enriched by Him who knew His work from the beginning. This explains why Saint Paul the Apostle did not claim to be superior to the Gentiles save in his knowledge of Jesus crucified. In fact, all the Gentiles needed to acquire was the knowledge of the Incarnation and the Redemption considered as an accomplished fact; for they had already received the deposit of all the remain-

ism must deny the possibility of salvation outside the Redemption brought about by Jesus. However that may be, although a religious perspective may be contested *ab extra*, that is to say, in the light of another religious perspective deriving from a different aspect of the same truth, it remains incontestable *ab intra* inasmuch as its capacity to serve as a means of expressing the total truth makes of it a key to that truth. Moreover it must never be forgotten that the restrictions inherent in the dogmatist point of view express in their own way the divine Goodness, which wishes to prevent men from going astray and which gives them what is accessible and indispensable to everyone, having regard to the mental predispositions of the human collectivity concerned.[5]

It will be understood from what has just been said that any seeming contradiction or depreciation of the Mosaic Law that may be found in the words of Christ or the teaching of the Apostles is in reality but an expression of the superiority of esoterism over exoterism[6] and does not therefore apply at the same level as this Law,[7]

---

ing truths. . . . It is well to consider that this divine Revelation, which idolatry had rendered unrecognizable, had nevertheless been preserved in its purity and perhaps in all its perfection in the mysteries of Eleusis, Lemnos, and Samothrace." This "knowledge of the Incarnation and the Redemption" implies before all else a knowledge of the renewal effected by Christ of a means of grace that in itself is eternal, like the Law that Christ came to fulfill but not to destroy. This means of grace is essentially always the same and the only means that exists, although its modes may vary in accordance with the different ethnic and cultural environments to which it reveals itself; the Eucharist is a universal reality like Christ himself.

5. In an analogous sense it is said in Islam that "the divergence of the scholars is a blessing" (*Ikhtilâf al-'ulamâ'i rahmah*).

6. This is brought out in a particularly clear manner by the words of Christ concerning Saint John the Baptist. From an exoteric point of view, it is obvious that the Prophet who stands nearest to the Christ-God is the greatest among men, and on the other hand that the least among the Blessed in Heaven is greater than the greatest man on earth, always by reason of this same proximity to God. Metaphysically, the words of Christ express the superiority of what is principial over what is manifested, or, from an initiatic point of view, of esoterism over exoterism, Saint John the Baptist being in this case regarded as the summit and fulfillment of the latter, which explains furthermore why his name is identical with that of Saint John the Evangelist, who represents Christianity in its most inward aspect.

7. In Saint Paul's Epistle to the Romans, one finds the following passage: "For circumcision verily profiteth, if thou keep the law: but if thou be a breaker of the law, thy circumcision is made uncircumcision. Therefore if the uncircumcised keep the

at least not *a priori*, that is, as long as this hierarchic relationship is not itself conceived in dogmatic mode. It is perfectly obvious that the main teachings of Christ transcend this viewpoint, and that is indeed the reason for their existence. They therefore likewise transcend the Law; in no other way could one explain the attitude of Christ with respect to the law of retaliation, or with regard to the woman taken in adultery, or to divorce. In fact the turning of the other cheek is not a thing that any social collectivity could put into practice with a view to maintaining its equilibrium,[8] and it has no meaning except as a spiritual attitude; the spiritual man alone firmly takes his stand outside the logical chain of individual reactions, since for him a participation in the current of these reactions is tantamount to a fall from grace, at least when such participation involves the center or the soul of the individual, though not when it remains purely an outward and impersonal act of justice such as

---

righteousness of the law, shall not his uncircumcision be counted for circumcision? And shall not uncircumcision which is by nature, if it fulfill the law, judge thee, who by the letter and circumcision dost transgress the law? For he is not a Jew, which is one outwardly; neither is that circumcision, which is outward in the flesh: But he is a Jew, which is one inwardly; and circumcision is that of the heart, in the spirit, and not in the letter; whose praise is not of men but of God" (Rom. 2:25-29). The same idea reappears in a more concise form in the following passage from the Koran: "And they say: Become Jews or Nazarenes in order that you may be guided; answer: No, we follow the way of Abraham who was pure (or 'primordial', *hanîf*) and who was not one of those who associate (creatures with Allah or effects with the Cause or manifestations with the Principle). (Receive) the baptism of Allah (and not that of men); and who indeed baptizes better than Allah? and it is He whom we adore" (*Sûrah* "The Cow" [2]:135, 138). The "baptism" referred to here expresses the same fundamental idea that Saint Paul expresses by the word "circumcision".

8. This is so clearly true that Christians themselves have never turned this injunction of Christ into a legal obligation, which proves once again that it is not situated on the same level as the Jewish Law and consequently is neither intended nor able to take its place. There is a *hadîth* that shows the compatibility existing between the spiritual point of view affirmed by Christ and the social point of view, which is that of the Mosaic Law. It is related that the first thief among the Muslim community was led before the Prophet in order that his hand might be cut off according to the Koranic law; but the Prophet turned pale. He was asked, "Hast thou some objection?" He answered: "How should I have nothing to object to! Must I be the ally of Satan in enmity against my brothers? If you wish God to forgive your sin and conceal it, you also must conceal the sin of others. For once the transgressor has been brought before the monarch, the punishment must be accomplished."

that envisaged by the Mosaic Law. But it was precisely because this impersonal character of the law of retaliation had been lost and replaced by passions that it was necessary for Christ to express a spiritual truth which, although condemning only a false pretension, appeared to condemn the Law itself. All this is clearly evidenced in Christ's answer to those who wished to stone the woman taken in adultery, and who, instead of acting impersonally in the name of the Law, would have acted personally in the name of their own hypocrisy. Christ did not therefore speak from the standpoint of the Law, but from that of inward, supra-social, and spiritual realities; and his point of view was exactly the same on the question of divorce. Perhaps the most striking proof to be found in Christ's teachings of the purely spiritual and therefore supra-social and extra-moral character of his Doctrine is contained in the following saying: "If any man come to me and hate not his father, and mother, and wife and children, and brethren, and sisters, yea, and his own life also, he cannot be my disciple" (Luke 14:26). It is clearly impossible to oppose such teaching to the Mosaic Law.

Christianity accordingly possesses none of the normal characteristics of an exoterism instituted as such, but presents itself as an exoterism in fact rather than as one existing in principle. Moreover, even without referring to Scriptural passages, the essentially initiatic character of Christianity is apparent from certain features of the first importance, such as the Doctrine of the Trinity, the Sacrament of the Eucharist, and, more particularly, the use of wine in this rite, or again from the use of purely esoteric expressions such as "Son of God" and especially "Mother of God". If exoterism is "something that is at the same time indispensable and accessible to all",[9] Christianity cannot be exoteric in the usual sense of the word, since it is in reality by no means accessible to everyone, although in fact, by virtue of its religious application, it applies to everyone. This inaccessibility of the Christian dogmas is expressed by calling them "mysteries", a word which has a positive meaning only in the initiatic domain to which moreover it belongs, but which, when applied in the religious sphere, seems to attempt to justify or conceal the fact that Christian dogmas carry with them no direct intellectual

9. Definition given by René Guénon in his article "Création et Manifestation" (*Études Traditionnelles*, October, 1937).

proof, if such a manner of speaking is permissible. For example, the divine Unity is a truth that is immediately evident and therefore capable of exoteric or dogmatic formulation, for this idea, in its simplest expression, is one that is accessible to every man whose mind is sound; on the other hand, the Trinity, inasmuch as it corresponds to a more differentiated point of view and represents a particular development of the Doctrine of Unity among others that are equally possible, is not strictly speaking capable of exoteric formulation, for the simple reason that a differentiated or derived metaphysical conception is not accessible to everyone. Moreover, the Trinity necessarily corresponds to a more relative point of view than that of Unity, in the same way that "Redemption" is a reality more relative than "Creation". Any normal man can conceive of the divine Unity to some extent, because this is the most universal and therefore in a certain sense the simplest aspect of Divinity; on the other hand, the Trinity can be understood only by those who are capable of conceiving the Divinity under other more or less relative aspects, that is, by those who are able, through spiritual participation in the divine Intellect, to move as it were in the metaphysical dimension; but that, precisely, is a possibility which is very far from being accessible to everyone, at least in the present state of humanity upon this earth. When Saint Augustine said that the Trinity was incomprehensible, he was necessarily speaking—doubtless in conformity with the tendencies of the Roman world—from the rational point of view of the individual, a point of view which, when applied to transcendent truths, cannot but reveal its own inadequacy. The only thing that is completely incomprehensible, from the standpoint of pure intellectuality, is that which is totally unreal, in other words pure nothingness, which is the same thing as impossibility and which, being nothing, cannot become an object of understanding.

Let it be added that the esoteric nature of the Christian dogmas and sacraments is the underlying cause of the Islamic reaction against Christianity. Because the latter had mixed together the *haqîqah* (esoteric Truth) and the *sharî'ah* (exoteric Law), it carried with it certain dangers of disequilibrium that have in fact manifested themselves during the course of the centuries, indirectly contributing to the terrible subversion represented by the modern world, in conformity with the words of Christ: "Give not that which is holy unto the dogs, neither cast ye your pearls before swine, lest they trample them under their feet, and turn again and rend you."

*   *   *

Since Christianity seems to confuse two domains that should normally remain separate, just as it confuses the two Eucharistic species which respectively represent these domains, it may be asked whether things might have been otherwise and whether this confusion is simply the result of individual errors? Assuredly not, and for the following reasons. The inward and esoteric truth must of necessity sometimes manifest itself in broad daylight, this being by virtue of a definite possibility of spiritual manifestation and without regard to the shortcomings of a particular human environment; in other words, the "confusion" in question[10] is but the negative consequence of something which in itself is positive, namely, the Christic manifestation itself. It is to this manifestation as well as to all other analogous manifestations of the Word, whatever their degree of universality, that the following inspired words relate: "And the light shineth in darkness; and the darkness comprehended it not." It was necessary that Christ, by metaphysical or cosmological definition as it were, should break the shell represented by the Mosaic Law, though without denying it; being himself the living kernel of this Law, he had every right to do so, for he was "more true" than it, and this is one of the meanings of his words, "Before Abraham was, I am." It may also be said that if esoterism does not concern everyone, it is for the reason, analogically speaking, that light penetrates some substances and not others; but on the other hand, if esoterism must manifest itself openly from time to time, as happened in the case of Christ, and at a lesser degree of universality in the case of al-Hallaj, it is, still by analogy, because the sun illuminates everything without distinction. Thus, if the "Light shineth in darkness" in the

10. The most general example of this "confusion", which might also be called a "fluctuation", is the mingling in the Scriptures of the New Testament of the two degrees of inspiration that Hindus denote respectively by the terms *Shruti* and *Smriti*, and Muslims by the terms *nafas ar-Rûh* and *ilqâ ar-Rahmâniyah*: the latter expression, like the word *Smriti*, denotes a derived or secondary inspiration, while the first expression, like the word *Shruti*, refers to Revelation properly so called, that is, to the divine Word in a direct sense. In the Epistles, this mingling even appears explicitly on several occasions; the seventh chapter of the First Epistle to the Corinthians is particularly instructive in this respect.

principial or universal sense we are concerned with here, this is because in so doing it manifests one of its possibilities, and a possibility, by definition, is something that cannot not be, being an aspect of the absolute necessity of the divine Principle.

These considerations must not lead us to overlook a complementary though more contingent aspect of the question. There must also exist on the human side, that is, in the environment in which such a divine manifestation is produced, a sufficient reason for its production; now for the world to which Christ's mission was addressed, this open manifestation of truths that should normally remain hidden—under certain conditions of time and place at least—was the only possible means of bringing about the reorientation of which that world had need. This is sufficient to justify that element in the spiritual radiation of Christ, as we have defined it, which would be abnormal and illegitimate under more ordinary circumstances. This laying bare of the "spirit" hidden in the "letter" could not, however, entirely do away with certain laws that are inherent in all esoterism without changing the nature of the latter entirely: thus, Christ spoke only in parables, "that it might be fulfilled which was spoken by the prophet, saying, I will open my mouth in parables; I will utter things which have been kept secret from the foundation of the world" (Matt. 13:35). Nonetheless, a radiation of this nature, though inevitable in the particular case in question, constitutes "a two-edged sword", if one may use such an expression here. But there is another thing to be considered, namely, that the Christian way is essentially a "way of Grace", being in this respect analogous to the "bhaktic" ways of India and certain ways to be found in Buddhism. In methods like these, by reason of their very nature, the distinction between an outer and an inner aspect is attenuated and sometimes even ignored, in the sense that "Grace", which is initiatic in its kernel or essence, tends to bestow itself in the largest measure possible, which it is enabled to do by virtue of the simplicity and universality of the symbolism and means proper to it. It may also be said that while the difference separating the "way of Merit" from the "way of Knowledge" is of necessity very great, in view of the fact that these two ways refer respectively to meritorious action and intellectual contemplation, the "way of Grace" occupies in a certain sense a position midway between the two; the inward and outward applications go hand in hand in the same radiation of Mercy, while in the sphere of spiritual realization the differences will be of degree rather than of principle; every intelligence and every will is able to participate in one and the same Grace according to the measure of its possibilities, in the same way that the sun illuminates everything without distinction, while acting differently on different substances.

Now apart from the fact that a synthetic mode of radiation such as that just described—with its laying bare of things a normal exoterism must keep under a veil—was the only possible way to give effect to the spiritual reorientation of which the Western world stood in need, it must be added that this mode also possesses a providential aspect in relation to cyclic evolution, in the sense of being included in the divine Plan concerning the final development of the present cycle of humanity. From another point of view one may also recognize, in the disproportion between the purely spiritual quality of the Christic Gift and the overly heterogeneous nature of the environment into which it was received, the mark of an exceptional mode of divine Mercy, which constantly renews itself for the sake of creatures: in order to save one of the "sick" parts of humanity, or rather "a humanity", God consents to be profaned; but on the other hand—and this is a manifestation of His Impersonality, which by definition lies beyond the religious perspective—He makes use of this profanation, since "it must needs be that offences come", in order to bring about the final decay of the present cycle of humanity necessary for the exhausting of all the possibilities included in this cycle, necessary therefore for the equilibrium of the cycle as a whole and the accomplishment of the glorious and universal radiation of God.

The dogmatist point of view is compelled, under penalty of having to admit that the actions of its personal God, the only one it takes into consideration, contradict one another, to define the apparently contradictory acts of the impersonal Divinity—when it cannot deny them purely and simply as it does in the case of the diversity of traditional forms—as "mysterious" and "unfathomable", while naturally attributing these "mysteries" to the Will of the personal God.

*   *   *

The existence of a Christian esoterism, or rather the eminently esoteric character of primitive Christianity, appears not only from New Testament texts, those in which certain of Christ's words possess no exoteric meaning, or from the nature of the Christian rites—to speak only of what is more or less accessible "from without" in the Latin Church—but also from the explicit testimony of ancient authors. Thus in his work on the Holy Spirit, Saint Basil speaks of a "tacit and mystical tradition maintained down to our own times and of a secret instruction that our fathers observed without discussion and which we follow by dwelling in the simplicity of their silence. For they understood how necessary was silence in order to maintain the respect and veneration due to our Holy Mysteries. And in fact it was not proper to make known in writing a doctrine containing things that catechumens are not permitted to contemplate". Again, according to Saint Dionysius the Areopagite, "Salvation is possible only for deified souls, and deification is nothing else but the union and resemblance we strive to have with God. The things that are bestowed uniformly and all at once, so to speak, on the blessed Essences dwelling in Heaven, are transmitted to us as it were in fragments and through the multiplicity of the varied symbols of the divine oracles. For it is on these divine oracles that our hierarchy is founded. And by these words we mean not only what our inspired Masters have left us in the Holy Epistles and in their theological works, but also what they transmitted to their disciples by a kind of spiritual and almost heavenly teaching, initiating them from person to person in a bodily way no doubt, since they spoke, but, I venture to say, in an immaterial way also, since they did not write. But since these truths had to be translated into the usages of the Church, the Apostles expressed them under the veil of symbols and not in their sublime nakedness, for not everyone is holy, and, as the Scriptures say, Knowledge is not for all."[11]

*　*　*

11. We may also quote a contemporary Catholic author, Paul Vulliaud: "We have put forward the view that the process of dogmatic enunciation during the first centuries was one of successive Initiation, or, in a word, that there existed an exoterism and an esoterism in the Christian religion. Historians may not like it, but one finds incontestable traces of the *lex arcani* at the origin of our religion. . . . In order

We have seen that Christianity is a "way of Grace" or a "way of Love" (the *bhakti-mârga* of the Hindus), and this definition calls for some further explanation of a general kind. The most pronounced dif-

to grasp quite clearly the doctrinal teaching of the Christian Revelation it is necessary to admit, as we have already insisted, the twofold nature of the gospel preaching. The rule enjoining that the dogmas should be revealed only to Initiates continued in operation long enough to enable even the blindest and most refractory observers to detect undeniable traces of it. Sozomen, a historian, wrote concerning the Council of Nicaea that he wished to record it in detail, primarily 'in order to leave for posterity a public monument of truth'. He was advised to remain silent concerning 'that which must not be known except by priests and the faithful'. The 'law of the secret' was in consequence perpetuated in certain places even after the universal conciliar promulgation of Dogma. Saint Basil, in his work *On the True and Pious Faith*, relates how he avoided making use of terms such as 'Trinity' and 'consubstantiality', which, as he said, do not occur in the Scriptures, although the things which they denote are to be found there. . . . Tertullian says, opposing Praxeas, that one should not speak in so many words of the Divinity of Jesus Christ and that one should call the Father 'God' and the Son 'Lord'. . . . Do not such locutions, practiced habitually, seem like the signs of a convention, since this reticence of language is found in all the authors of the first centuries and is of canonical application? The primitive discipline of Christianity included an examination at which the 'competent' (those who asked for baptism) were admitted to election. This examination was called the 'scrutiny'. The Sign of the Cross was made on the ears of the catechumen with the word *ephpheta*, for which reason this ceremony came to be called 'the scrutiny of the opening of the ears'. The ears were opened to the 'reception' (*cabâlâh*) or 'tradition' of the divine truths. . . . The Synoptico-Johannine problem . . . cannot be resolved except by recalling the existence of a twofold teaching, exoteric and achromatic, historical and theologico-mystical. . . . There is a parabolic theology. It formed part of that inheritance which Theodoret calls, in the preface to his *Commentary on the Song of Songs*, the 'paternal inheritance', which signifies the transmission of the sense applicable to the interpretation of the Scriptures. . . . Dogma, in its divine part, constituted the revelation reserved to the Initiates, under the 'Discipline of the Secret'. Tentzelius claimed to have traced back the origin of this 'law of the secret' to the end of the second century. . . . Emmanuel Schelstrate, librarian of the Vatican, observed it with good reason in apostolic times. In reality, the esoteric manner of transmitting divine truths and interpreting texts existed among both Jews and Gentiles, as it later existed among Christians. . . . If one obstinately refuses to study the initiatic processes of Revelation, one will never arrive at an intelligent, subjective assimilation of Dogma. The ancient liturgies are not sufficiently put to use, and in the same way Hebrew scholarship is absolutely neglected. . . . The Apostles and the Fathers have preserved in secret and silence the 'Majesty of the Mysteries'; Saint Dionysius the Areopagite has of set purpose cultivated the use of obscure words; as Christ assumed the title 'Son of Man', so he calls baptism 'Initiation to *Theogenesis*'. . . . The discipline of the secret was fully justified. Neither the Prophets nor Christ him-

18

ference between the New Covenant and the Old is that in the latter the divine aspect of Rigor predominated, whereas in the former it is on the contrary the aspect of Mercy which prevails. Now the way

self revealed the divine secrets with such clearness as to make them comprehensible to all" (Paul Vulliaud, *Études d'Ésotérisme catholique*). Lastly we should like to quote, for the sake of documentation and despite the length of the text, an author of the early nineteenth century: "In the beginning Christianity was an initiation comparable to those of the pagans. When speaking of this religion Clement of Alexandria exclaims: 'O truly sacred mysteries! O pure light! Amid the gleam of torches falls the veil which covers God and Heaven. I become holy from the moment I am *initiated*. It is the Lord himself who is the hierophant; He sets His *seal* upon the adept whom he enlightens; and to reward his faith he commends him eternally to His Father. Those are the orgies of my mysteries. *Come and seek admission to them.*' These words might be taken in a merely metaphorical sense, but the facts prove that they must be interpreted literally. The Gospels are full of calculated reticences and of allusions to Christian initiation. Thus one may read: 'He that hath ears, let him hear.' Jesus, when addressing the multitude, always made use of parables. 'Seek,' he said, 'and ye shall find; knock, and it shall be opened unto you.' The meetings were in secret, and people were admitted only under stated conditions. Complete understanding of the doctrine was achieved only after passing through three grades of instruction. The Initiates were consequently divided into three classes. The first class comprised the *hearers*, the second the *catechumens* or the *competent*, and the third the *faithful*. The hearers were novices, who were prepared, by means of certain practices and instructions, for the communication of the dogmas of Christianity. A portion of these dogmas was disclosed to the catechumens who, after the prescribed purifications, received baptism or *initiation to theogenesis* (divine generation), as Saint Dionysius calls it in his *Ecclesiastical Hierarchy*; from that time onward they became *servants of the faith* and had free access to the churches. In the mysteries there was nothing secret or hidden from the faithful; all was accomplished in their presence; they could see all and hear all; they had the right to be present during the whole liturgy; it was enjoined upon them that they should watch attentively lest any profane person or initiate of inferior rank should slip in among them; and the *sign of the cross* served them as a sign of recognition. The mysteries were divided into two parts. The first was called the *mass of the catechumens* because members of that class were allowed to attend it; it included all that is said from the beginning of the divine office up to the recitation of the creed. The second part was called the mass of the faithful. It included the preparation of the *sacrifice*, the sacrifice itself, and the giving of thanks which follows. When this mass was about to begin a deacon cried in a loud voice: *Sancta sanctis; foris canes!* 'The holy things are for the holy; let the dogs go out!' Thereupon they expelled the catechumens and the penitents, the latter being members of the faithful who, having some serious fault on their conscience, had been subjected to the penances prescribed by the Church, and thus were unable to be present at the celebration of the *awful mysteries*, as Saint John Chrysostom calls them. The faithful, once alone, recited the symbol of the faith, in order to ensure that all present had received initiation and so that one might safely hold converse before them of Mercy is in a certain sense easier than the way of Rigor because, while corresponding at the same time to a more profound reality, it also benefits from a special Grace: this is the "justification by Faith", whose "yoke is easy and burden light", and which renders the "yoke of Heaven" of the Mosaic Law unnecessary. Moreover this "justification by Faith" is analogous—and its whole esoteric significance rests on this—to "liberation by Knowledge", both being to a greater or less extent independent of the "Law", that is to say, of works.[12] Faith is in fact nothing else than the "bhaktic" mode of Knowledge and of intellectual certitude, which means that Faith is a passive act of the intelligence, its immediate object being not the truth as such, but a symbol of the truth. This symbol will yield up its secrets in propor-

openly and without enigmas concerning the great mysteries of the religion and especially of the Eucharist. The doctrine and the celebration of this sacrament was guarded as an inviolable secret; and if the doctors referred to it in their sermons or books, they did so only with great reserve, by indirect allusion and enigmatically. When Diocletian ordered the Christians to deliver their sacred books to the magistrates, those among them who obeyed this edict of the emperor from fear of death were driven out of the community of the faithful and were looked upon as traitors and apostates. Saint Augustine gives us some idea of the grief of the Church at seeing the sacred Scriptures handed over to unbelievers. In the eyes of the Church it was regarded as a terrible profanation when a man who had not been initiated entered the temple and witnessed the holy mysteries. Saint John Chrysostom mentions a case of this kind to Pope Innocent I. Some barbarian soldiers had entered the Church of Constantinople on Easter Eve. 'The female catechumens, who had just undressed in order to be baptized, were compelled by fear to flee in a state of nakedness; the barbarians did not allow them time to cover themselves. The barbarians then entered the places where the sacred things are kept and venerated, and some of them, *who had not yet been initiated into our mysteries,* saw all the most sacred things that were there.' In the seventh century, the constant increase in the number of the faithful led to the institution by the Church of the minor orders, among which were numbered the porters, who succeeded the deacons and subdeacons in the duty of guarding the doors of the churches. About the year 700, everyone was admitted to the spectacle of the liturgy; and of all the mystery which in early times surrounded the sacred ceremonial, there remained only the custom of reciting secretly the canon of the mass. Nevertheless even today, in the Greek rite, the officiating priest celebrates the divine office behind a curtain, which is drawn back only at the moment of the elevation; but at this moment those assisting should be prostrated or inclined in such a manner that they cannot see the holy sacrament" (F. T. B. Clavel, *Histoire pittoresque de la Franc-Maçonnerie et des Sociétés secrètes anciennes et modernes*).

12. A distinction analogous to the one that sets in opposition "Faith" and the "Law" is to be found within the initiatic realm itself; to "Faith" correspond here the various spiritual movements founded upon the invocation of a divine Name

tion to the greatness of the Faith, which in its turn will be determined by an attitude of trust or emotional certitude, that is, by an element of *bhakti* or love. Insofar as Faith is a contemplative atti-

(the Hindu *japa*, the Buddhist *buddhânusmriti, nien-fo*, or *nembutsu*, and the Muslim *dhikr*); a particularly characteristic example is provided by Shri Chaitanya, who threw away all his books in order to devote himself exclusively to the "bhaktic" invocation of *Krishna*, an attitude comparable to that of the Christians, who rejected the "Law" and "works" in the name of "Faith" and "Love". Similarly, to cite yet another example, the Japanese Buddhist schools called *Jôdo* and *Jôdo-Shinshû*, whose doctrine, founded on the *sûtra*s of Amitabha, is analogous to certain doctrines of Chinese Buddhism and proceeds, like them, from the "original vow of Amida", reject the meditations and austerities of the other Buddhist schools in order to devote themselves exclusively to the invocation of the sacred Name of *Amida*: here ascetic effort is replaced by simple confidence in the Grace of the Buddha Amida, a Grace which he bestows out of his Compassion on those who invoke him, independently of any "merit" on their part. "The invocation of the holy Name must be accompanied by an absolute sincerity of heart and the most complete faith in the goodness of Amida, whose wish it is that all creatures should be saved. In place of virtues, in place of knowledge, Amida, taking pity on the men of the 'Latter Days', has allowed that there be substituted faith in the redemptive value of his Grace, in order that they may be delivered from the sufferings of the world." "We are all equal by the effect of our common faith and of our confidence in the Grace of Amida Buddha." "Every creature, however great a sinner it may be, is certain of being saved and enfolded in the light of Amida and of obtaining a place in the eternal and imperishable Land of Happiness, if only it believes in the Name of Amida Buddha and, abandoning the present and future cares of the world, takes refuge in the liberating Hands so mercifully stretched out towards all creatures, reciting his Name with an entire sincerity of heart." "We know the Name of *Amida* through the preaching of *Shâkya-Muni*, and we know that included in this Name is the power of Amida's wish to save all creatures. To hear this Name is to hear the voice of salvation saying: 'Have confidence in Me, and I shall surely save you,' words which Amida addresses to us directly. This meaning is contained in the Name *Amida*. Whereas all our other actions are more or less stained with impurity, the repetition of the *Namu-Amida-Bu* is an act devoid of all impurity, for it is not we who recite it but Amida himself who, giving us his own Name, makes us repeat It." "When once belief in our salvation by Amida has been awakened and strengthened, our destiny is fixed: we shall be reborn in the Pure Land and shall become Buddhas. Then, it is said, we shall be entirely enfolded in the Light of Amida, and, living under his loving direction, our life will be filled with joy unspeakable, the gift of the Buddha" (*Les Sectes bouddhiques japonaises*, by E. Steinilber-Oberlin and Kuni Matsuo). "The original vow of Amida is to receive in his Land of Felicity whoever shall pronounce his Name with absolute confidence: happy then are those who pronounce his Name! A man may possess faith, but if he does not pronounce the Name his faith will be of no use to him. Another may pronounce the Name while thinking of that alone, but if his faith is not sufficiently deep, his re-birth will not

tude, its subject is the intelligence; it can therefore be said to constitute a virtual Knowledge; but since its mode is passive, it must compensate for this passivity by a complementary active attitude, that is
to say, by an attitude of the will the substance of which is precisely
trust and fervor, by virtue of which the intelligence will receive spiritual certitudes. Faith is *a priori* a natural disposition of the soul to
admit the supernatural; it is therefore essentially an intuition of the
supernatural brought about by Grace, which is actualized by means
of the attitude of fervent trust.[13] When, through Grace, Faith
becomes whole, it will have been dissolved in Love, which is God;
that is why, from the theological standpoint, the Blessed in Heaven
no longer have Faith, since they behold its object, namely, God, who

take place. But he who believes firmly in re-birth as the goal of *nembutsu* (invocation) and who pronounces the Name, the same will without any doubt be reborn
in the Land of Reward" (*Essays in Zen Buddhism*, Vol. 3, by Daisetz Teitaro Suzuki).
It will not have been difficult to recognize the analogies to which we desired to
draw attention: *Amida* is none other than the divine Word. *Amida-Buddha* can
therefore be translated, in Christian terms, as "God the Son, the Christ", the Name
"Christ Jesus" being equivalent to the Name *Buddha Shâkya-Muni*; the redemptive
Name *Amida* corresponds exactly to the Eucharist and the invocation of that Name
to communion; lastly, the distinction between *jiriki* (individual power, that is, effort
with a view to merit) and *tariki* ("power of the other", that is, grace apart from
merit)—the latter being the way of *Jôdo-Shinshû*—is analogous to the Pauline distinction between the "Law" and "Faith". It may be added that if modern
Christianity is suffering in some measure from a decline of the intellectual element, this is precisely because its original spirituality was of a "bhaktic" nature, and
an exteriorization of *bhakti* leads inevitably to a regression of intellectuality in favor
of sentimentality.

13. The life of the great *bhakta* Shri Ramakrishna provides a very instructive example of the "bhaktic" mode of Knowledge. The saint wished to understand the identity between gold and clay; but instead of starting out from a metaphysical *datum*
which would have enabled him to perceive the vanity of riches, as a *jnânin* would
have done, he kept praying to Kali to cause him to understand this identity by a revelation: "Every morning, for many long months, I held in my hand a piece of
money and a lump of clay and repeated: *Gold is clay, and clay is gold*. But this
thought brought no spiritual work into operation within me; nothing came to
prove to me the truth of such a statement. After I know not how many months of
meditation, I was sitting one morning at dawn on the bank of the river, imploring
our Mother to enlighten me. All of a sudden the whole universe appeared before
my eyes clothed in a sparkling mantle of gold. . . . Then the landscape took on a
duller glow, the color of brown clay, even lovelier than the gold. And while this
vision engraved itself deeply on my soul, I heard a sound like the trumpeting of
more than ten thousand elephants, who clamored in my ear: *Clay and gold are but*

is Love or Beatitude. It should be added that from an initiatic point of view, as expressed for example in the teaching of the Hesychast tradition, this vision can and even should be obtained in this life.

Another aspect of Faith that may be mentioned here is the connection between Faith and miracles, a connection that explains the great importance of miracles not only in the case of Christ, but in Christianity as such. In Christianity, by contrast with Islam, the miracle plays a central and quasi-organic part, and this is not unconnected with the "bhaktic" nature of the Christian way. Miracles would in fact be inexplicable apart from the place that they hold in Faith; possessing no persuasive value in themselves—for otherwise satanic miracles would be a criterion of truth—they nevertheless possess this value to an exceptional degree in association with all the other factors that enter into the Christic Revelation. In other words, if the miracles of Christ, the Apostles, and the saints are precious and venerable, this is solely because they are associated with other criteria which *a priori* permit of their being invested with the value of divine "signs". The essential and primordial function of a miracle is either to awaken the grace of Faith—which assumes a natural disposition to admit the supernatural, whether consciously or not, on the part of the person affected by this grace—or to perfect a Faith already acquired. To define still more exactly the function of the miracle, not only in Christianity but in all religious forms—for none of them disregard miraculous facts—it may be said that a miracle, apart from its symbolical character, which links it with the object of Faith itself, is able to evoke an intuition that becomes an element of certitude in the soul of the believer. Lastly, if miracles can awaken Faith, Faith can in turn bring about miracles, for "Faith can move mountains". This reciprocal relationship also shows that these two things are connected cosmologically and that there is

one thing for you. My prayers were answered, and I threw far away into the Ganges the piece of gold and the lump of clay." In the same connection, we may quote the following reflections of an Orthodox theologian: "A dogma that expresses a revealed truth, which appears to us an unfathomable mystery, must be lived by us by means of a process whereby, instead of assimilating the mystery to our own mode of understanding, we must on the contrary watch for a profound change, an inward transformation of our spirit, so as to make us fit for the mystical experience" (Vladimir Lossky, *Essai sur la théologie mystique de l'Église d'Orient*).

nothing arbitrary in this connection, for the miracle establishes an immediate contact between the divine Omnipotence and the world, while Faith establishes in its turn an analogous but passive contact between the microcosm and God; mere ratiocination, that is, the discursive operation of the mental faculty, is as far removed from Faith as are natural laws from miracles, while intellectual knowledge will see the miraculous in the natural and vice versa.

As for Charity, which is the most important of the three theological virtues, it possesses two aspects, one passive and the other active. Spiritual Love is a passive participation in God, who is infinite Love; but love is on the contrary active in relation to created things. Love of one's neighbor, insofar as it is a necessary expression of the Love of God, is an indispensable complement to Faith. These two modes of Charity are affirmed by the Gospel teaching regarding the Supreme Law, the first mode implying consciousness of the fact that God alone is Beatitude and Reality, and the second consciousness of the fact that the ego is only illusory, the "me" of others being identified in reality with "myself";[14] if I must love my "neighbor" because he is "me", this implies that I must love myself *a priori*, not being other than my "neighbor"; and if I must love myself, whether in "myself" or in my "neighbor", it is because God loves me and I ought to love what He loves; and if He loves me it is because He loves His creation, or in other words, because Existence itself is Love and Love is as it were the perfume of the Creator inherent in every creature. In the same way that the Love of God, or the Charity that has as its object the divine Perfections and not our own well-being, is Knowledge of the one and only divine Reality, in which the apparent reality of the created is dissolved—a knowledge that implies the identification of the soul with its uncreated Essence,[15] which is yet another aspect of the symbolism of Love—so the love of one's neighbor is basically nothing else than knowledge of the indifferentiation before God of all that is created. Before

14. This realization of the "not-I" explains the important part played in Christian spirituality by humility; a similar part is played in Islamic spirituality by "poverty" (*faqr*) and in Hindu spirituality by "childlikeness" (*bâlya*); the symbolism of childhood in the teaching of Christ will be recalled here.

15. "We are entirely transformed into God," says Meister Eckhart, "and changed into Him. Just as, in the sacrament, the bread is changed into the body of Christ,

passing from the created to the Creator, or from manifestation to the Principle, it is in fact necessary to have realized the indifferentiation, or let us say the "nothingness", of all that is manifested. It is toward this that the ethic of Christ is directed, not only by the indistinction that it establishes between the "me" and the "not me", but also, in the second place, by its indifference with regard to individual justification and social equilibrium. Christianity is thus situated outside the "actions and reactions" of the human order; by primary definition, therefore, it is not exoteric. Christian charity neither has nor can have any interest in "well-being" for its own sake, because true Christianity, like every orthodox religion, considers that the only true happiness human society can enjoy is its spiritual well-being, its flower being the presence of the saint, the goal of every normal civilization; for "the multitude of the wise is the welfare of the world" (Wisd. of Sol. 6:24). One of the truths overlooked by moralists is that when a work of charity is accomplished through love of God, or in virtue of the knowledge that "I" am the "neighbor" and that the "neighbor" is "myself"—a knowledge that implies this love—the work in question has for the neighbor not only the value of an outward benefit, but also that of a benediction. On the other hand, when charity is exercised neither from love of God nor by virtue of the aforesaid knowledge, but solely with a view to human "well-being" considered as an end in itself, the benediction inherent in true charity does not accompany the apparent benefaction, either for the giver or for the receiver.

*　　*　　*

As for the monastic orders their presence can be explained only by the existence, in the Western as well as the Eastern Church, of an initiatic tradition going back—as Saint Benedict and the Hesychasts alike testify—to the Desert Fathers and so to the Apostles and to Christ. The fact that the cenobitism of the Latin Church can be traced back to the same origins as that of the Greek Church—the

so am I changed into Him, in such wise that He makes me one with His Being and not simply like to it; by the living God, it is true that there is no longer any distinction."

latter, however, consisting of a single community and not different orders—clearly proves that the first is esoteric in essence like the second; moreover, the eremitical life is considered by both to mark the summit of spiritual perfection—Saint Benedict said so expressly in his Rule—and it may therefore be concluded that the disappearance of the hermits marks the decline of the Christic flowering. Monastic life, far from constituting a self-sufficient way, is described in the Rule of Saint Benedict as a "commencement of religious life", while for "him who hastens his steps towards the perfection of monastic life, there are the teachings of the Holy Fathers, the carrying out of which leads man to the supreme end of religion";[16] now these teachings contain in a doctrinal form the very essence of Hesychasm.

The organ of the spirit, or the principal center of spiritual life, is the heart; here again the Hesychast doctrine is in perfect accord with the teaching of every other initiatic tradition. But what is more important from the standpoint of spiritual realization is the teaching of Hesychasm on the means of perfecting the natural participation of the human microcosm in the divine Metacosm, that is, the transmutation of this participation into supernatural participation and finally into union and identity: this means consists in the "inward prayer" or "Prayer of Jesus". This "prayer" surpasses in principle all the virtues in excellence, for it is a divine act in us and for that reason the best of all possible acts. It is only by means of this prayer that the creature can be really united with his Creator; the goal of this prayer is consequently the supreme spiritual state, in which man transcends everything pertaining to the creature and,

---

16. We would like to quote the remainder of this passage, which is taken from the last chapter of the book, entitled "That the Practice of Justice is Not Wholly Contained in This Rule": "What page is there of the Old or New Testament, what divinely authorized word therein, that is not a sure rule for the conduct of man? Again, what book of the holy catholic Fathers does not resolutely teach us the right road to attain our Creator? Furthermore, what are the Discourses of the Fathers, their Institutions and their lives (those of the Desert Fathers), and what is the Rule of our holy Father Basil, if not a pattern for monks who live and obey as they ought, and authentic charters of the virtues? For us who are lax, who lead blameful lives and are full of negligence, herein is indeed cause to blush with confusion. Whoever then thou mayest be who pressest forward toward the heavenly homeland, accomplish first, with the help of Christ, this poor outline of a rule that we have traced; then at last, with the protection of God, wilt thou reach those sublimer heights of doctrine and virtue the memory of which we have just evoked."

being directly united with the Divinity, is enlightened by the divine Light. This supreme state is "holy silence", symbolized by the black color given to certain Virgins.[17]

To those who consider "spiritual prayer" a simple and even superfluous practice, the Palamite doctrine replies that this prayer represents on the contrary the most exacting way possible, but that in return it leads to the highest pinnacle of perfection, on condition—and this is essential and reduces to nothing the shallow suspicions of moralists—that the activity of prayer is in harmony with all the rest of one's human activities. In other words, the virtues—or conformity to the divine Law—constitute the essential condition without which spiritual prayer would be ineffective; we are therefore a long way from the naïve illusion of those who imagine that it is possible to attain God by means of merely mechanical practices, without any other commitment or obligation. "Virtue"—so the Palamite teaching maintains—"disposes us for union with God, but Grace accomplishes this inexpressible union." If the virtues are able in this way to play the part of modes of knowledge, it is because they retrace by analogy "divine attitudes"; there is in fact no virtue which does not derive from a divine Prototype, and therein lies their deepest meaning: "to be" is "to know".

Lastly, we must emphasize the fundamental and truly universal significance of the invocation of the divine Name. This Name, in the Christian form—as in the Buddhist form and in certain initiatic branches of the Hindu tradition—is a name of the manifested Word,[18] in this case the Name of "Jesus", which, like every revealed divine Name when ritually pronounced, is mysteriously identified with the Divinity. It is in the divine Name that there takes place the mysterious meeting of the created and the Uncreated, the contingent and the Absolute, the finite and the Infinite. The divine Name is thus a manifestation of the Supreme Principle, or to speak still

---

17. This "silence" is the exact equivalent of the Hindu and Buddhist *nirvâna* and the Sufic *fanâ*; the "poverty" (*faqr*) in which "union" (*tawhîd*) is achieved refers to the same symbolism. Regarding this real union—or this re-integration of the finite in the Infinite—we may also mention the title of a book by Saint Gregory Palamas: *Witnesses of the Saints: Showing that Those who Participate in Divine Grace Become, Conformably with Grace Itself, without Origin and Infinite.* We may also recall in this connection the following adage of Muslim esoterism: "The Sufi is not created."

18. We are thinking here of the invocation of Amida Buddha and of the formula *Om mani padme hum,* and as regards Hinduism, of the invocation of Rama and Krishna.

more plainly, it is the Supreme Principle manifesting itself; it is not therefore in the first place a manifestation, but the Principle itself.[19] "The sun shall be turned into darkness, and the moon into blood, before the great and the terrible day of the Lord come," says the prophet Joel, but "whosoever shall call on the name of the Lord shall be delivered,"[20] and we may also recall the beginning of the first Epistle to the Corinthians, addressed to "all that in every place call upon the name of Jesus Christ our Lord", and the injunction contained in the first Epistle to the Thessalonians to "unceasing prayer", on which Saint John Damascene comments as follows: "We must learn to invoke God's Name more often than we breathe, at all times and everywhere and during all our labors. The Apostle says: 'Pray without ceasing,' which is to say that we must remember God at all times, wherever we are and whatever we are doing."[21] It is not without reason therefore that the Hesychasts consider the invocation of the Name of Jesus as having been bequeathed by Jesus to the Apostles: "It is thus"—according to the *Century* of the Monks Kallistos and Ignatios—"that our merciful and beloved Lord Jesus Christ, at the time when he came to his Passion freely accepted for us, and also at the time when, after his Resurrection, he visibly showed himself to the Apostles, and even at the moment when he

---

19. Similarly, according to the Christian perspective, Christ is not in the first place man, but God.

20. The Psalms contain a number of references to the invocation of the Name of God: "I cried unto the Lord with my voice, and He heard me out of His holy hill." "Then called I upon the Name of the Lord; O Lord, I beseech Thee, deliver my soul." "The Lord is nigh unto all them that call upon Him, to all that call upon Him in truth." Two passages also contain a reference to the Eucharistic mode of invocation: "Open thy mouth wide, and I will fill it." "Who satisfieth thy mouth with good things, so that thy youth is renewed like the eagle's." So also Isaiah: "Fear not: for I have redeemed thee, I have called thee by thy name; thou art mine." "Seek ye the Lord while He may be found, call ye upon Him while He is near." And so Solomon in the Book of Wisdom: "I called upon God, and the spirit of wisdom came to me."

21. In this commentary by Saint John Damascene, the words "invoke" and "remember" are used to describe or illustrate the same idea; it will be recalled that the Arabic word *dhikr* signifies both "invocation" and "remembrance"; in Buddhism also "to think of Buddha" and "to invoke *Buddha*" are expressed by one and the same word (*buddhânusmriti*; the Chinese *nien-fo* and the Japanese *nembutsu*). On the other hand, it is worth noting that the Hesychasts and the Dervishes use the same word to describe invocation: the recitation of the "prayer of Jesus" is called by the

was about to re-ascend to the Father . . . bequeathed these three things to his disciples (the invocation of his Name, Peace, and Love, which respectively correspond to faith, hope, and charity). . . . The beginning of all activity of the divine Love is the confident invocation of the saving Name of our Lord Jesus Christ, as he himself said (John 15:5): 'Without me ye can do nothing.' By the confident invocation of the Name of our Lord Jesus Christ, we steadfastly hope to obtain his Mercy and the true Life hidden in him. It is like unto another divine Wellspring, which is never exhausted (John 4:14) and which yields up these gifts when the Name of our Lord Jesus Christ is invoked, without imperfection, in the heart." We may also quote the following passage from an Epistle (*Epistula ad Monachos*) of Saint John Chrysostom: "I have heard the Fathers say: Who is this monk who forsakes and belittles the rule? He should, when eating and drinking, when seated or serving others, when walking or indeed when doing anything whatsoever, invoke unceasingly: 'Lord Jesus Christ, Son of God, have mercy on me.'[22]

Hesychasts "work", while the Dervishes name every form of invocation "occupation" or "business" (*shughl*).

22. This formula is often contracted to the Name of Jesus alone, particularly by those who are more advanced in the way. "The most important means in the life of prayer is the *Name of God*, invoked in prayer. Ascetics and all who lead a life of prayer, from the anchorites of the Egyptian desert to the Hesychasts of Mount Athos . . . insist above all on the importance of the Name of God. Apart from the Offices there exists for all the Orthodox a rule of prayer, composed of psalms and different orisons; for the monks it is much more considerable. But the most important thing in prayer, the thing that constitutes its very heart, is what is named the Prayer of Jesus: 'Lord Jesus Christ, Son of God, have mercy on me, a sinner.' The repetition of this prayer hundreds of times, and even indefinitely, is the essential element of every monastic rule of prayer; it can, if necessary, replace the Offices and all the other prayers, since its value is universal. The power of the prayer does not reside in its content, which is simple and clear (it is the prayer of the tax-collector), but in the sweet Name of Jesus. The ascetics bear witness that this Name contains the force of the presence of God. Not only is God invoked by this Name; He is already present in the invocation. This can certainly be said of every Name of God; but it is true above all of the divine and human Name of Jesus, which is the proper Name of God and of man. In short, the Name of Jesus present in the human heart communicates to it the force of the deification accorded to us by the Redeemer" (S. Bulgakov, *L'Orthodoxie*). "The Name of Jesus", says Saint Bernard, "is not only light; it is also nourishment. All food is too dry to be assimilated by the soul if it is not first flavored by this condiment; it is too insipid unless this salt relieves its tastelessness. I have no taste for thy writings if I cannot read this Name

Persevere unceasingly in the Name of our Lord Jesus that thy heart may drink the Lord and the Lord may drink thy heart, to the end that in this manner the two may become One."

there; no taste for thy discourse if I do not hear it resounding therein. It is honey for my mouth, melody for my ears, joy for my heart, but it is also a medicine. Does any one among you feel overcome with sadness? Let him then taste Jesus in his mouth and heart, and behold how before the light of his Name all clouds vanish and the sky again becomes serene. Has one among you allowed himself to be led into a fault, and is he experiencing the temptation of despair? Let him invoke the Name of Life, and Life will restore him" (*Sermon 15 on the Song of Songs*).

3

"Our Father Who Art in Heaven"

In the monotheistic Semitic world, Christ was the only one to call God "my Father". Doubtless he was not the first to use this symbolism of paternity, examples of which we find in fact in the Torah: "I (*Yahweh*) will be his father, and he shall be my son" (2 Sam. 7:14); "like as a father pitieth his children, so the Lord pitieth them that fear Him" (Ps. 103:13); "thou, O Lord, art our father" (Isa. 63:16); "but now, O Lord, thou art our father; we are the clay, and thou our potter; and we all are the work of thy hand" (Isa. 64:8); "for I (*Yahve*) am a father to Israel, and Ephraim is my firstborn" (Jer. 31:9); "have we not all one father? hath not one God created us?" (Mal. 2:10).

All this according to the Torah;[1] Christ, however, made of this symbolism a central idea—the very Name of God, so to speak. In calling God "Father", Christ attests to the "Sovereign Good": he refers on the one hand to the essentiality of divine Goodness,[2] and on the other hand to the reciprocity between the Creator and the creature "made in His image"; this means that Christ grants priority, not to divine Power and the aspect of Lordship, but to divine Love and the aspect of Paternity, precisely; as a result, man is presented, not as a simple slave, but as a child who, in relation to his Father, has rights which are granted him by that Father, and which stem from his being a "valid interlocutor" and "image of God".

In Christ's language, there is clearly a distinction to be made between "our Father" and "my Father": the relation of filiation is

---

1. The expression "Our Father" is also to be found in the Talmud and in Jewish liturgy; it is used ten times a year in the liturgy and in connection with the expression "Our King".

2. "Verily, my Mercy precedeth my Wrath," according to a *hadîth*; this indicates that Goodness pertains to the Essence. And similarly, according to the Koran: "Your Lord hath prescribed for Himself Mercy" (*Sûrah* "Cattle" [6]:54).

principial and potential in the former case, and fully actual and effective in the second. The ordinary man is a "child of God" in the respect we have just indicated, that is, by the simple fact that he is a man and hence an "interlocutor"; but Christ is "child" or "son of God" in still another respect, which is superimposed onto the preceding; it is, geometrically speaking, what the vertical dimension is to the horizontal, or what the sphere is to the circle: he is "child" or "son" by his person and not by the simple fact that he belongs to the human species, nor by virtue of an initiation or a spiritual orientation capable of actualizing a potentiality of *theosis*. For the *Avatâra* is a cosmic phenomenon which implies by definition every spiritual perfection—as well as every physical perfection—but which no realization on the part of an ordinary man could produce; the *yogin*, the *sannyâsin*, the *jnânin* can "realize" *Brahma*, but he will never be Rama or Krishna.

At this point we would like to digress and say the following: on the one hand, the Gospel says of the Holy Virgin that she is "full of grace" and that "the Lord is with thee", and that "henceforth all generations shall call me blessed";[3] on the other hand, Christ inherited from the Virgin his entire human nature, from the psychic as well as the physical point of view, so that his sacramental body and blood are fundamentally those of the Virgin. Now a person who possesses such prerogatives—to the point of being called "Mother of God"—necessarily has an "avataric" character, expressed theologically by the idea of the "Immaculate Conception": thus the cult of Mary is not merely a matter of tradition; it clearly results from Scripture.[4]

Theology is right to acknowledge that in Jesus there is a human nature and a divine nature and that in a certain respect both natures are united in a single person, that of Christ. The distinction, however, between a "nature"—human or divine—having its own will

3. The Koran says of Mary: "Verily, God hath chosen thee and made thee pure, and hath preferred thee above all the women of the world" (*Sûrah* "The Family of Imran" [3]:42).

4. Protestantism ignores this cult because its aim is to concentrate solely on the Christ-Savior, and because it minimizes the import of the passages we have quoted by referring to other passages apparently less favorable to Mary. The *upâya*, the "saving means", does not always conform to historical facts—very far from it—as is amply proven by religious divergences.

while not being a "person" and a unique and indivisible "person" having two incommensurable and in principle divergent wills: this distinction greatly risks being reduced in the final analysis to a question of terminology. Be that as it may, we have no difficulty in acknowledging that the pitfalls implied in the definition of the God-Man surpass the resources of a thought which intends to avoid every misunderstanding at every level; and the same observation applies to certain implicit "clauses"—no doubt unusable dogmatically—in Trinitarian theology.

*   *   *

Unquestionably, the Christian notion of "child of God" indicates an element of esoterism, which asserts itself, not in relation to all exoterism, since the notion also comprises an exoteric application, but—from the Christian point of view—in relation to the "Old Law", which seems to be formalistic and to some extent social rather than intrinsically moral; this is to say that the "New Law" represents in its own fashion the perspective of "inwardness", which transcends the perspective of formal prescriptions and observances, while imposing on man an esoterically practicable but socially unrealistic *ascesis*. Aside from the natural prerogatives of human deiformity, it could be said that it is by the spiritual attitude of inwardness or essentiality that the "servant" of the "Lord" becomes effectively the "child" of the "Father", which—as a human being—he was potentially or virtually.

Let us specify the following points: the alimentary prescriptions or the prohibitions concerning the Sabbath are plainly outward rules; by their very nature and quantity they constitute an "objective formalism"—willed by God in view of certain temperaments—but not necessarily a "subjective formalism", the latter being more or less a reduction of the religion to these observances. Be that as it may, the supreme Commandment—in Israel and everywhere else— is the love of God; this love may require us always to be aware of the profound and underlying reasons for given prescriptions, just as it may require only zeal in obedience to the Law; but neither our comprehension nor our zeal confers a quality of inwardness on the prescriptions themselves, which by their nature are external. Thus esoterism, in the Hindu world above all, is fully conscious of the relative and conditional character of the rules of conduct; to deny this character is precisely "subjective formalism".[5]

The Jew is child of God on account of the Election of Israel; the Christian is such on account of the Redemption. The Jew feels he is a child of God in relation to the "pagans", whereas the Christian feels that way even with regard to the Jews, whose perspective seems to him "exterior", or even "carnal". As for Islam, it has neither the notion of "Father" nor therefore that of "child", but it does have that of "Friend" (*Walî*), which is applied both to God and to man: to God, who "lends assistance", and to the saints, who "help" God; but Islam does not for all that give up the notion of "slave", since for Islam this notion is equivalent to that of "creature". Besides, the primacy accorded the idea of "Lord"—and the complementary idea of "servant"—also has its merits, by the nature of things; its result is a profound resignation to the "Will of God", a resignation which refuses to ask God why He permits a given trial or does not grant a given favor, and which wisely combines a need for explanation with a sense of proportions.[6]

* * *

"Our Father who art in Heaven": the specification "in Heaven" indicates transcendence in relation to the earthly state, considered first from the objective and macrocosmic point of view and then from the subjective and microcosmic standpoint. Indeed the "earth" or "world" can be our individual and more or less sensorial soul as well as the ambience in which we live and which determines us, just as "Heaven" can be our spiritual virtualities as well as the paradisal worlds; for "the kingdom of God is within you".

5. A practice can be termed "formalistic", not because it is based upon a form—otherwise every spiritual practice would pertain to formalism—but because its immediate object belongs to the outward, hence *a fortiori* formal, order.

6. If the human complement of the "Lord" (*Rabb*) is logically the "servant" or "slave" (*'abd*), the complement of Allah as such—and He presents Himself as *a priori* the "Clement" (*Rahmân*) and the "Merciful" (*Rahîm*)—will be man as "vicar on earth" (*khalîfah fi'l-'ard*).

"Hallowed be Thy Name": the verb "hallow" is almost synonymous with "worship" and consequently with "pray" or "invoke". To worship God is to be conscious of His transcendence, hence of His absolute primacy on the human plane; and to have this awareness is to think of Him always, in conformity with the parable of the unjust judge as well as with the injunction of the Epistle.[7] And this is crucial: "But thou, when thou prayest, enter into thy closet, and when thou hast shut thy door, pray to thy Father, which is in secret"; according to the Hesychasts, this chamber is the heart, whose door, open to the world, must be closed. This is quite characteristic of the Christian message, which is a message of contemplative inwardness and sacrificial love precisely, inwardness being the consequence— esoteric in varying degrees—of the perspective of love.[8]

"Thy kingdom come": if the hallowing of the divine Name is connected with man's prayer, the coming of the divine Kingdom is linked to God's response; and this we may paraphrase as follows: "Let Thy Name be uttered in a holy manner, that Thy Grace may descend upon us." It could also be said that the first of the two sayings refers to transcendence and the second to immanence: for as the "kingdom of God" is "within you", our first concern ought to be to await it where it is most immediately accessible to us; for not only is it impossible for us to realize it *hic et nunc* in the outward world, but every valid and holy work must begin within ourselves, independently of the outward result. And it is not by chance that the saying concerning the Kingdom comes after that about the hallowing of the Name: the unitive dimension in fact presupposes the devotional dimension; the mystery of transcendence must precede and introduce that of immanence.

* * *

7. "And shall God not avenge his own elect, which cry day and night unto Him, though he bear long with them? I tell you He will avenge them speedily" (Luke 18:7). "Pray without ceasing [*sine intermissione*]" (1 Thess. 5:17).

8. The injunction "use not vain repetitions" further reinforces this analogy; the "vain" or "many" repetitions indicate outwardness, which can be interpreted at different levels.

This confronting of the relationships of transcendence and immanence leads us to specify a metaphysically crucial point. God is one, and as a result the Transcendent comprises a dimension of immanence just as the Immanent comprises a dimension of transcendence: for on the one hand, the divine Presence in the depths of the sanctified heart, or in the pure Intellect, does not lose its transcendence by the fact of its immanence, since the ego is not identified *tale quale* with the Self; and on the other hand, the transcendence of the creative Principle does not preclude the objective and "existentiating" immanence of the same Principle in creation. In other words: to speak of transcendence is to speak first of all about the macrocosm, and to speak of immanence is to speak *a priori* about the microcosm; however, each pole always includes the other, as is shown graphically by the Far Eastern symbol of the *yin-yang*, whose testimony we never tire of invoking in our doctrinal expositions.

On the one hand, there is no transcendence without immanence; for the very perception of transcendence implies immanence in the sense that the knowing subject is situated at the level of the object known: one can know divine truth only "by the Holy Spirit", which is immanent in the Intellect;[9] otherwise man would not be "made in the image of God". On the other hand, there is no immanence without transcendence, since the ontological, and in principle mystical, continuity between the immanent Divinity and the individual consciousness in no way excludes the discontinuity between these two poles, which in truth are incommensurable. We may also express ourselves by specifying that union goes from God to man, but not from man to God. Geometrically speaking, what relates to man is the perspective of the concentric circles, which symbolize the modes in the hierarchical arrangement of conformation to the Center; by contrast, what relates to God is the image of the radii, which project the Center in the direction of our emptiness, reintegrating us by that very fact into its Plenitude.

9. As Meister Eckhart noted, who was not afraid of words, to say the least.

* * *

But let us return, after this digression, to the idea of the divine "Father". This term, as we have said, has a meaning that differs according to whether it relates to man as such or to Christ alone; but it also has a meaning that differs according to whether it is conceived "vertically" or "horizontally", that is, according to whether it relates to "Beyond-Being" or to Being. In the first case, "Father" is the pure Absolute, and nothing can be associated with Him; the two other "Persons" already pertain to Relativity, of which they represent the summit; far from pertaining to the manifested world, they constitute, together with the Absolute pure and simple, what we may call the "divine Order". In the second case—which alone has been retained by dogmatic theology—the "Father" is situated at the same level of ontological reality as the other two *hypostases*, whence the Trinity "Power", "Wisdom", "Love", if one may express it thus.[10] While it is true that this ontological and "horizontal" Trinity does not coincide with the "pure Absolute", it is nonetheless absolute from the point of view of creatures; thus man, when he prays, should not concern himself with the "degrees of reality" comprised in the principial Order, on pain of speaking into the void.

It may be objected that religion has no reason for including the idea of "Beyond-Being", since its aim is the salvation of souls and not metaphysical knowledge, and indeed, as far as its saving function is concerned, religion can do without the idea in question; but in another respect, that of its claim to absoluteness, it must include it, lest it mislead—or exclude—certain souls or certain intelligences. One is therefore right in thinking that the word "Father" expresses all that it is capable of expressing, at all levels of doctrine and degrees of understanding. What explains certain impasses of dogmatic theology and its recourse to the unsatisfactory notion of mystery is precisely a plurality of unequal perspectives, this plurality being inevitable since religion must contain everything, without thereby having to renounce its specific function.

---

10. In Vedantic terms: the "vertical" Trinity corresponds to *Brahma, Îshvara, Buddhi*; and the "horizontal" Trinity—which is to be found in each of these terms—corresponds to *Sat, Chit, Ânanda*.

4

Some Observations

In the perspective of *gnosis*, Christ, "Light of the world", is the universal Intellect, as the Word is the "Wisdom of the Father". Christ is the Intellect of microcosms as well as that of the macrocosm; he is thus the Intellect in us[1] as well as the Intellect in the Universe and *a fortiori* in God; in this sense, it can be said that there is no truth or wisdom that does not come from Christ, and this is obviously independent of all consideration of time and place.[2] Just as "the light shineth in darkness; and the darkness comprehended it not", so too the Intellect shines in the darkness of passions and illusions. The relationship of the Son to the Father is analogous to the relationship of pure Love to Being or of the Intellect to the "Self", and that is why we are, in the Intellect or in sanctifying Grace, "brothers" of Christ.

But Christ is likewise prefigured in the whole creation; this also has an aspect of incarnation, and another of crucifixion. On a lesser scale, humanity, and with it the human individual, is an image of Christ and comprises both aspects: man is "incarnation" by his Intellect and his freedom, and "crucifixion" by his miseries.

---

1. The Word "was the true Light, which lighteth every man" (John 1:9).

2. "Now faith," says Saint Paul, "is the substance of things hoped for, the evidence of things not seen. . . . Through faith we understand that the worlds were framed by the word of God, so that things which are seen were not made of things which do appear" (Hebrews 11:1, 3); this proves that faith is, to say the least, not contrary to *gnosis*; doubtless not all faith is metaphysical knowledge, but all metaphysical knowledge, being an "evidence of things not seen", is of the domain of faith. *Gnosis* is the perfection of faith in the sense that it combines this knowledge with the corresponding realization; it is wisdom and sanctity: sanctifying wisdom and sapiential sanctity. The most external expression of the element "realization" is works, which on the one hand prove and on the other give life to faith, and without which it is "dead, being alone" (James 2:17).

*   *   *

From the doctrinal point of view, Christian *gnosis* is nothing else than Trinitarian metaphysics,[3] with its microcosmic application: our pure existence corresponds to the Father, our pure intelligence to the Son, and our pure will to the Holy Spirit. The vertical line of the cross denotes the relationship of the Father to the Son, while the horizontal line symbolizes the Holy Spirit; the latter "proceeds from the Father and is delegated by the Son", which signifies that the Spirit, which is at once Beatitude and Will, proceeds from the Father, then also from the Son (*Filioque*) insofar as he represents the Father, but not insofar as he is distinct from Him. The Father is Beyond-Being, the Son is Being, and the Spirit is Beatitude and Manifestation; when the perspective is limited to ontology, the Father is Being as such, and the Son the "Consciousness" of Being. To say that the Spirit is Beatitude and Manifestation—whatever the level of the perspective, ontological or supra-ontological—means that It is at once the "inner life" and the "creative projection" of Divinity: It is thus an "expansion" or "spiration" *in divinis* at the same time as a "springing forth" *ex divinis*; It is, on the one hand, "internal" or "contemplative" Beatitude, and on the other hand, "external" or "active" Beatitude. That is why in the sign of the cross the Holy Spirit "occupies" the whole of the horizontal line; it could even be said that, in the making of this sign, the words *Spiritus Sanctus* designate the Spirit *in divinis,* and the word *Amen* the Spirit "in creation", if such an expression can be allowed.

The Spirit "as creation" is none other than the Virgin in three aspects, macrocosmic, microcosmic, and historical: first, It is Universal Substance, then It is the soul in a state of sanctifying grace, and finally It is the human manifestation of these aspects, the Virgin Mary. In this sense, it can be said that the word *Amen* is a name of the Virgin, perfect creature—or perfect creation—and that, if the vertical line of the sign of the cross denotes the relationship of the Father and the Son, the horizontal line will denote the relationship

---

3. Analogously, the metaphysics of Islam is unitary in the sense that it proceeds by principial reductions to Unity, while the metaphysics of Judaism is at once unitary and denary (Decalogue, *Sephiroth*).

of Husband and Spouse. The whole soul of the Virgin is one great *Amen*; there is nothing in it which is not an acquiescence in the Will of God.

*   *   *

Christian art comprises essentially three images: the Virgin and Child, the Crucifixion, and the Holy Visage: the first image relates to the Incarnation, the second to the Redemption, and the third to the Divinity of Christ. Man recapitulates these three symbols or mysteries respectively by purity, which is the vehicle of "Christ in us", by death to the world, and by sanctity or wisdom.

Strictly speaking, art forms part of the liturgy—in the broadest sense—for like liturgy it is "public work" (λειτουργία);[4] hence, it cannot be left to the arbitrary disposition of men. Art, like the liturgy properly so called, constitutes the terrestrial "garment" of God; it both envelops and unveils the divine Presence on earth.[5]

*   *   *

The Church of Peter is visible, and continuous like water; that of John—instituted on Calvary and confirmed at the sea of Tiberias—is invisible, and discontinuous like fire. John became "brother" of

---

4. According to Saint Augustine, the liturgy is essentially simple, so that this simplicity is almost a criterion of authenticity; if it were otherwise, says the Bishop of Hippo, the liturgy would be lower than the Jewish Law, which, after all, was given by God and not by the liturgists; further, he stresses the fact that Christian feasts are few in number.

5. We have had occasion at various times to underline the sacred, hence immutable, character of religious art: it is not a purely human thing, and above all it does not consist in seeking impossible mysteries in non-existent profundities, as is the intention of modern art, which, instead of adapting "our times" to the truth, aims at adapting the truth to "our times". In relation to artistic or artisanal—therefore also "liturgical"—expression, the terms "Christian" and "medieval" are in fact synonymous; to repudiate Christian art on the pretext that Christianity stands above "cultures" is a failure to see the context and the value of this art; it is to repudiate elements of truth and also, thereby, of sanctity.

41

Christ and "son" of the Virgin, and he is moreover the Prophet of the Apocalypse; Peter is charged to "feed my sheep", but his Church seems to have inherited also his denials, whence the Renaissance and its direct and indirect consequences; nevertheless, "the gates of hell shall not prevail against it". John "tarries till I come", and this mystery remains closed to Peter;[6] one may see here a prefiguration of the schism between Rome and Byzantium. "Feed my sheep": there is nothing in these words that excludes the interpretation put upon them by the Greeks, namely, that the Bishop of Rome is *primus inter pares* and not *pontifex maximus*.

*   *   *

The Holy Spirit is given by Confirmation, through the medium of fire, for oil is none other than a form of liquid fire, as is wine; the difference between Baptism and Confirmation could be defined by saying that the first has a negative—or "negatively positive"—function, since it "takes away" the state of the fall, while the second sacrament has a purely positive function in the sense that it "gives" a light and a power that are divine.[7]

This transmission acquires a new "dimension" and receives its full efficacy through the vows that correspond to the "Evangelical counsels"; these vows—true initiatic leaven—denote at the same time a death and a second birth, and they are in fact accompanied by symbolic funeral rites; the consecration of a monk is a sort of bur-

---

6. It is significant that the Celtic Church, that mysterious springtime world which appears like a sort of last prolongation of the golden age, held itself to be attached to Saint John.

7. According to Tertullian, "The flesh is anointed that the soul may be sanctified; the flesh is signed that the soul may be fortified; the flesh is placed in shadow by the laying on of hands that the soul may be illumined by the Holy Spirit." As for Baptism, the same author says that "the flesh is washed that the soul may be purified". According to Saint Dionysius, Baptism, Eucharist, and Confirmation refer respectively to the ways of "purification", "illumination", and "perfection"; according to others, it is Baptism which is called an "illumination"; this clearly does not contradict the foregoing perspective, since all initiation "illumines" by definition: the taking away of "original sin" opens the way to a "light" pre-existing in Edenic man.

ial.[8] By poverty, man severs himself from the world; by chastity he severs himself from society; and by obedience, he severs himself from himself.[9]

*   *   *

The whole of Christianity rests on these words: Christ is God. Likewise, on the sacramental plane: the bread "is" his body, and the wine "is" his blood.[10] There is, furthermore, a connection between the Eucharistic and the onomatological mysteries: the Named one is "really present" in his Name; that is to say, he "is" his Name.

The Eucharist is in a sense the "central" means of grace in Christianity; it must therefore express integrally what characterizes that tradition, and it does so in recapitulating not only the mystery of Christ as such, but also its double application to the "greater" and the "lesser" mysteries; the wine corresponds to the first, and the bread to the second, and this is clearly shown not only by the respective natures of the sacred elements, but also by the following symbolic facts: the miracle of the bread is "quantitative", in the sense that Christ multiplied what already existed, whereas the miracle of the wine is "qualitative", for Christ conferred on the water a quality that it did not have, namely, that of wine. Or again, the body of the crucified Redeemer had to be pierced in order that blood might flow out; blood thus represents the inner aspect of the sacrifice, which is moreover underlined by the fact that blood is liquid, hence "non-formal", while the body is solid, hence "formal"; the body of Christ had to be pierced because, to use the language of Meister Eckhart, "if you want the kernel, you must break the shell". The

---

8. These funeral rites remind one of the symbolic cremation which, in India, inaugurates the state of *sannyâsa*.

9. The married man can be chaste "in spirit and in truth", and the same necessarily holds good for poverty and obedience, as is proven by the example of Saint Louis and other canonized monarchs. The reservation expressed by the words "in spirit and in truth", or by the Pauline formulation "the letter killeth, but the spirit giveth life", has a capital importance in the Christian perspective, but it also contains—and moreover providentially—a "two-edged sword".

10. For Clement of Alexandria, the body of Christ, or the Eucharistic bread, concerns active life or faith, and the blood or the wine, contemplation and *gnosis*.

water that flowed from Christ's side and proved his death is like the negative aspect of the transmuted soul: it is the "extinction" which, according to the point of view, either accompanies or precedes the beatific plenitude of the divine blood; it is the "death" which precedes "Life", and which is as it were its external proof.

* * *

Christianity rests also on the two supreme commandments, which contain "all the law and the prophets". In *gnosis*, the first commandment—total love of God—implies awakened consciousness of the Self, whereas the second—love of neighbor—refers to seeing the Self in what is "not-I". Likewise for the injunctions of *oratio et jejunium*: all Christianity depends on these two disciplines, "prayer and fasting".

Oratio et jejunium: "fasting" is first of all abstention from evil, and then the "void for God" (*vacare Deo*) in which "prayer"—the "remembrance of God"—is established, and which is filled by the victory already won by the Redeemer.

Prayer culminates in a constant recalling of divine Names, insofar as it is a question of an articulated "remembrance". The *Golden Legend*, so rich in precious teachings, contains stories that bear witness to this: a knight wished to renounce the world and entered the Cistercian order; he was illiterate and, further, incapable of retaining, from all the teachings he received, anything but the words *Ave Maria*; these words "he kept with such great recollectedness that he pronounced them ceaselessly for himself wherever he went and whatever he was doing". After his death, a beautiful lily grew on his grave, and on each petal was written in golden letters *Ave Maria*; the monks opened the grave and saw that the root of the lily was growing from the knight's mouth. To this story we have only one word to add concerning the "divine quality" of the Name of the Virgin: he who says Jesus says God; and equally he who says Mary says Jesus, so that the *Ave Maria*—or the Name of Mary—is, of the divine Names, the one which is closest to man.

The *Golden Legend* recounts also that the executioners of Saint Ignatius of Antioch were astonished by the fact that the saint pronounced the Name of Christ without ceasing: "I cannot keep from doing so," he told them, "for it is written in my heart." After the saint's death, the pagans opened his heart and there saw, written in golden letters, the Name of Jesus.[11]

* * *

God is Love, and He is Light, but He is also, in Christ, sacrifice and suffering, and this too is an aspect or extension of Love. Christ has two natures, divine and human, and he offers also two ways, *gnosis* and charity: the way of charity, insofar as it is distinguished from *gnosis*, implies pain, for perfect love desires to suffer; it is in suffering that man best proves his love; but there is also in this as it were a price to be paid for the "intellectual easiness" of such a perspective. In the way of *gnosis*, where the whole emphasis is on pure contemplation and the chief concern is with the glorious aspect of Christ rather than with his grievous humanity—and where there is in certain respects a participation in the divine nature, which is ever blissful and immutable—suffering does not apply in the same way; that is, it does not, in principle, have to exceed the demands of a general *ascesis*, such as the Gospel designates by the term *jejunium*; a quasi-

11. The same fact is recounted of a Dominican saint, Catherine dei Ricci. Apart from the *Ave Maria* and the Name of Jesus, mention should be made of the double invocation *Jesu Maria*, which contains as it were two mystical dimensions, as also of *Christe eleison*, which is in effect an abridgement of the "Jesus Prayer" of the Eastern Church; it is known that the mystical science of ejaculatory prayer was transmitted to the West by Cassian, who appears retrospectively as the providential intermediary between the two great branches of Christian spirituality, while in his own time he was, for the West, the representative of the mystical tradition as such. And let us recall here equally these liturgical words: *Panem celestem accipiam et nomen Domini invocabo* and *Calicem salutaris accipiam et nomen Domini invocabo*. In Greek and Slavic monasteries, a knotted rope forms part of the investiture of the Small Schema and the Great Schema; it is conferred ritually on the monk or the nun. The Superior takes this rosary in his left-hand and says: "Take, brother N., the sword of the Spirit, which is the word of God, to pray to Jesus without ceasing, for you must constantly have the Name of the Lord Jesus in the mind, in the heart, and on the lips, saying: 'Lord Jesus Christ, Son of God, have mercy on me, a sinner.'" In the same order of ideas, we would draw attention to the "act of love"—the perpetual prayer of the heart—revealed in our times to Sister Consolata of Testona. (See *Jesus Appeals to the World*, by Lorenzo Sales.)

impersonal detachment here takes precedence over an individual desire for sacrifice. All Christian spirituality oscillates between these two poles, although the aspect of charity-suffering greatly preponderates in practice—and for obvious reasons—over the aspect *gnosis*-contemplation.

The question "What is God?" or "What am I?" outweighs, in the soul of the gnostic, the question "What does God want of me?" or "What must I do?", although these questions are far from being irrelevant, since man is always man. The gnostic, who sees God "everywhere and nowhere", does not base himself in the first place on alternatives outside himself, although he cannot escape them; what matters to him above all is that the world is everywhere woven of the same existential qualities and poses in all circumstances the same problems of remoteness and proximity.

*   *   *

The insistence, in the Christian climate, on the virtue of humility—or rather the manner of this insistence or the display of this virtue—leads us to return to this problem, which is at once moral and mystical.[12]

Humility has two aspects, which are prefigured in the Gospel by the washing of the feet, on the one hand, and by the cry of abandonment on the cross, on the other. The first humility is effacement: when we are brought, rightly or wrongly, to see a quality in ourselves, we must first attribute it to God and secondly see in ourselves either the limits of this quality or the defects that could neutralize it; and when we are brought to see a defect in others, we must first try to find its trace or the responsibility for it in ourselves and secondly exert ourselves to discover qualities that can compensate for it. But truth—provided it is within our reach—surpasses every other value, so that to submit to truth is the best way to be humble; virtue is good because it is true, and not inversely. Christ humbled himself in washing the feet of his disciples; he abased himself by serving while he was yet the Master, but not by calumniating him-

12. We have already spoken of it in our *Spiritual Perspectives and Human Facts*.

self; he did not say: "I am worse than you," and he gave no example of virtue contrary to truth or intelligence.[13]

The second—the great—humility is spiritual death, the "losing of life" for God, the extinction of the ego; this is what saints have had in view in describing themselves as "the greatest of sinners"; if this expression has a meaning, it applies to the ego as such, and not to such and such an ego. Since all sin comes from the ego and since without it there would be no sin, it is indeed the ego that is the "most vile" or the "lowest of sinners"; when the contemplative has identified his "I" with the principle of individuation, he perceives as it were in himself the root of all sin and the very principle of evil; it is as if he had assumed, after the example of Christ, all our imperfections, in order to dissolve them in himself, in the light of God and in the burnings of love. For a Saint Benedict or a Saint Bernard, the "degrees of humility" are stages in the extinction of the passionate "I", stages marked by symbolic attitudes, disciplines which further the transmutation of the soul; the key to this wisdom is that Christ was humbled on the cross through identifying himself, in the night of abandonment, with the night of the human ego, and not through identifying himself with such and such an "I"; he felt himself forsaken, not because he was Jesus, but because he had become man as such; he had to cease being Jesus that he might taste all the straitness, all the separation from God, of the pure ego and thereby of our state of fall.[14]

That we may not be able to determine our place in the hierarchy of sinners by no means signifies that we have not the certitude of

13. Christ gave other teachings on humility, for example when he said that he had not come to be served but to serve, or when he said that "whosoever therefore shall humble himself as this little child, the same is greatest in the kingdom of heaven"; now the true nature of all children is purity and simplicity, not rivalry. Let us recall also the parable of the uppermost rooms at feasts. According to Saint Thomas Aquinas, humility demands neither that we should submit what is divine in us to what is divine in another, nor that we should submit what is human in us to what is human in another, nor still less that the divine should submit to the human; but there is still the question, sometimes delicate but never insoluble, of the right definition of things.

14. The saying of Christ: "Why callest thou me good? There is none good but one, that is, God" belongs to the greater humility we have here in view; it is the same when Christ cites little children as examples. If it were necessary to take literally the

being "vile", not only as ego in general, but also, and therefore, as a particular ego; to believe oneself "vile" for the sole reason that one is "I" would empty humility of its content.

Humility in Christianity is conceived as a function of love, and this is one of the factors conferring upon it its characteristic texture. "The love of God," says Saint Augustine, "comprises all the virtues."

* * *

"And the light shineth in darkness; and the darkness comprehended it not." The message of Christ, by its form, is addressed *a priori* to the passional element in man, to the element of corruptibility in his nature, but it remains gnostic or sapiential in Christ himself and therefore in Trinitarian metaphysics, not to speak of the sapiential symbolism of Christ's teachings and parables. But it is in relation to the general form—the volitional perspective—of the message that Christ could say: "They that are whole have no need of the physician, but they that are sick: I came not to call the righteous, but sinners to repentance" (Mark 2:17). Again, when Christ says: "Judge not, that ye be not judged," he is referring to our passional nature and not to pure intelligence, which is neutral and is identified with those "that are whole". If Christ shall come to "judge the quick and the dead", this again relates to the Intellect—which alone has the right to judge—and to the equation "Christ-Intellect".

The volitional perspective, to which we have just alluded, is affirmed in the clearest possible way in Biblical history: we see there a people, at once passionate and mystical, struggling in the grip of a Law that crushes and fascinates them, and this prefigures in a providential way the struggles of the passional soul—of every soul insofar as it is subject to passions—with the truth, which is the final end of the human state. The Bible always speaks of "that which happens" and almost never of "that which is", though it does so implicitly, as the Cabalists point out; we are the first to recognize this, but

mystical conviction of being the "vilest of sinners", it would not be possible to explain how saints who have had this conviction should speak about the evil of some heretic; moreover it would be absurd to ask men to have an acute sense of the least defects of their nature and at the same time to be incapable of discerning these defects in another.

it alters nothing in the visible nature of these Scriptures, nor in the human causes behind this nature. From another angle, Judaism had hidden what Christianity was called upon to make openly manifest;[15] on the other hand, the Jews had openly manifested, from the moral point of view, what Christians later learned to hide; the ancient crudity was replaced by an esoterism of love, no doubt, but also by a new hypocrisy.

It is necessary to take account equally of this: the volitional perspective has a tendency to retain the ego because of the idea of moral responsibility, whereas *gnosis*, on the contrary, tends to reduce it to the cosmic powers of which it is a combination and a conclusion. And again: from the point of view of will and passion, men are equal; but they are not so from the point of view of pure intellection, for the latter introduces into man an element of the absolute which, as such, exceeds him infinitely. To the moralizing question "Who art thou that judgest another?"—a question by which some would like to obliterate all "wisdom of serpents" or all "discerning of spirits" in a vague and charitable psychologism—one would have the right to reply "God" in every case of infallible judgment; for intelligence, insofar as it is "relatively absolute", escapes the jurisdiction of virtue, and consequently its rights surpass those of man regarded as passional and fallible ego; God is in the truth of every truth. The saying that "no one can be judge and party in his own cause" can be applied to the ego only insofar as the ego limits or darkens the mind, for it is arbitrary to attribute to the intelligence as such a fundamental limit with respect to an order of contingencies; to assert, as certain moralists would, that man has no right to judge, amounts to saying that he has no intelligence, that he is only will or passion, and that he has no kind of likeness to God.

The sacred rights of the Intellect appear moreover in the fact that Christians have not been able to dispense with Platonic wisdom, and that later the Latins found the need for recourse to Aristotelianism, as if thereby recognizing that *religio* could not do without the element of wisdom, which a too exclusive perspective of

15. Commentators on the Torah state that the impediment of speech from which Moses suffered was imposed on him by God so that he would not be able to divulge the Mysteries which, precisely, the Law of Sinai had to veil and not to unveil; but these Mysteries were at root none other than the "Christic Mysteries".

love had allowed to fall into discredit.[16] But if knowledge is a profound need of the human spirit, it is by that very fact also a way.

To return to our earlier thought, it could also be expressed as follows: contrary to what is the case in *gnosis*, love scarcely has the right to judge another; it takes all upon itself and excuses everything, at least on the level where it is active, a level the limits of which vary according to individual natures; "pious fraud"[17]—out of charity—is the price of volitional individualism. If *gnosis* for its part discerns essentially—and on all levels—both spirits and values, this is because its point of view is never personal, so that in *gnosis* the distinction between "me" and "other", and the subtle and paradoxical prejudices attaching to this, scarcely have meaning; but here too the application of the principle depends on the limitations imposed on us by the nature of things and of ourselves.

Charity with regard to our neighbor, when it is the act of a direct consciousness and not just a moral sentiment, implies seeing ourselves in the other and the other in ourselves; the scission between *ego* and *alter* must be overcome in order that the division between Heaven and earth may be healed.

* * *

16. The ancient tendency to reduce *sophia* to a "philosophy", that is, an "art for art's sake" or a "knowledge without love", hence a pseudo-wisdom, has necessitated the predominance in Christianity of the contrary viewpoint. Love, in the sapiential perspective, is the element that surpasses simple ratiocination and makes knowledge effective; this cannot be over-emphasized.

17. Veracity, which in the end has more importance than moral conjectures, implies in short the use of logic in a manner that is consequential, that is to say: putting nothing above the truth and not falling into the contrary fault of believing that to be impartial means not to consider anyone right or wrong. One must not stifle discernment for the sake of impartiality, for objectivity consists, not in absolving the wrong and accusing the good, but in seeing things as they are, whether that pleases us or not; it is consequently to have a sense of proportion as much as a sense of subtle shades of meaning. It would be pointless to say such elementary things if one did not meet at every turn this false virtue, which distorts the exact vision of facts and which could dispense with its scruples if only it realized sufficiently the value and efficacy of humility before God.

According to Saint Thomas, it is not in the nature of free will to choose evil, although this possibility derives from having freedom of agency associated with a fallible creature. Will and liberty are thus connected; in other words, the Doctor introduces into the will an intellectual element and makes the will participate, quite properly, in intelligence. Will does not cease to be will by choosing evil—we have said this on other occasions—but it ceases fundamentally to be free, and so intellective; in the first case, it is the dynamic faculty, passional power—animals also have a will—and in the second, the dynamization of discernment. It could be added that neither does intelligence cease to be itself when in error, but in this case the relationship is less direct than for the will; the Holy Spirit (Will, Love) is "delegated" by the Son (Intellect, Knowledge), and not inversely.

Christian doctrine does not claim that moral effort produces metaphysical knowledge, but it does teach that restoring the fallen will—extirpating the passions—releases the contemplativity latent in the depths of our theomorphic nature; this contemplativity is like an aperture, which divine Light cannot but accede to, whether as Justice or *a fortiori* as Mercy; in *gnosis*, this process of mystical alchemy is accompanied by appropriate concepts and states of consciousness.[18] Seen from this angle, the primacy of love is not opposed to the perspective of wisdom, but illumines its operative aspect.[19]

---

18. Knowledge is then "sanctifying" and is not limited to satisfying some more or less justifiable need for explanation; it accords fully with the Pauline doctrine of charity. The implacability of such knowledge is not arrogance, but purity. *Gnosis* makes of knowledge something effective, ontological, "lived". Outside of *gnosis*, it is not a question of extirpating the passions, but of directing them towards Heaven.

19. The Augustinian-Platonic doctrine of knowledge is still in perfect accord with gnosis, while Thomistic-Aristotelian sensationalism, without being false on its own level and within its own limits, is in accord with the demands of the way of love, in the specific sense of the term *bhakti*. But this reservation is far from applying to the whole of Thomism, which is identified, in many respects, with truth unqualified. It is necessary to reject the opinion of those who believe that Thomism, or any other ancient wisdom, has an effective value only when we "re-create it in ourselves"—we "men of today"!—and that if Saint Thomas had read Descartes, Kant, and the philosophers of the nineteenth and twentieth centuries, he would have expressed himself differently; in reality, he would then only have had to refute a thousand more errors. If an ancient saying is right, there is nothing to do but accept it; if it

*   *   *

The morality that offers the other cheek—so far as morality can here be spoken of—means, not an unwonted solicitude toward one's adversary, but complete indifference toward the fetters of this world, or more precisely a refusal to let oneself be caught up in the vicious circle of terrestrial causations. The man who wants to be right at any price on the personal plane loses serenity and moves away from the "one thing needful"; the affairs of this world bring with them only disturbances, and disturbances take one further from God. But peace, like every spiritual attitude, can disassociate itself from external activity; holy anger is internally calm, and the unavoidable role of the office of judge—unavoidable because motivated by higher and non-personal interests—is compatible with a mind free from attachment and hatred. Christ opposes the passions and personal interest, but not the performance of duty or the collective interest; in other words, he is opposed to personal interest when that interest is passionate or harmful to the interests of others, and he condemns hatred even when it serves a higher interest.

The "non-violence" advocated by the Gospels symbolizes—and renders effective—the virtue of the mind preoccupied with "what is" rather than with "what happens". As a rule, man loses much time and energy in questioning himself about the injustice of his fellows as well as about possible hardships of destiny; whether there is human injustice or divine punishment, the world—the "current of forms" or the "cosmic wheel"—is what it is: it simply follows its course; it is conformable to its own nature. Men cannot not be unjust insofar as they form part of this current; to be detached from the current and to act contrary to the logic of facts and of the bondage that it engenders is bound to appear madness in the eyes of the world, but it is in reality to adopt here below the point of view of eternity. And to adopt this point of view is to see oneself from a great distance: it is to see that we ourselves form a part of this world

is false, there is no reason to take notice of it; but to want to "rethink" it through a veil of new errors or impressions quite clearly has no interest, and any such attempt merely shows the degree to which the sense of intrinsic and timeless truth has been lost.

of injustice, and this is one more reason for remaining indifferent amid the uproar of human quarrelling. The saint is the man who acts as if he had died and returned to life; having already ceased to be "himself", in the earthly sense, he has absolutely no intention of returning to that dream, but maintains himself in a kind of wakefulness, which the world, with its narrowness and impurities, cannot understand.

Pure love is not of this world of oppositions; it is by origin celestial, and its end is God; it lives as it were in itself, by its own light and in the beam of God-Love, and that is why charity "seeketh not her own, is not easily provoked, thinketh no evil; rejoiceth not in iniquity, but rejoiceth in the truth; beareth all things, believeth all things, hopeth all things, endureth all things" (1 Cor. 13:5-7).

5

Delineations of Original Sin

The idea of original sin situates the cause of the human fall in an act; consequently, this fall consists in committing evil acts, sins precisely. The disadvantage of this idea—which nonetheless is providential and efficacious—is that a man who commits no outright transgressions may believe himself perfect, as if it sufficed to do no evil to deserve Heaven; Christian doctrine counters this temptation by stressing that every man is a sinner; to doubt it is to add two more sins, those of presumption and heresy. In such a climate, one almost feels obligated, if not to sin, at least to see sins everywhere; it is true that there is a definite number of mortal sins, but the venial sins are innumerable, and they become serious when they are habitual, for then they are vices.

Be that as it may, an obligatory *mea culpa* that has nothing concrete in view is not a panacea and hardly makes us better; but what is altogether different is to be conscious of the presence in our soul of a tendency to "outwardness" and "horizontality", which constitutes, if not original sin properly so called, at least the hereditary vice that is derived from it.

In connection with the idea of sin-as-act, let us note in passing that there are behaviors which are sins objectively without being so subjectively, and that there are others which are sins subjectively without being so objectively: a given saint neglects a religious duty because he is in ecstasy; a given hypocrite accomplishes it because he wishes to be admired. This is said in order to recall that an act is valid according to its intention; however, it is not enough for the intention to be subjectively good: it must also be so objectively.

But let us return to our subject: to affirm that every man is a "sinner" does not amount to saying that no man is capable of abstaining from evil actions, but it certainly means that all men—with the rarest exceptions—succumb to the temptations of "outwardness" and "horizontality"; where there is no temptation of excess in the direction of either the outward or the horizontal, there is no longer either concupiscence or impiety.[1] Assuredly, every man has the right to a certain solidarity with his ambience, as is proven by our faculties of sensation and action, but this right is limited by our complementary duty of inwardness, without which we would not be men, precisely; this means that the pole of attraction which is the "kingdom of God within you" must in the final analysis prevail over the seductive magic of the world.[2] This is expressed by the supreme Commandment, which, while teaching us what we must do, also teaches us what we are.

*   *   *

The concept of the sin of omission[3] allows us to grasp more firmly the problem of hereditary sin, that sin which exists in us before our actions. If the requirement of the supreme Commandment is to love God "with all thy heart, and with all thy soul, and with all thy strength, and with all thy mind", it follows that the contrary attitude is the supreme sin, in varying degrees since one has to distinguish between hatred of God and simple indifference; nevertheless, God says in the Apocalypse: "So then because thou art lukewarm, and neither cold nor hot, I will spew thee out of my mouth." If we wish to give the word "sin" its broadest or deepest meaning, we would say that it expresses above all an attitude of the heart; hence a "being" and not simply a "doing" or "not doing"; in this case, the Biblical myth symbolizes a "substance" and not simply an "accident".

---

1. Which evokes the case of "pneumatics" and above all the mystery of the "Immaculate Conception".

2. According to Shankara, the one who is "liberated in this life" (*jîvan-mukta*) is not he who stands apart from all that is human; it is he who, when he "laughs with those who laugh and weeps with those who weep", remains the supernaturally unaffected witness of the "cosmic play" (*lîlâ*).

3. According to the Apostle James, he that "knoweth to do good, and doeth it not" commits a sin; this is the very definition of sin by omission, but at the same time it goes beyond the framework of a formalistic and exoteric morality.

Thus, original "sin" for the Hindus is "nescience" (*avidyâ*): ignorance that "*Brahma* is real, the world is illusory", and that "the soul is not other than *Brahma*"; all actions or attitudes contrary to intrinsic and vocational Law (*Dharma*) result from this blindness of heart.

*   *   *

Above we said "horizontality" and "outwardness". To be "horizontal" is to love only terrestrial life, to the detriment of the ascending and celestial path; to be "exteriorized" is to love only outward things, to the detriment of moral and spiritual values. Or again: horizontality is to sin against transcendence, thus to forget God and consequently the meaning of life; and outwardness is to sin against immanence, thus to forget our immortal soul and consequently its vocation. In assuming that the original sin was an act—whatever the form given it by a particular mythology—we shall say, on the one hand, that this act had as its effect the two kinds of neglect just mentioned and, on the other hand, that this neglect predisposes to the indefinite repetition of the original transgression; every sinful action repeats the drama of the forbidden fruit. Primordial perfection was made of "verticality" and "inwardness" as is attested by those two distinctive characteristics of man which are vertical posture and language, the latter coinciding with reason.

Transcendence is objective inasmuch as it concerns the divine Order in itself; immanence is subjective inasmuch as it refers to the divine Presence in us; nonetheless there is also a subjective transcendence, that which within us distinguishes the divine Self from the human "I", and an objective immanence, namely, the divine Presence in the world surrounding us. To be truly conscious of "God-as-Object" is also to be conscious of His immanence, and to be conscious of "God-as-Subject" is also to be conscious of His transcendence.

Inwardness and verticality, outwardness and horizontality:[4] these are the dimensions that constitute man in all his greatness and all

4. In accordance with the principle of the double meaning of symbols, inwardness and verticality are not solely positive, any more than outwardness and horizontality are solely negative. Inwardness means not only depth, but also subjectivism, ego-

his littleness. To say transcendence is to say both metaphysical Truth and saving Divinity; and to say immanence is to say transpersonal Intellect and divine Selfhood: verticality in the face of "our Father who art in heaven", and inwardness in virtue of the "kingdom of God which is within you", whence a certitude and a serenity that no stratagem of the powers of darkness can take away from us.

* * *

Eve and Adam succumbed to the temptation to wish to be more than they could be; the serpent represents the possibility of this temptation. The builders of the Tower of Babel, as well as the Titans, Prometheus, and Icarus, wished to put themselves improperly in God's place; they too suffered the humiliating chastisement of a fall. According to the Bible, the forbidden tree was one of discernment between "good" and "evil"; now this discernment, or this difference, pertains to the very nature of Being; consequently its source could not be in the creature; to claim it for oneself is to wish to be equal to the Creator, and that is the very essence of sin—of all sin. Indeed, the sinner decides what is good, counter to the objective nature of things; he willingly deludes himself about things and about himself; whence the fall, which is nothing other than the reaction of reality.

The great ambiguity of the human phenomenon resides in the fact that man is divine without being God: Koranically speaking, man gives all the creatures their names, and that is why the angels must prostrate before him—except for the supreme Angel,[5] which indicates that man's divinity, and consequently his authority and autonomy, are relative, although "relatively absolute". Thus the fall of man as such could not be total, as is proven *a priori* by the nature and destiny of the patriarch Enoch, father of all "pneumatics", so to speak.

---

ism, hardness of self; verticality means not only ascension, but also the fall. Similarly, but inversely, outwardness means not only superficiality and dispersion, but also movement towards a center that liberates; and horizontality means not only baseness, but also stability.

5. Or the Archangels, which amounts to the same thing; it is the divine Spirit that is mirrored directly at the center or summit of universal Manifestation.

For exoterist ideology, esoterism—*gnosis*—can originate only from darkness, since it seems to claim the prerogative of the forbidden tree, spontaneous and autonomous discernment between "good and evil". But this is to overlook the essential, namely, that *aliquid est in anima quod est increatum et increabile . . . et hoc est Intellectus.*[6] The fall was, precisely, the rupture between reason and Intellect, the ego and the Self; one could speculate forever on the modes and degrees of this rupture, which on the one hand involves the human species and on the other hand could not be absolute.

---

6. Meister Eckhart: "There is something in the soul which is uncreated and uncreatable . . . and this is the Intellect."

6

The Dialogue between Hellenists and Christians

Like most inter-traditional polemics, the dialogue which opposed Hellenism to Christianity was to a great extent unreal. The fact that each was right on a certain plane—or in a particular "spiritual dimension"—resulted in each emerging as victor in its own way: Christianity by imposing itself on the whole Western world, and Hellenism by surviving in the very heart of Christianity and conferring on Christian intellectuality an indelible imprint.

The misunderstandings were nonetheless profound, and it is not difficult to see why this was so if divergences of perspective are taken into account. From the point of view of the Hellenists, the divine Principle is at the same time one and multiple; the gods personify the divine qualities and functions and, at the same time, the angelic prolongations of these qualities and functions; the idea of immanence prevails over that of transcendence, at least in exoterism. The universe is an order that is so to speak architectural, deployed from the Supreme Principle by way of intermediaries, or of hierarchies of intermediaries, down to earthly creatures; all the cosmic principles and their rays are divine, or semi-divine, which amounts to saying that they are envisaged in relation to their essential and functional divinity. If God gives us life, warmth, and light, He does so by way of Helios or inasmuch as He is Helios; the sun is like the hand of God, and is thus divine; and since it is so in principle, why should it not be so in its sensible manifestation? This way of looking at things is based on the essential continuity between the Cause and the effect, and not on an existential discontinuity or accidentality; the world being the necessary and strictly ordered manifestation of Divinity, it is, like Divinity, eternal; it is, for God, a way of deploying Himself "outside Himself". This eternity does not imply that the world cannot undergo eclipses, but if it inevitably does so, as all mythologies teach, it is so that it may rise again in accordance with an eternal rhythm; it therefore cannot not be. The very absoluteness of the Absolute necessitates relativity; *Mâyâ* is "without origin", say the Vedantists. There is no "gratuitous creation" nor any creation *ex nihilo*; there is a necessary manifestation *ex divino*, and this manifestation is free within the framework of its necessity, and necessary within the framework of its liberty. The world is divine through its character as a divine manifestation, or by way of the metaphysical marvel of its existence.

There is no need to describe here, on account of a concern for symmetry, the Christian outlook, which is that of Semitic monotheism and is for that reason familiar to everyone. On the other hand, it seems indispensable before proceeding further to clarify the fact that the Hellenistic conception of the "divinity of the world" has nothing to do with the error of pantheism, for the cosmic manifestation of God in no way detracts from the absolute transcendence appertaining to the Principle in itself, and in no way contradicts what is metaphysically acceptable in the Semitic and Christian conception of a *creatio ex nihilo*. To believe that the world is a "part" of God and that God, by His Selfhood or by His very essence, spreads Himself into the forms of the world, would be a truly "pagan" conception—such as has no doubt existed here and there, even among the men of old—and in order to keep clear of it, one must possess a knowledge that is intrinsically what would be represented on the plane of ideas by a combination between the Hellenistic "cosmosophy" and the Judeo-Christian theology, the reciprocal relationship of these two outlooks playing the part of a touchstone with respect to total truth. Metaphysically speaking, the Semitic and monotheistic "creationism", as soon as it presents itself as an absolute and exclusive truth, is nearly as false as pantheism; it is so "metaphysically", because total knowledge is in question and not the opportuneness of salvation alone, and "nearly" because a half-truth which tends to safeguard the transcendence of God at the expense of the metaphysical intelligibility of the world is less erroneous than a half-truth which tends to safeguard the divine nature of the world at the expense of the intelligibility of God.

If the Christian polemicists did not understand that the outlook of the Greek sages was no more than the esoteric complement of the Biblical notion of creation, the Greek polemicists did not understand the compatibility between the two outlooks any better. It is true that one incomprehension sometimes begets another, for it is difficult to penetrate the profound intention of a foreign concept when that intention remains implicit, and when in addition it is presented as destined to replace truths which are perhaps partial, but which are in any case evident to those who accept them traditionally. A partial truth may be insufficient from one point of view or another; it is nonetheless a truth.

* * *

In order properly to understand the significance of this dialogue, which in some respects was but a confrontation between two monologues, one must take account of the following: as far as the Christians were concerned there was no knowledge possible without love; that is to say that in their eyes *gnosis* was valid only on condition that it was included within a unifying experience; by itself, and apart from the living experience of spiritual reality, an intellectual knowledge of the Universe had no meaning to them; but eventually the Christians had to recognize the rights of a knowledge that was theoretical, and thus conceptual and proleptic, which they did by borrowing from the Greeks certain elements of their science, not without sometimes heaping abuse on Hellenism as such, with as much ingratitude as inconsistency. If a simple and rather summary formulation be permissible, one could say that for the Greeks truth is that which is in conformity with the nature of things; for the Christians truth is that which leads to God. This Christian attitude, to the extent that it tended to be exclusive, was bound to appear to the Greeks as "foolishness"; in the eyes of the Christians the attitude of the Greeks consisted in taking thought for an end in itself, outside of any personal relation to God; consequently it was a "wisdom according to the flesh", since it cannot by itself regenerate the fallen and impotent will, but on the contrary by its self-sufficiency draws men away from the thirst for God and for salvation. From the Greek point of view, things are what they are whatever we may make of them; from the Christian—to speak schematically and *a priori*—only our relationship to God makes sense. The Christians could be reproached for an outlook that was too much concerned with the will and too self-interested, and the Greeks on the one hand for too much liveliness of thought and on the other for too rational and too human a perfectionism; it was in some respects a dispute between a love-song and a mathematical theorem. It could also be said that the Hellenists were predominantly right in principle and the Christians right in fact, at least in a particular sense that can be discerned without difficulty.

As for the Christian gnostics, they necessarily admitted the doctrinal anticipations of the divine mysteries, but on condition—it cannot be too strongly emphasized—that they remained in a quasi-organic connection with the spiritual experience of *gnosis*-love; to know God is to love Him, or rather, since the Scriptural point of departure is love: to love God perfectly is to know Him. To know was indeed *a priori* to conceive of supernatural truths, but to do so while making our whole being participate in this understanding; it was thus to love the divine quintessence of all *gnosis*, that quintessence which is "love" because it is at once union and beatitude. The school of Alexandria was as fully Christian as that of Antioch, in the sense that it saw in the acceptance of Christ the *sine qua non* of salvation; its foundations were perfectly Pauline. In Saint Paul's view a conceptual and expressible *gnosis* is a knowing "in part" (*ex parte*), and it shall be "done away" when "that which is perfect is come",[1] namely, the totality of *gnosis*, which, through the very fact of its totality, is "love" (*caritas*, ἀγάπη), the divine prototype of human *gnosis*. In the case of man there is a distinction—or a complementarism—between love and knowledge, but in God their polarity is surpassed and unified. In the Christian perspective this supreme degree is called "love", but in another perspective—notably in the Vedantic—one can equally well call it "knowledge", while maintaining, not that knowledge finds its totalization or its exaltation in love, but on the contrary that love (*bhakti*), being individual, finds its sublimation in pure knowledge (*jnâna*), which is universal; this second mode of expression is directly in conformity with the sapiential perspective.

* * *

The Christian protest is unquestionably justified insofar as it is directed to the "humanist" side of "classical" Hellenism and to the

---

1. 1 Corinthians 13:10.

mystical ineffectuality of philosophy as such. On the other hand, it is in no way logical to reproach the Greeks with a divinization of the cosmos on the pretext that there can be no "entry" of God into the world, while admitting that Christ, and he alone, brings about just such an entry; indeed, if Christ can bring it about, it is precisely because it is possible and because it is realized *a priori* by the cosmos itself; the "avataric" marvel of Christ retraces, or humanizes, the cosmic marvel of creation or of "emanation".

From the point of view of the Platonists—in the widest sense— the return to God is inherent in the fact of existence: our being itself offers the way of return, for that being is divine in its nature, otherwise it would be nothing; that is why we must return, passing through the strata of our ontological reality, all the way to pure Substance, which is one; it is thus that we become perfectly "ourselves". Man realizes what he knows: a full comprehension—in the light of the Absolute—of relativity dissolves it and leads back to the Absolute. Here again there is no irreducible antagonism between Greeks and Christians: if the intervention of Christ can become necessary, it is not because deliverance is something other than a return, through the strata of our own being, to our true Self, but because the function of Christ is to render such a return possible. It is made possible on two planes, the one existential and exoteric and the other intellectual and esoteric; the second plane is hidden in the first, which alone appears in the full light of day, and that is the reason why for the common run of mortals the Christian perspective is only existential and separative, not intellectual and unitive. This gives rise to another misunderstanding between Christians and Platonists: while the Platonists propound liberation by Knowledge because man is an intelligence,[2] the Christians envisage in their general doctrine a salvation by Grace because man is an existence— as such separated from God—and a fallen and impotent will. Once again, the Greeks can be reproached for having at their command

---

2. Islam, in conformity with its "paracletic" character, reflects this point of view— which is also that of the *Vedânta* and of all other forms of *gnosis*—in a Semitic and religious mode, and realizes it all the more readily in its esoterism; like the Hellenist, the Muslim asks first of all: "What must I know or admit, seeing that I have an intelligence capable of objectivity and of totality?" and not *a priori*: "What must I want, since I have a will that is free, but fallen?"

but a single way, inaccessible in fact to the majority, and for giving the impression that it is philosophy that saves, just as one can reproach the Christians for ignoring liberation by Knowledge and for assigning an absolute character to our existential and volitive reality alone and to the means appropriate to that aspect of our being, or for taking into consideration our existential relativity alone and not our "intellectual absoluteness"; nevertheless the reproach to the Greeks cannot concern their sages, any more than the reproach to the Christians can impugn their *gnosis*, nor in a general way their sanctity.

The possibility of our return to God—wherein are different degrees—is universal and timeless: it is inscribed in the very nature of our existence and of our intelligence; our powerlessness can only be accidental, not essential. That which is principially indispensable is an intervention of the *Logos*, but not in every case the intervention of a particular manifestation of the *Logos*, unless we belong to it by reason of our situation and, by virtue of that fact, it chooses us; as soon as it chooses us, it holds the place of the Absolute as far as we are concerned, and then it "is" the Absolute. It could even be said that the imperative character that Christ assumes for Christians—or for men providentially destined for Christianity—retraces the imperative character inherent in the *Logos* in every spiritual way, whether of the West or of the East.

*   *   *

One must react against the evolutionist prejudice which would have it that the thought of the Greeks "attained" to a certain level or a certain result, that is to say, that the triad Socrates-Plato-Aristotle represents the summit of an entirely "natural" thought, a summit reached after long periods of effort and groping. The reverse is the truth, in the sense that all the said triad did was to crystallize rather imperfectly a primordial and intrinsically timeless wisdom, actually of Aryan origin and typologically close to the Celtic, Germanic, Mazdean, and Brahmanic esoterisms. There is in Aristotelian rationality and even in the Socratic dialectic a sort of "humanism" more or less connected with artistic naturalism and scientific curiosity, and thus with empiricism. But this already too contingent dialectic—though we must bear in mind that the Socratic dialogues belong to spiritual "pedagogy" and have something of the provisional in them—must not lead us into attributing a "natural" character to intellections that are "supernatural" by definition, or "naturally supernatural". On the whole, Plato expressed sacred truths in a language that had already become profane—profane because more rational and discursive than intuitive and symbolist, or because it followed too closely the contingencies and humors of the mirror that is the mind—whereas Aristotle placed truth itself, and not merely its expression, on a profane and "humanistic" plane. The originality of Aristotle and his school resides no doubt in giving to truth a maximum of rational bases, but this cannot be done without diminishing that truth, and it has no purpose save where there is a regression of intellectual intuition; it is a "two-edged sword" precisely because truth seems henceforth to be at the mercy of syllogisms. The question of knowing whether this constitutes a betrayal or a providential re-adaptation is of small importance here, and could no doubt be answered in either sense.[3] What is certain is that Aristotle's teaching, so far as its essential content is concerned, is still much too true to be understood and appreciated by the protagonists of the "dynamic" and relativist or "existentialist" thought of our epoch. This last half-plebeian, half-demonic kind of thought is in contradiction with itself from its very point of departure, since to say that everything is relative or "dynamic", and therefore "in motion", is to say that there exists no point of view from which that

---

3. With Pythagoras one is still in the Aryan East; with Socrates-Plato one is no longer wholly in that East—which in reality is neither "Eastern" nor "Western", that distinction having no meaning for an archaic Europe—but neither is one wholly in the West; whereas with Aristotle Europe begins to become specifically "Western" in the current and cultural sense of the word. The East—or a particular East—forced an entry with Christianity, but the Aristotelian and Caesarean West finally prevailed, only to escape in the end from both Aristotle and Caesar, but by the downward path. It is opportune to observe here that all modern theological attempts to "surpass" the teaching of Aristotle can follow only the same downward path, in view of the falsity of their motives, whether implicit or explicit. What is really being sought is a graceful capitulation before evolutionist scientism, before the machine, before an activist and demagogic socialism, a destructive psychologism, abstract art and surrealism, in short before modernism in all its forms—that modernism which is less and less a "humanism" since it de-humanizes, or that individualism which is ever more infra-individual. The moderns, who are neither Pythagoreans nor Vedantists, are surely the last to have any right to complain of Aristotle.

fact can be established; Aristotle had in any case fully foreseen this absurdity.

The moderns have reproached the pre-Socratic philosophers—and all the sages of the East as well—with trying to construct a picture of the universe without asking themselves whether our faculties of knowledge are equal to such an enterprise; the reproach is perfectly vain, for the very fact that we can put such a question proves that our intelligence is in principle adequate to the needs of the case. It is not the "dogmatists" who are naïve, but the skeptics, who have not the least idea in the world of what is implicit in the "dogmatism" they oppose. In our day some people go so far as to claim that the goal of philosophy can only be the search for a "type of rationality" adapted to the comprehension of "human reality"; the error is the same, but a coarser and meaner version of it, and more insolent as well. How is it that they cannot see that the very idea of inventing an intelligence capable of resolving such problems proves, in the first place, that this intelligence exists already—for it alone could conceive of any such idea—and shows in the second place that the goal aimed at is of an unfathomable absurdity? But our present purpose is not to prolong this subject; it is simply to call attention to the parallelism between the pre-Socratic—or more precisely the Ionian—wisdom and oriental doctrines such as the *Vaisheshika* and the *Sânkhya*, and to underline, on the one hand, that in all these ancient visions of the Universe the implicit postulate is the innateness of the nature of things in the Intellect[4] and not a supposition or other logical operation, and on the other hand, that this notion of innateness furnishes the very definition of that which the skeptics and empiricists think they must disdainfully characterize as "dogmatism"; in this way they demonstrate that they are ignorant, not only of the nature of intellection, but also of the nature of dogmas in the proper sense of the word. The admirable thing about the Platonists is obviously not their "thought"; it is the content of their thought, whether called "dogmatic" or otherwise.

---

4. In the terminology of the ancient cosmologists one must allow for symbolism: when Thales saw in "water" the origin of all things, we have every reason to believe that it is the Universal Substance—the *Prakriti* of the Hindus—that is in question and not the sensible element. It is the same with the "air" of Anaximenes of Miletus or of Diogenes of Apollonia, or with the "fire" of Heraclitus.

The Sophists inaugurate the era of individualistic rationalism and unlimited pretensions; thus they open the door to all arbitrary totalitarianisms. It is true that profane philosophy also begins with Aristotle, but in a rather different sense, since the rationality of the Stagirite tends upwards and not downwards, as does that of Protagoras and his like; in other words, if a dissipating individualism originates with the Sophists—not forgetting allied spirits such as Democritus and Epicurus—Aristotle on the other hand opens the era of a rationalism still anchored in metaphysical certitude, but nonetheless fragile and ambiguous in its very principle, as we have had occasion to point out more than once.

However that may be, if one wants to understand the Christian reaction, one must take account of all these aspects of the spirit of Greece, and at the same time of the Biblical, mystical, and "realizational" character of Christianity. Greek thought appeared in the main as a promethean attempt to appropriate to itself the light of Heaven, rashly breaking through the stages on the way to Truth; but at the same time it was largely irresistible because of the self-evidence of its content: that being so, one must not lose sight of the fact that in the East sapiential doctrines were never presented in the form of a "literature" open to all, but that on the contrary their assimilation required a corresponding spiritual method, and this is the very thing that had disappeared and could no longer be found among the Greeks of the classical epoch.

* * *

It has been said and said again that the Hellenists and the Orientals—"Platonic" spirits in the widest sense—have been blameworthy in "arrogantly" rejecting Christ, or that they are trying to escape from their "responsibilities"—once again and always!—as creatures toward the Creator in withdrawing into their own center where they claim to find, in their own pure being, the essence of things and the divine Reality; they thus dilute, it is alleged, the quality of creature and at the same time that of Creator with a sort of pantheistic impersonalism, which amounts to saying that they destroy the relationship of "obligation" between the Creator and the creature. In reality "responsibilities" are relative as we ourselves are relative in our existential particularity; they cannot be less rela-tive—or "more absolute"—than the subject to which they are relat-ed. One who, by the grace of Heaven, succeeds in escaping from the tyranny of the ego is by that very circumstance discharged from the responsibilities that the ego entails. God shows Himself as creative Person insofar as—or in relation to the fact that—we are "creature" and individual, but that particular reciprocal relationship is far from exhausting all our ontological and intellectual nature; that is to say, our nature cannot be exhaustively defined by "duty", "rights", or other such related ideas. It has been said that the "rejec-tion" of the Christic gift on the part of the "Platonic" spirit consti-tutes the subtlest and most luciferian perversity of the intelligence; this argument, born of a misguided instinct of self-preservation, though understandable on its own plane, can easily and far more pertinently be turned against those who make use of it: for if we are obliged at all costs to find some mental perversion somewhere, we shall find it with those who want to substitute for the Absolute a per-sonal and therefore relative God, and temporal phenomena for metaphysical principles, not in connection with a childlike faith making no demands of anyone, but within the framework of the most exacting erudition and the most totalitarian intellectual pre-tension. If there is such a thing as abuse of the intelligence, it is to be found in the substitution of the relative for the Absolute, or the accident for the Substance, on the pretext of putting the "concrete" above the "abstract";[5] it is not to be found in the rejection—in the name of transcendent and immutable principles—of a relativity presented as absoluteness.

The misunderstanding between Christians and Hellenists can in large part be condensed to a false alternative: in effect, the fact that God resides in our deepest "being"—or in the transpersonal depth of our consciousness—and that we can in principle realize Him with the help of the pure and theomorphic Intellect, in no way excludes the equal and simultaneous affirmation of this immanent and impersonal Divinity as objective and personal, nor the fact that we can do nothing without His grace, despite the essentially "divine" character of the Intellect in which we participate naturally and supernaturally.

---

5. It is really an abuse of language to qualify as "abstract" everything that is above the phenomenal order.

It is perfectly true that the human individual is a concrete and definite person, and responsible before a Creator, a personal and omniscient Legislator; but it is quite as true—to say the least of it—that man is but a modality, so to speak external and coagulated, of a Divinity at once impersonal and personal, and that human intelligence is such that it can in principle be conscious of this fact and thus realize its true identity. In one sense it is evidently the fallen and sinful individuality that is "ourselves"; in another sense it is the transcendent and unalterable Self: the planes are different; there is no common measure between them.

When the religious dogmatist claims for some terrestrial fact an absolute import—and the "relatively absolute" character of the same fact is not here in question—the Platonist or the Oriental appeals to principial and timeless certitudes; in other words, when the dogmatist asserts that "this is", the gnostic immediately asks: "By virtue of what possibility?" According to the gnostic, "everything has already been"; he admits the "new" only insofar as it retraces or manifests the "ancient", or rather the timeless, uncreated "idea". The function of celestial messages is in practice and humanly absolute, but they are not for that reason the Absolute, and as far as their form is concerned they do not pass beyond relativity. It is the same with the intellect at once "created" and "uncreated": the "uncreated" element penetrates it as light penetrates air or ether; this element is not the light, but is its vehicle, and in practice one cannot dissociate them.

There are two sources of certitude: on the one hand the innateness of the Absolute in pure intelligence, and on the other the supernatural phenomenon of grace. It is amply evident—and cannot be too often repeated—that these two sources can be, and consequently must be, combined to a certain extent, but in fact the exoterists have an interest in setting them against each other, and they do so by denying to intelligence its supernatural essence and by denying the innateness of the Absolute, as well as by denying grace to those who think differently from themselves. An irreducible opposition between intellection and grace is as artificial as it could be, for intellection is also a grace, but it is a static and innate grace; there can be absolutely no reason why this kind of grace should not be a possibility and should never be manifested, seeing that by its very nature it cannot not be. If anyone objects that in such matters it is not a matter of "grace" but something else, the answer must be that in that case grace is not necessary, since there are only two alternatives: either grace is indispensable, and if so intellection is a grace, or intellection is not a grace, and if so grace is not indispensable.

If theologians admit, with the Scriptures, that one cannot enunciate an essential truth about Christ "but by the Holy Spirit", they must also admit that one cannot enunciate an essential truth about God without the intervention of that same Spirit; the truths of the wisdom of Greece, like the metaphysical truths of all peoples, are therefore not to be robbed of their "supernatural" and in principle salvific character.

From a certain point of view, the Christian argument is the historicity of the Christ-Savior, whereas the Platonic or "Aryan" argument is the nature of things or the Immutable. If, to speak symbolically, all men are in danger of drowning as a consequence of the fall of Adam, the Christian saves himself by grasping the pole held out to him by Christ, which no one else can hold out, whereas the Platonist saves himself by swimming; but neither course weakens or neutralizes the effectiveness of the other. On the one hand there are certainly men who do not know how to swim or who are prevented from doing so, but on the other hand swimming is undeniably among the possibilities open to man; the whole thing is to know what counts most in a situation whether individual or collective.[6] We have seen that Hellenism, like all directly or indirectly sapiential doctrines, is founded on the axiom man-intelligence rather than man-will, and that is one of the reasons why it had to appear as inoperative in the eyes of a majority of Christians; but only "of a majority" because the Christian gnostics could not apply such a reproach to the Pythagoreans and Platonists; the gnostics could not do otherwise than admit the primacy of the Intellect, and for that reason the idea of divine Redemption meant to them something very different from and more far-reaching than a mysticism derived from history and a sacramental dogmatism. It is necessary to repeat once more—as others have said before and better—that sacred facts are true because they retrace on their own plane the nature of

---

6. In other words: if one party cannot logically deny that there are men who save themselves by swimming, no more can the other party deny that there are men who are saved only because a pole is held out to them.

things, and not the other way round: the nature of things is not real or normative because it evokes certain sacred facts. The principles, essentially accessible to pure intelligence—if they were not so man would not be man, and it is almost blasphemy to deny that human intelligence considered in relation to animal intelligence has a supernatural side—the universal principles confirm the sacred facts, which in their turn reflect those principles and derive their efficacy from them; it is not history, whatever it may contain, that confirms the principles. This relationship is expressed by the Buddhists when they say that spiritual truth is situated beyond the distinction between objectivity and subjectivity, and that it derives its evidence from the depths of Being itself, or from the innateness of Truth in all that is.

In the sapiential perspective divine Redemption is always present; it pre-exists all terrestrial alchemy and is its celestial model, so that it is always thanks to this eternal Redemption—whatever may be its vehicle on earth—that man is freed from the weight of his vagaries and even, *Deo volente*, from that of his separative existence; if "my words shall not pass away" it is because they have always been. The Christ of the gnostics is he who is "before Abraham was" and from whom arise all the ancient wisdoms; a consciousness of this, far from diminishing a participation in the treasures of the historical Redemption, confers on them a scope that touches the very roots of Existence.

7

The Complexity of Dogmatism

Every confession of faith claims the guarantee of perpetual assistance by the Holy Spirit, and rightly so inasmuch as a confession of faith that is valid in itself—hence having the power to save, if not to lead to every mystical summit—could not contain an intrinsically false dogma or a totally inoperative rite; but this assistance is nonetheless always relative, given that Revelation itself is relative in relation to absolute Truth, the *sophia perennis*; otherwise there would not be different Revelations;[1] the assistance of the Holy Spirit is total only for the total Truth. One thing that should not be forgotten is that the purpose of religions is the divine will to save men steeped in passion, and not to present an explanation of universal Principles and of the world; in consequence, the Holy Spirit claimed by Christianity is more a savior than a metaphysician, at least as regards its manifestation within the sphere of religion; it is more concerned with warding off that which, in connection with a particular mentality, is detrimental to salvation than with rectifying doctrinal errors that are more or less a matter of indifference in this respect.[2]

Intrinsically "orthodox" dogmas, that is, those disposed in view of salvation, differ from one religion to another; consequently they cannot all be objectively true. However, all dogmas are symbolically

---

1. Let us note, however, that archaic traditions do not have exclusivist dogmas; Hinduism, in particular, combines a multiform symbolism with one of the best articulated and most explicit metaphysical doctrines.

2. Thus it is illogical, to say the least, to wish to contrast the "wisdom of Christ", whose purpose is to save and not to explain, with the "wisdom of this world"—that of Plato, for example—whose purpose is to explain and not to save; besides, the fact that Platonic wisdom is not dictated by an intention to save does not imply that it is of "this world" or "according to the flesh", or even that it does not contain any liberating virtue within the methodic context that it requires.

true and subjectively efficacious, which is to say that their purpose is to create human attitudes that contribute in their way to the divine miracle of salvation. This, in practice, is the meaning of the Buddhist term *upâya*, "skillful means" or "spiritual stratagem", and it is thanks to this efficient intention—or this virtually liberating "truth"—that all dogmas are justified and are in the final analysis compatible despite their antagonisms. Thus the denial of purgatory by Protestants results, not from an exhaustive cosmology, to be sure, but from a psychological or mystical economy based upon the saving power of faith; obviously, faith does not save by itself, but does so in connection with the divine Mercy which, in Protestantism, is crystallized in the unique Sacrifice of Christ. In such perspectives, the dogmatic concept does not contain its end within itself, that is, in its capacity to inform; it is merely a means in view of a result, and in this case it can be said without hesitation that "the end justifies the means"; this observation applies to all religious concepts that are objectively contestable, on condition, of course, that they issue from archetypal truths and pertain to intrinsically orthodox systems. The abrupt contrast between the dogmas of Christianity and Islam is, within the context of Semitic monotheism, the most salient example of these formal antinomies; it is clearly impossible for both parties to be right, or for them to be right in the same respect, but it is possible—and necessarily so—for each to be right in its own way, from the point of view of the respective "saving psychology", and thus by virtue of the results.

In eschatological logic, the Catholic dogma of purgatory results from the idea of justification through works, whereas the Protestant denial of purgatory results from the idea of justification through faith. On the Catholic side, it will be objected that the denial of purgatory leads to lukewarmness and thus compromises salvation; on the Protestant side, it will be thought on the contrary that the idea of purgatory compromises saving trust (the *prapatti* of the Hindus) and leads to the excesses of penitentialism and the abuse of indulgences; in both cases the reproaches are unjust, even though each side contains an element of truth. Be that as it may, if the Protestant denial of purgatory leads to complacency and unconcern, as the Catholics think, and if from the Protestant point of view the idea of purgatory leads to the cult of works to the detriment of faith, Hindus and Buddhists, with no less reason, could express analogous objections against the monotheistic idea of an eternal hell: they could make the point that this concept not only is absurd in itself since it abuses the notion of eternity, but also favors despair and in the final analysis unbelief and indifference. The transmigrationists will therefore think that the Protestant rejection of purgatory is neither worse nor better than the monotheistic rejection of transmigration, a concept which also, and necessarily, possesses psychological, moral, and mystical virtues.

Thus it is proper to distinguish between "informative" dogmas, which have a direct import, and "functional" dogmas, whose import is indirect: the first communicate metaphysical, cosmological, or eschatological information; the second determine moral and spiritual attitudes. Although purely functional dogmas, if taken literally, may possibly be erroneous, in the final analysis they rejoin the truth by their fruits.

* * *

It will be understood that all this does not mean divergent dogmas are equivalent simply because they are justified in one way or another, for two contradictory theses cannot be right in the same respect; all we wish to point out here is the distinction between informative and functional dogmas, although the dividing line between them is not absolute. If the objection were raised that the denial of purgatory by the Protestants is false since purgatory exists, we would reply, in the first place, that for the true "believer"—and for him alone— this denial means in practice that Paradise is accessible through the merits of Christ and, second, that the Orthodox also reject the idea of a place of expiation because, according to them, souls can no longer gain merit after death, even though they may benefit from the prayers of the Church, which adds an element of compensation; for the Orthodox, as for Muslims, "purgatory" is the hell from which the divine Mercy has removed particular souls.[3] Next we

---

3. To the objection that their dogma is false, the Protestants would reply that they do not deny hell and that God always has the power to save whom He wills, which rejoins the opinion of the Orthodox Church and Islam; besides, certain Anglicans accept the idea of purgatory. Let us add that this idea, aside from other motiva-

would make the point that, if the Protestant rejection of purgatory is false—or to the extent it is false—the Hindu and Buddhist idea of reincarnation, taken literally and not metaphysically, is also false; now the immense majority of Hindus and Buddhists take reincarnation quite literally, not in an arbitrary manner, but in accordance with the literal meaning of their Scriptures,[4] which is inadequate as regards cosmic reality, but not as regards a specific spiritual psychology.[5] From the point of view of this psychology, the question is not that of knowing what some dogma includes or excludes, but what we draw from it.

Another materially inexact, but not functionally pointless, dogma concerns the reduction of animals to dust after the "resurrection of the body": our objection is that the subjectivity of a superior animal is far too personal to be reducible to nothingness; now "nothingness" here is in fact synonymous with "transmigration". Since transmigration is not admissible in Semitic monotheism, one replaces it by "nothingness" and thus extricates oneself from a doctrinal responsibility which a monotheistic theology, having to remain centered upon man and the human, could not assume.

A classic example, so to speak, of a functional dogma is the denial in the Koran of the crucifixion of Christ; it is true that this denial has been interpreted by some Muslims as meaning simply that Christ was not vanquished, just as Abraham, thrown into the

---

tions, is justified because the sector in hell where the door remains open from above differs necessarily, by that very fact, from the sector without such an opening, and this for quasi-metaphysical reasons.

4. Where there is a literal meaning, there is also a legitimate possibility of a literal interpretation: since the Law of Manu teaches that a given sin entails a given rebirth among animals, there are necessarily men who believe it, despite the cosmological transpositions of the symbolism made by others. This gives us an opportunity to insert the following remark: according to certain sources, devotional Buddhism teaches that women have no access to the Paradise of Amitabha until they undergo a masculine rebirth; this opinion is not only illogical within the framework of Amidism, but contrary to numerous accounts issuing from this school.

5. The idea of reincarnation is equivalent—qualitatively and not by its content—to the conviction that the earth is flat and that the sun circles the earth; in both cases there is "naïvety" through lack of experience and also lack of imagination; but this "optical illusion" can nonetheless be given a symbolic and psychological use.

furnace, was not vanquished by the fire,[6] and as Daniel, in the lions' den, was not vanquished by the beasts; however, general feeling upholds the literal meaning of the passage.[7] Aside from the fact that the denial of the Cross closes the door to the Christian perspective, which Islam quite evidently did not have to repeat, this denial contributes indirectly to the spiritual attitude pertaining to the Muslim perspective; the function here sanctifies the means, namely, the symbolism.

* * *

The naïvety of certain concepts that have become dogmatic in practice can be explained on the one hand by the natural symbolism of things and on the other by a wise concern for self-protection; for if the truth has, in the final analysis, the function of rendering man divine, it could not at the same time have the function of dehumanizing him. For example, it could not have the aim of causing us to experience the pangs of the infinitely great or the infinitely small, as modern science intends to do; to reach God, we have the right to remain children, and we even have no choice, given the limits of our nature.

A classic example of naïve dogma is the Biblical story of creation, followed by that of the first human couple: if we are skeptical—therefore atrophied—we clash with the childishness of the literal meaning, but if we are intuitive—as every man ought to be—we are sensitive to the irrefutable truths of the images; we feel that we bear these images within ourselves, that they have a universal and timeless validity. The same observation applies to myths and even to fairy tales: while describing principles—or situations—concerning the universe, they describe at the same time psychological and spiritual realities of the soul; and in this sense it can be said that the symbolisms of religion or of popular tradition are common experiences for us, both on the surface and in depth.

6. "We (*Allâh*) said: O fire, be coolness and peace for Abraham!" (*Sûrah* "The Prophets" [21]:69).

7. It should be noted that the idea that Christ was not crucified but was taken directly to Heaven existed already at the time of the Apostles, which proves that the intentions behind this idea cannot be reduced to an exclusively Islamic function.

8

Christian Divergences

On the basis of what was said in the preceding chapter, we may broach the question of the divergence between Catholicism and Protestantism, by showing first of all that it is improper to apply the logic of one confession to another, at least from the standpoint of intrinsic values, though not from the standpoint of a particular symbolism or a particular mode of efficacy.

Religious or confessional phenomena are ruled by two great principles, namely, "apostolic succession" and the "mandate of Heaven"; to the first pertains sacramental regularity, and to the second the extra-canonical intervention of Grace. "Mandate of Heaven" is a Confucian phrase, which signifies that investiture, and consequently authority, descends directly from Above, without the intermediary of a sacramental means, by virtue of an archetypal reality that must manifest itself in a given world and in response to earthly conditions that call forth this descent. Such was the case with the emperors of China—it is really the Throne that created the emperor—and also, as Dante observed in his treatise on monarchy, with the Roman, and later the Christian and Germanic, emperors; and quite paradoxically, the papacy itself is an example of this kind of investiture, since what creates a pope is an election and not a sacrament.[1] In the framework of Christianity as a whole, the Reformation, while appearing logically and technically as a heresy—though let us not forget that Rome and Byzantium anathematize each other—possesses in itself a justification and hence an efficacy, which it draws from a spiritual archetype that was, if not

---

1. Let it be noted that Baptism—*mutatis mutandis*—pertains partially to the same principle, since it does not necessarily require priesthood; nevertheless it is not unconnected to the initiatic sphere, since it brings about the remission of original sin and thus transforms a primordial potentiality into a virtuality.

entirely ignored by Rome, at least certainly "restrained".[2]

In other words, the phenomenon of the Reformation, exactly like other analogous manifestations—notably in Hinduism and Buddhism—results from the principle of the "mandate of Heaven", hence from the providential intervention of the archetype of a spiritual possibility. For this reason, this phenomenon is altogether independent of the rule of "apostolic succession" and "sacramental technique", and this independence—the confessional or exoteric mentality being what it is—explains precisely the vehemence of the Lutheran and other denials. The sometimes naïve character of the formulations plays no part here, for such is the general tone of exoteric ostracism; and it is symbolism, no more and no less.

* * *

Protestants and Amidists—although still other examples could be cited—consider that it is faith that saves, not of itself, but by virtue of a Redemption, historical or mythological, as the case may be; and since they can neither admit that works add something to the Grace granted by Heaven nor contest that moral effort is humanly indispensable, they see the motivation for this effort in our gratitude toward the saving Power. Now one of two things: either gratitude is necessary, in which case it is not faith alone that saves; or it is faith that saves, in which case gratitude is not necessary. But if one goes to the root of things, it will be perceived that "gratitude" and "sincerity" are synonymous here: that is, sincerity forms a part of faith; thus it is only sincere faith—proven precisely by moral effort and works—which is faith as such in the eyes of God. In other words, sincerity necessarily manifests itself through our desire to please Heaven, which, having saved us from evil, obviously expects us to practice good; and this consistency may be termed "gratitude".

It is known that the idea of Redemption, whatever its "mythical" expression, results from the idea of man's fundamental corruption;

---

2. See *Christianity/Islam: Essays on Esoteric Ecumenicism,* "The Question of Evangelicalism".

now this Augustinian and Lutheran concept, which implies the conclusion that man is totally incapable of righteousness in the eyes of God, is like a theological "caricature" of the very contingency of the human being, by virtue of which we can have no quality or power outside God. In Augustinianism, what cuts the Gordian knot is grace combined with faith; metaphysically, it is also *gnosis*, which participates in the Sovereign Good, or it is the Sovereign Good that is manifested in and by *gnosis*. And predestination is what we are, outside all temporal mechanism.

It is true that the anthropological pessimism of Saint Augustine did not apply to the first human couple before the fall, but to humanity marked by the fall. Adam and Eve, being creatures, were obviously contingent, not absolute; but the fall derives from contingency, precisely, and manifests it at an inferior level, that of illusion and sin. It is here that a divergence of perspective intervenes: according to some, fallen man always remains man; in him there is something inalienable, without which he would cease to be human; according to others, fallen man is defined by the fall, which necessarily penetrates and corrupts all his initiatives, and this is the point of view of Saint Augustine, but to a less "totalitarian" degree than for Luther, for the Bishop of Hippo admits that under certain conditions we may be deserving of merit, whereas Luther denies this and instead substitutes the as it were impersonal mystery of faith. But aside from this difference in degree, the ancient Churches and the Reformation both make use—and Amidism in fact does the same—of the idea of our fundamental helplessness as the springboard of a method founded upon saving faith.

* * *

In this order of ideas, it is possible to distinguish between two ways of looking at things. According to the first it will be said: if a man makes no effort to transcend himself, he follows his passions and becomes lost; if he does not advance toward his salvation, he moves away from it, for he who does not advance, retreats—whence the obligation of sacrifice, asceticism, and meritorious works. According to the second way, the contrary will be said: man is saved in advance by religion, which is why religion exists; it suffices therefore to have faith and to observe the rules; in other words, every believer, by definition, finds himself included in saving Grace; it suffices not to step out of it; that is, to keep one's faith while abstaining from vices and crimes—whence the obligation of moral equilibrium on the basis of faith.

The first of these perspectives, which is that of Catholicism for example, is dynamic, so to speak: its symbol could be the star, whose rays are either centripetal or centrifugal, according to whether man strives toward his salvation or on the contrary retreats from it. This dramatic alternative is addressed first to passional men—or to men insofar as they are passional—and then to those whose nature requires a mystical way that is combative and sublime, hence "heroic". The second of these two perspectives, which is among others that of Protestantism, is static and balanced, so to speak: its symbol could be the circle, which on the one hand includes and on the other excludes, according to whether man remains within the precincts of salvation or on the contrary leaves them. This alternative, which in fact is reassuring, is addressed in the first place to men predisposed to trust in God, but trusting neither in their capacity to save themselves nor in priestly complications, and then, more particularly, to contemplatives of a calm type, who love simplicity and peace.

The two perspectives necessarily combine, despite their difference of accentuation; each of them gives rise to characteristic abuses: either to dramaticism and the cult of suffering in the first case, or to complacency and lukewarmness in the second.[3] In any case, an abuse can serve as an argument only in a very relative manner; there are no abuses possible in the archetypes.

In the same vein of thought, we may note the following: the Reformers argue that Redemption suffices to guarantee salvation to those of the baptized whose faith is sincere and is accompanied,

---

3. In authentic Protestantism, complacency is excluded by intensity of faith and by the sense of duty, hence by that "categorical imperative" which is virtue and morality. In Catholicism, Thomist intellectuality is capable of checking the excesses of a "baroque" sentimentalism; moreover, medieval art, which is truly celestial, has in principle an analogous function, since it introduces an element of intellectuality and serenity into religious sentiment, for "those who have ears to hear". It could be added that it is possible to love "our cathedrals" out of patriotism, hence unintelligently and without understanding their message.

consequently, by an impeccable morality; this in fact is all that is needed, in Christianity, to satisfy the requirements of the necessary minimum. But when they reject monastic asceticism, which to them seems a useless luxury and even a lack of faith, they lose sight of the fact that asceticism stems not from the dimension of the indispensable, but from that of love, and sometimes from that of fear; for on the one hand it is necessary to love God with all our faculties, and on the other it is better to go to Heaven "with fewer members" than to hell "with all our members". The Reformers had in their favor at least two extenuating circumstances, one secondary and one essential: first that Catholics have attitudes which, by their over-accentuation and narrow-mindedness, inevitably provoked reactions,[4] and second that in the economy of the Protestant perspective love of God coincides with the active joy of gratitude, hence with the happiness that comes from piety and virtue. Now this perspective is capable of a deepening which transcends ordinary measures and which pertains to the sphere of holy "peace", not holy "passion".

* * *

After these generalities, some considerations concerning ritual divergences are called for. It is not exact to say that the Lutheran Communion is only a "memorial", that it denies the ontological relation between Calvary and the rite; it is Zwingli and the liberal Protestants, not Luther, who thus minimize the Eucharistic mystery; for the German Reformer believed in the Real Presence in both species. In denying transubstantiation—not inherence or consubstantiation—he refers moreover to Saint Paul, who speaks of "the

---

4. The confusion between the elementary requirements of what is strictly necessary and the possible feats of mystical excess—the first dimension relating to salvation as such, and the second to the degrees of beatitude—is also found in the Muslim world, despite the sober and reassuring realism of the Koran and the *Sunnah*, without which the Revelation would not be "good tidings" (*bushrâ*). The confusion in question seems to stem from an overly passional need for absoluteness, which instead of being qualitative becomes quantitative, and which in addition readily confuses legalism with virtue and delights in exaggerations whose sole motive is to please God, as if He could, out of blindness, be biased favorably towards such things, *quod absit.*

bread which we break" (1 Cor. 10:16), and who says: "so let him eat of that bread" (1 Cor. 11:28); that is to say, the Apostle speaks of "bread" and not the "appearance of bread". Even Calvin affirms that "Christ, with the plenitude of his gifts, is no less present, in Communion, than if we were seeing him with our eyes and touching him with our hands." What actualizes the ontological relation between the Mass and Calvary is the Real Presence, independently of the question of transubstantiation; that one may conceive of transubstantiation as a change of substance—an elliptical idea if ever there was one—is an entirely different question.

The Lutheran Communion pertains in the final analysis to the same ritual economy as Muslim prayer; it is like a minimal fragment of the Catholic Mass from the point of view of content or grace, but it is something else from the point of view of the container or form, so that the Catholic objections do not apply to it, except for the self-defense of Catholicism. The Catholic Eucharist offers graces commensurate with the spiritual possibilities of a Saint Bernard; the Lutheran Communion, given that "in my Father's house are many mansions", offers a viaticum commensurate with ordinary believers of good will—*et in terra pax hominibus bonae voluntatis*—exactly as is the case with Muslim prayer, the only "sacrament" of exoteric Islam, which proves that the Lutheran rite is eschatologically sufficient in its religious context. All Catholics must take Communion, but not all of them are Saint Bernard; and the very transcendence of the Eucharist entails terrible dangers, as Saint Paul attests. No doubt Luther closed a door, but he opened another; if he lessened the Eucharistic Grace, he nonetheless, by considerably simplifying and centralizing worship, too dispersed in Roman practice, opened the door to a particular spiritual climate, which also possesses its mystical virtuality—on condition of its being turned to account by a Christo-centric fervor whose sap is faith, and thus by a comportment that is not "meritorious" or "heroic", but "normal" and "Biblical". For sanctity does not coincide purely and simply with "heroism of virtue"; it also comprises modes akin to quietism, where moral equilibrium, joined to contemplative union, plays a preponderant role.[5]

5. We were told this by a monk of the Eastern Church.

What matters in the Lutheran Communion is the fact that the bread communicates Christ's will to save us, or the fact that he has saved us, which here amounts to the same thing; like certain Muslim theologians, Luther aims not at everywhere "dotting the i's"—which is the Roman tendency—but at believing in the literal wording of Scripture[6] and acknowledging that a given enigma is true "without asking oneself how" (*bilâ kayfa*);[7] whence his refusal to accept transubstantiation, which in his opinion adds nothing to the Real Presence, any more than does the Gnostic idea of an immaterial and merely "apparent" body add something to the Divinity of Christ.

Perhaps it is necessary to specify here that for Lutherans there is only one saving Sacrifice, that of Calvary: Communion does not "renew" it; it is not a new sacrifice; it merely actualizes for believers the unique Sacrifice. For Catholics, however, each Mass is a new sacrifice, "bloodless" no doubt and "relative" in comparison with the blood Sacrifice, but nonetheless having a truly sacrificial character; Protestants see in this conception a multiplication of the Sacrifice— multiple Masses being put in place of the one Sacrifice—whereas for the Catholics these Masses are precisely "relative", as we have just said; this does not satisfy the Protestants, given their archetypist insistence on the unicity of Christ and their horror of "secondary causes", as Muslims would say. On the whole, the Catholic Mass is comparable to the image of the sun reflected in a mirror: without pretending to be the sun, it "repeats" it in a certain fashion, and in practice the Catholics readily overemphasize this repetition, despite theological specifications that are not always kept in mind by the religious sensibility; whereas the Lutheran Communion is comparable—or aims at being comparable—not to the reflected image of the sun, but simply to its ray. The relentlessness of the Lutheran battle against the Mass is explainable by the idea that the Catholic rite becomes *de facto* too independent of its unique and indivisible pro-

---

6. *Alles geglaubt oder nichts geglaubt*: "to believe all or nothing".

7. It is curious to note that the problems of evil and predestination, which are insoluble within monotheistic and theological logic, led Luther and others to perfectly Asharite reasonings, to Gordian knots which they could not cut except by means of that *deus ex machina* which is "faith", a movement that is *a priori* volitive and sentimental, yet in essence intuitive and, in privileged cases, capable of opening the door to *gnosis*.

totype, to the point of seeming to substitute itself for it; obviously, Catholics cannot accept this reproach, any more than the Islamic reproach of tritheism, but they should be able to understand that at the basis of these grievances there lies an intention of method much more than of doctrine, of mystical attitude much more than of theological adequacy.

On the Catholic side—let us insist upon this once again—it seems to have been forgotten that the majesty of the Eucharistic sacrifice implies certain practical consequences concerning the handling of the rite. The concrete and demanding character of this majesty has been patently forgotten by submitting the sacrifice to all kinds of intentions, applications, or modalities that are too contingent—we would almost say too casual—and thus profaning it in the final analysis;[8] it is as if the sense of the divine dignity of the rite were concentrated upon the Eucharistic species only, particularly the host, which is exposed and worshiped in the monstrance, but which is mistreated in being given to anyone and under ridiculous conditions. Be that as it may, Lutherans reject the Masses on account of the historic and sacramental uniqueness of the Sacrifice, just as the Asharites reject secondary causes on account of the princial and efficient uniqueness of God; in both cases there is ostracism in virtue of an idea of absoluteness.

Before going further, it is perhaps necessary to recall the Eucharistic theses of Catholicism and Orthodoxy; for Catholics, the Eucharistic presence of Christ is produced, not by "impanation" nor by "consubstantiation", but by "transubstantiation", meaning that the "substance of the bread no longer remains", which they justify— abusively in our view[9]—with the consecrating words of Christ; according to this theory, the "substantial form of the species no

8. Experience proves that the "first communion" of children—obligatory for all and socially conventional—is a double-edged sword, for if on the one hand it benefits children who are really pious, on the other hand it exposes the sacrament to a profanation, which could not be in the interest of unworthy children, even if they are relatively innocent.

9. As regards the pure doctrine, for we do not deny the possibility of a certain psychological opportuneness for a particular ethnic group. This kind of justification also obviously applies to the Reformation—not in the sense of a profusion of "strategic" specifications in this case, but on the contrary in the name of simplicity and pious inarticulation.

longer remains", not even their "raw material". The Orthodox, for their part, either do not admit transubstantiation, or they do not admit that it implies "a substance that changes and accidents that do not change"; their intention is to remain faithful—quite wisely—to the Eucharistic teaching of Saint John Damascene, according to whom "the Holy Spirit intervenes and does what transcends all word and thought. . . . And if you inquire as to how this happens, let it suffice you to know that it happens through the Holy Spirit . . . that the word of God is true, effective, and all-powerful, the manner of it remaining unfathomable."[10]

*   *   *

Catholicism is Catholicism, and Protestantism is Protestantism; by this truism we mean to say that a purely formal Protestantizing tendency has no organic connection with the archetype that motivated and brought about the Reformation, all the more so in that it is the archetype that chooses the man and not inversely; it is not enough to imitate or improvise gestures in order to be concretely in conformity with a spiritual archetype and consequently in harmony with the divine Will. It is possible that Heaven could will a phenomenon such as the Lutheran Communion; but it is impossible that it could will the Lutheranization of the Catholic Mass, for God cannot contradict Himself on one and the same plane, the very one that would imply an intrinsic contradiction; the fact that God brings about the manifestation of the Islamic possibility in no way means that He wishes Christianity to be Islamized, any more than He desires that Islam be Christianized. The principle of the spiritual economy of archetypes means that one and the same form may be valid in a particular confessional context but not in another, except for an adaptation that stems from the archetype itself and not from a purely human enterprise.

According to Catholic logic, the Lutheran Communion is invalid, not only because the rite has been changed, but also because the officiant is not a priest; whereas from the Lutheran—or

---

10. *Exposé précis de la Foi orthodoxe*, 4:13. The Reformers did not think otherwise.

general Protestant—point of view, the officiant is a priest thanks to the sacerdotal virtuality that man as such possesses by his deiform nature; Christ actualized this virtuality through the "mandate of Heaven" of which we have spoken above; that is, Heaven permits this Mandate to descend upon the officiant by virtue of his election by the Community, or by those whom the Community delegates, exactly as is the case—technically speaking—with the Roman pontiff.[11] Tradition—Protestants reason—may well confirm this Mandate, but does not create it; the officiant is not a pastor *ex opere operato*. Doubtless, the Western Church never went so far as to deny the laity a kind of indirect sacerdotal function, but it has not granted it the same degree of recognition as has the Eastern Church; on the contrary, it too much neglected it, the celibacy of priests helping to widen the gap between the tonsured and the laity, which, precisely, was avoided by the Orthodox.

* * *

And this leads us to another problem: what is the meaning of the fact that the Reformation rejects Tradition and intends to base itself on Scripture alone? It means that it is a question of a religious possibility that is marginal and clearly not fundamental: the argument here is that Scripture alone is absolutely certain and stable, whereas Tradition occasionally calls for caution and is often diverse and variable, as is shown by the diversity—and in some cases the doubtful character—of the liturgies.[12] Catholics, Orthodox, and Protestants are in agreement on the subject of Scripture, but not on that of Tradition; in Islam as well the abrupt divergences between Sunnites and Shiites have to do with Tradition and not with the Book. Quite obviously, the Catholics are right to maintain their point of view, which is fundamental, but that of the Protestants corresponds no less to a possibility in a particular theological, mystical,

---

11. And for the *'ulamâ—mutatis mutandis*—whose authority is also derived from a delegation, in virtue of the sacerdotal potentiality of man. We have noted above that Baptism, inasmuch as it can be conferred by a member of the laity, pertains to the same general principle.

12. Otherwise the Tridentine Mass would not have been necessary.

and moral context, though not outside it. What Christ termed "the commandments of men" certainly pertains to the element "Tradition"; the Talmud is incontestably "traditional". On the other hand, the total absence of any tradition is impossible; even Lutheranism, Calvinism, and *a fortiori* High Church Anglicanism are traditional in certain respects.

In this context, we cannot pass over in silence the following observation: on the Catholic side, there is a certain bureaucratization of the sacred, which goes hand in hand with a kind of militarization of sanctity, if one may be allowed to express oneself thus; in particular, there is a cult of monastic "Rules" and one of liturgical "rubrics". Protestantism intends to place itself in a more "evangelical" dimension, but it opposes Roman excesses with new excesses; only the Eastern Church maintains the Christic message in perfect equilibrium, all things considered. For the Eastern Church, Protestantism is a function of Catholicism; the one does not go without the other; they are the two poles of the Western disequilibrium.[13]

In other words: Tradition, considered in itself and outside any restrictive modality, is comparable to a tree; the root, the trunk, the branches, and the fruit are what they must be; each part comes in its season, and none of them wants to be another; this is what the Orthodox have understood perfectly, they who stop at the Seventh Council and wish to hear no talk of any "institutionalized Pentecost", if we may use such an expression out of a desire for clarity. It is not that a patriarch, with the agreement of other patriarchs, who are his equals, cannot undertake a particular, secondary adaptation required by particular circumstances—the contrary would be

---

13. One example, among others, of "Tradition" as a "commandment of men" is the cardinalate: whereas bishops and patriarchs derive from the Apostles, there is nothing in the New Testament that prefigures the cardinals. At the beginning of this papal institution, even the laity could obtain this dignity; after the 11th century, it was attributed only to the bishops, priests, and deacons who surrounded the Pope; in the 13th century, every cardinal received the rank of bishop and the red hat; finally, in the 17th century, the cardinals received the title of "Eminence". All this has a more imperial than sacerdotal character and scarcely accords with the principle "everywhere, always, by all" (*quod ubique, quod semper, quod ab omnibus creditum est*); having said this, we do not contest that such an institution may be required by the Roman or Latin mentality any more than we contest the requirements of the play of Providence.

opposed to the nature of things—but no patriarch can make a decision regarding a substantial change, such as the introduction of the
filioque or the celibacy of priests, and impose it upon all the patriarchs, who are his brothers.[14] As a result of the unstable, adventur-
ous, and innovative mentality of the Roman, German, and Celtic
Westerners, the Catholic West has not been able to realize fully an
equilibrium between the principles of growth and conservation, or
in other words it has needed an institution which grants pre-emi-
nence to the first principle over the second,[15] and which thus "tra-
ditionalizes" a possibility that in itself is problematic. Thus, we admit
that the Papacy—for that is what is at issue—was a providential
although ambiguous necessity,[16] but the Protestant phenomenon
benefits from the same justification, at least in a secondary way; in
other words, the very ambiguity of the Papacy necessarily gave rise
to the Protestant reaction and to the denominational scission of the
Latin West.

*   *   *

One of the great qualities of the Catholic Church—which it shares
with the Orthodox Church—is its sense of the sacred, which is litur-
gically and aesthetically expressed by its solemn Masses; in

14. The *filioque* could have found its place among the possible "theological opinions"; but it was not at all necessary—history proves it—to impose it tyrannically
upon the entire Church.

15. Let it be noted that the Mass of Pius V was not an innovation but a putting in
order; the abuse lay in a preceding disorder, not in the conservative measures of
the Pope.

16. "But be not ye called Rabbi: for one is your Master, even Christ; and all ye are
brethren. And call no man your father upon the earth: for one is your Father,
which is in Heaven. Neither be ye called masters: for one is your Master, even
Christ" (Matt. 23:8-10). But the Pope is placed in a quasi-absolute fashion above the
bishops, his brothers, and is called "Holy Father", and on the other side there are
the "Doctors of the Church"; these facts clash singularly with the passage of the
Gospel quoted and offer—to say the least—extenuating circumstances for the
Orthodox and Lutheran protestation against the Papacy as it has in fact presented
itself. In a certain sense, the Papacy is a Trojan horse, which introduces the spirit
of innovation into the Church.

Protestantism, this sense is concentrated uniquely on Scripture and prayer, which unquestionably entails a great impoverishment, not necessarily for the individual, but for the collectivity. It is true that the Anglican Church, the "High Church" in any case, has largely maintained a sense of the sacred, and Luther, who rejected all iconoclastic fanaticism, was also not insensitive to it; it is above all Calvinism that has put a rigid moralism in place of this sense, whereas liberal Protestantism—that typical product of the nineteenth century—has in the final analysis squandered everything, which is also and even more thoroughly what Catholic modernism does. Be that as it may, authentic Evangelicalism has to a certain extent replaced the sense of the sacred by the sense of inwardness, with analogous psychological consequences; for he who sincerely, "in spirit and in truth", loves to stand before God is not far from the reverential disposition of which we are speaking.

*   *   *

It has been said that the Protestant Reformation brought about an almost total destruction of sacred forms. Unquestionably it produced a certain void—although in Germanic countries there are temples that soberly prolong the Gothic forms—but is this void so much more deadly than the false plenitude of the Renaissance, and in particular the horrible profusion of the Baroque style?[17] In reality, the Protestant "destruction" goes hand in hand with a Catholic "destruction": on the one hand there is negation and impoverishment, and on the other rejection and falsification.

The Roman, Byzantine, and Gothic styles are not phases in an indefinite "evolution"; they are definitive crystallizations of legitimate modes of Christian art.[18] The center of the Western Christian

17. Which was the sentimentalist reaction to the pagan coldness of the Renaissance. The baroque style has been described by some as the "style of joy", whereas it is sad, owing to its dreamlike, hollow, and pompous unrealism, in short, to its lies and stupidity; the dress of the period attests to the same aberration.

18. There is "elaboration", to be sure, but not "evolution": once the "idea" has been fully manifested, the style no longer has to change, in spite of a diversity that is always possible and even necessary. In sacred art, unlimited evolution is as nonexistent as in biology: growth stops the moment the idea—the specific type—is fully realized.

world was the basilica of Constantine in Rome; now one fine day the Popes had the disastrous idea of destroying this venerable jewel of sacred art and replacing it by a gigantic, pagan, and glacial imperial palace, as pretentious within as without, and of adorning it with naturalistic works expressing all the sensual and marmoreal megalomania of the time.[19] The art of the Renaissance entails as its consequence the obligation to admire it—no Pope has the power to destroy the work of Bramante and Michelangelo—and it has thus imposed a lack of discernment which does not stop short at the aesthetic plane and the fruits of which are still being gathered today, indeed today more than ever before; the most general expression of this poisoning is what we may term "civilizationism", that is, the debasement of religion by means of an ideology of total and indefinite progress. Henceforth it is impossible to dissociate the Christian from the "civilized" man, in the narrow and somewhat ridiculous sense of this word; in this respect, Christians of the East have been the victims of Christians of the West, especially since Peter the Great. In any case, the Protestants cannot be held solely responsible for the modern deviation, even though it has been rightly pointed out that Calvinism has favored industrialism; but this takes nothing away from the fact that everything began with the Renaissance, and the Protestants had no part in that.[20] If we mention these things, it is not to enlarge upon a historical question which, strictly speaking, remains outside our subject matter, but to prevent a possible prejudice on the part of traditionalists who, sure of their principles—for which one cannot blame them—have had neither the idea nor the opportunity of verifying some of their apparently plausible, but in fact inadequate, conclusions. And in any case, no Church has ever opposed the so-called attainments of "human genius"—artistic, literary, scientific, technical, even political. What has been sought, on the contrary, is to attribute them to the "Christian genius", with a baffling lack of discernment and imagination.

---

19. And since the price of this monstrous edifice was the sale of indulgences, one should have renounced building it; it is a question of a sense of proportions as well as of moral sense, or a sense of *barakah*.

20. Besides, the French Revolution took place in a Catholic country; and likewise, before it, the enterprise of the Encyclopedists.

All things considered, we still have to add the following observations: civilizationism is practically synonymous with industrialism, and the essence of industrialism is the machine; now the machine produces and kills at one and the same time; it produces objects and kills the soul,[21] and this is to say nothing of its practical, and in the long run extremely serious, disadvantages, which are only too well known. Religion has accepted and almost "Christianized" the machine, and it is dying from this, whether through absurdity and hypocrisy, as in the past, or through capitulation and suicide, as today. It is as if there were only two sins, unbelief and unchastity; the machine is neither an unbeliever nor is it unchaste; therefore one may sprinkle it with holy water in good conscience.

* * *

It was in the climate of the Renaissance that the Reformation burst forth and spread with the force of a hurricane, and so it remains to this very day; and this allows us to apply the argument of Gamaliel to the Protestant phenomenon, namely, that a religious movement that does not proceed from God will not last.[22] This argument loses all its value, of course, when it is applied to an intrinsically false religious ideology, and *a fortiori* to philosophical or political ideologies, for in such cases the reason for their success is something else altogether: it does not stem from the power of a spiritual archetype, but simply from the seduction of error and the weakness of men.

Protestantism encompasses almost a third of Christianity—consequently its importance in the Western world is immense—and it is impossible to pass over it in silence when one is considering reli-

---

21. What distinguishes a traditional machine—such as the loom—from the modern machine is that it combines intelligible simplicity and an explicit and spiritually effective symbolism with an aesthetic quality, which for normal man is essential. The modern machine, on the contrary, does not have these qualities, and instead of serving man and contributing to his well-being, it enslaves and dehumanizes him.

22. The ostracizing spirit of Calvin—which contrasts with the generosity of Luther—is not an argument against the Reformation, for it is not Calvin who invented the Inquisition; in any case what is involved here is the exoterist, hence formalistic and intolerant, climate.

gions, denominations, and spiritualities. Let it be noted that without the Reformation there would have been no Council of Trent nor, consequently, the Catholic Counter-Reformation; now this functional necessity of Protestantism speaks in its favor and indirectly proves the relative—not absolute, but confessionally sufficient—legitimacy of this powerful movement; without it, the Roman Church would perhaps not have found the necessary impetus to recover and rebuild.[23] The fact that this scission in the midst of Western Christianity created at the same time favorable conditions for the final fall of the West takes nothing away from the positive meaning of the Protestant phenomenon, but shows in any case how the meshing of the positive and the negative are part of the ambiguous and ingenious play of Providence. The same observation applies *a priori* to Catholicism, certain aspects of which have contributed to the origin of the modern world, though this does not in the least take away from its quality as a great religious message and traditional civilization—hence its merits on the plane of intellectuality, sacred art, and sanctity.

*   *   *

Quite paradoxically, in Lutheranism there is at one and the same time an intention of esoterism and of exoterism, hence of interiorization and of exteriorization; on the one hand, Luther aimed at bringing everything back to the inward—"But thou, when thou prayest, enter into thy closet,[24] and when thou hast shut thy door, pray to thy Father which is in secret"—and on the other hand, he aimed at reducing everything to the "supernaturally natural" priesthood of man as such, hence of every man, or more precisely of every baptized man, for "all ye are brethren". With the first intention, the mystic of Wittenberg opens the door to certain esoteric possibilities, by the nature of things; with the second, he closes the

---

23. It is an interesting fact that the Fathers of the Council of Trent gave up condemning Luther expressly, which would have been required by conciliary custom; they preferred not to "close the door definitively to dialogue", which has a symbolical as well as a practical meaning.

24. That of the heart, according to the Hesychasts.

door to a certain type of sanctity, founded upon the "chivalric" notion of the "heroism of virtue", a notion which in itself is correct, but which becomes false when the aim is to reduce all possible sanctity to this type while disparaging everything that relates to quietism and *gnosis*. Be that as it may: in being inspired by the injunction of Christ to the Samaritan, to worship neither on Mount Gerizim nor in the Temple, but "in spirit and in truth", Luther wished to efface as much as possible the outward signs of worship—without being fanatical like Calvin—as if transcendence could not tolerate immanence; but at the same time he actualized a certain desire for esoterism, a paradox also manifested by Amidism and Shiism. The non-formal—or emptiness—is in fact a vehicle of the supraformal and of plenitude, as Saint Bernard understood quite well in emptying his chapels of all images and all adornments, and as Zen monks understood no less well in making use of an art of bareness, hence of emptiness.

Not unconnected to this question of an "esoterizing exoterism" is the fact that the Reformation, which issued from an ascetical religion, "rediscovered" the spiritual potential of sexuality, exactly as was the case in Buddhism, also ascetical, when Shinran, monk that he was, married and introduced marriage into his sect, the *Jôdo-Shinshû*.[25] The intrinsically sacred character of sexuality was not unknown to Judaism or to Hinduism, from which the two ascetical religions just mentioned issued respectively; however, neither Judaism nor Hinduism was unaware of the value of asceticism, which obviously keeps all its rights in every religious climate.[26] Man is so made that he naturally slides towards the outward and has need of a wound to bring him closer to "the kingdom of God which is within you", and this notwithstanding the complementary fact that the contemplative—and he alone—perceives traces of the Divine in

25. Let us not lose sight of the fact that Catholicism witnessed the blossoming of the more or less "erotic" mysticism of the knights, the troubadours, and the *Fedeli d'Amore*; Tantric Buddhism exhibits analogous features, but with a very different emphasis.

26. Judaism gave birth to the ascetical sect of the Essenes; as for Hinduism, it is unusual in that its compartmentalized structure and metaphysical amplitude enable it fully to turn to account every spiritual possibility: fully, that is, independently of every antagonistic religious context.

outward beauties, which amounts to saying that given his predisposition, these beauties have the capacity to interiorize him, in conformity with the principle of Platonic *anamnesis*. This means that the ambiguity of man is that of the world: everything manifests God—directly or indirectly, or in both ways at the same time—but nothing is God; thus everything can either bring us closer to Him or take us further from Him. Each religion, or each confession, intends to offer its solution to this problem in conformity with a particular psychological, moral, and spiritual economy.

*   *   *

Someone has asked us[27] why Protestantism, since it manifests *grosso modo* the same archetype as Amidism, does not, like Amidism, possess a method of ejaculatory prayer; now this archetype does not of itself imply that mode of prayer any more than that mode of prayer implies this archetype; rather it implies an emphasis upon faith and the assiduous practice of prayer, and in fact we find both of these elements in authentic Protestantism.

Another question that we have been asked concerns the formal homogeneity that every intrinsically orthodox confession possesses; now if Protestantism on the whole does not possess this homogeneity, each of its great branches—Lutheranism, Calvinism, Anglicanism—possesses it. In the same way, each of the ancient Churches is homogeneous, whereas Christianity as a whole is not, any more than are other religions, each of which comprises at least two more or less antagonistic denominations.

"For where two or three are gathered together in my Name, there I am in the midst of them", Christ said. Among all the possible meanings of this saying, there could also be this one: the first two who assemble are Catholicism and Orthodoxy, and the third, which is mentioned apart, is Protestantism. In fact, Christ could have said: "Where three are gathered", thereby placing the three confessions on the same level; but he said "two or three", which

27. Referring to the chapter "The Question of Evangelicalism" in our book *Christianity/Islam: Essays on Esoteric Ecumenicism*.

98

indicates a certain inequality, but always within the framework of religious legitimacy: inequality as regards completeness or plenitude, but at the same time legitimacy as regards love of Christ and spiritual authenticity, and thus an underlying fraternity despite the differences.

9

Keys to the Bible

In order to understand the nature of the Bible and its meaning, it is essential to have recourse to the ideas of both symbolism and revelation; without an exact and, in the measure necessary, sufficiently profound understanding of these key ideas, the approach to the Bible remains hazardous and risks engendering grave doctrinal, psychological, and historical errors. Here it is above all the idea of revelation that is indispensable, for the literal meaning of the Bible, particularly in the Psalms and in the words of Jesus, affords sufficient food for piety apart from any question of symbolism; but this nourishment would lose all its vitality and all its liberating power without an adequate idea of revelation or of suprahuman origin.

Other passages, particularly in Genesis, though also in texts such as the Song of Songs, remain an enigma in the absence of traditional commentaries. When approaching Scripture, one should always pay the greatest attention to rabbinical and cabalistic commentaries and—in Christianity—to the patristic and mystical commentaries; then will it be seen how the word-for-word meaning practically never suffices by itself and how apparent naïveties, inconsistencies, and contradictions resolve themselves in a dimension of profundity for which one must possess the key. The literal meaning is frequently a cryptic language that more often veils than reveals and that is only meant to furnish clues to truths of a cosmological, metaphysical, and mystical order; the Oriental traditions are unanimous concerning this complex and multidimensional interpretation of sacred texts. According to Meister Eckhart, the Holy Spirit teaches all truth; admittedly, there is a literal meaning that the author had in mind, but as God is the author of Holy Scripture, every true meaning is at the same time a literal meaning; for all that is true comes from the Truth itself, is contained in it, springs from it, and is willed by it. And so with Dante in his *Convivio*: "The

Scriptures can be understood, and ought to be explained, principally in four senses. One is called literal. . . . The second is called allegorical. . . . The third sense is called moral. . . . The fourth sense is called anagogical, that is, beyond sense (*sovrasenso*); and this is when a Scripture is spiritually expounded, which, while true in its literal sense, refers beyond it to the higher things of the eternal Glory, as we may see in that Psalm of the Prophet, where he says that when Israel went out of Egypt Judea became holy and free. Which, although manifestly true according to the letter, is nonetheless true in its spiritual meaning, namely, that the soul, in forsaking its sins, is made holy and free in its powers" (*Trattato Secondo*, I).

As regards Biblical style—setting aside certain variations that are of no importance here—it is important to understand that the sacred or suprahuman character of the text could never be manifested in an absolute way through language, which perforce is human; the divine quality referred to appears rather through the wealth of superposed meanings and in the theurgic power of the text when it is thought and pronounced and written.

Equally important is the fact that the Scriptures are sacred, not because of their subject matter and the way in which it is dealt with, but because of their degree of inspiration, or what amounts to the same, their divine origin; it is this that determines the contents of the book, and not the reverse. The Bible can speak of a multitude of things other than God without being the less sacred for it, whereas other books can deal with God and exalted matters and still not be the divine Word.

The apparent incoherence in certain sacred texts results ultimately from the disproportion between divine Truth and human language: it is as if this language, under the pressure of the Infinite, were shattered into a thousand disparate pieces or as if God had at His disposal no more than a few words to express a thousand truths, thus obliging Him to use all sorts of ellipses and paraphrases. According to the Rabbis, "God speaks succinctly"; this also explains the syntheses in sacred language that are incomprehensible *a priori*, as well as the superposition of meanings already mentioned. The role of the orthodox and inspired commentators is to intercalate in sentences, when too elliptic, the implied and unexpressed clauses, or to indicate in what way or in what sense a certain statement should be taken, besides explaining the different symbolisms, and so forth. It is the orthodox commentary and not the word-for-word meaning of the Torah that acts as law. The Torah is said to be "closed", and the sages "open" it; and it is precisely this "closed" nature of the Torah that renders necessary from the start the Mishnah or commentary that was given in the tabernacle when Joshua transmitted it to the Sanhedrin. It is also said that God gave the Torah during the day and the Mishnah during the night and that the Torah is infinite in itself, whereas the Mishnah is inexhaustible as it flows forth in duration. It should also be noted that there are two principal degrees of inspiration, or even three if the orthodox commentaries are included; Judaism expresses the difference between the first two degrees by comparing the inspiration of Moses to a bright mirror and that of the other prophets to a dark mirror.

The two keys to the Bible are, as already stated, the ideas of symbolism and revelation. Too often revelation has been approached in a psychological, hence purely naturalistic and relativistic, sense. In reality revelation is the fulgurant irruption of a knowledge that comes, not from an individual or collective subconscious, but on the contrary from a supraconsciousness, which though latent in all beings nonetheless immensely surpasses its individual and psychological crystallizations. In saying that "the kingdom of God is within you", Jesus Christ means not that Heaven—or God—is of a psychological order, but simply that access to spiritual and divine realities is to be found at the center of our being, and it is from this center precisely that revelation springs forth when the human ambience offers a sufficient reason for it to do so and when therefore a predestined human vehicle presents itself, namely, one capable of conveying this outflow.

But clearly the most important basis for what we have just spoken of is the admission that a world of intelligible light exists, both underlying and transcending our consciousness; the knowledge of this world, or this sphere, entails as a consequence the negation of all psychologism and likewise all evolutionism. In other words, psychologism and evolutionism are nothing but makeshift hypotheses to compensate for the absence of this knowledge.

To affirm then that the Bible is both symbolistic and revealed means, on the one hand, that it expresses complex truths in a language that is indirect and full of imagery and, on the other, that its source is neither the sensorial world nor the psychological or rational plane, but rather a sphere of reality that transcends these planes and immensely envelops them, while yet in principle being accessible to man through the intellective and mystical center of his being, or through the "heart", if one prefers, or pure "Intellect". It is the Intellect which comprises in its very substance the evidence for the sphere of reality that we are speaking of and which thus contains the proof of it, if this word can have a meaning in the domain of direct and participative perception. Indeed the classical prejudice of scientism, or the fault in its method if one wishes, is to deny any mode of knowledge that is suprasensorial and suprarational, and in consequence to deny the planes of reality to which these modes refer and which constitute, precisely, the sources both of revelation and of intellection. Intellection—in principle—is for man what revelation is for the collectivity; in principle, we say, for in fact man cannot have access to direct intellection—or *gnosis*—except by virtue of a pre-existing scriptural revelation. What the Bible describes as the fall of man or the loss of Paradise coincides with our separation from total intelligence; this is why it is said that "the kingdom of God is within you", and again: "Knock, and it shall be opened unto you." The Bible itself is the multiple and mysterious objectification of this universal Intellect or *Logos*: it is thus the projection, by way of images and enigmas, of what we carry in a quasi-inaccessible depth at the bottom of our heart; and the facts of sacred History—where nothing is left to chance—are themselves cosmic projections of the unfathomable divine Truth.

10

Evidence and Mystery

God created the world out of nothing; this is the teaching of the Semitic theologies, and by it they answer the following difficulty: if God had made the world out of a pre-existing substance, that substance would be either itself created or else divine. The creation is not God; it cannot therefore emanate from Him; there is an unbridgeable hiatus between God and the world; neither can become the other; the orders of magnitude or of reality, or of perfection, are incommensurable.

The main concern of this reasoning is not a disinterested perception of the nature of things, but the safeguarding of a simple and unalterable notion of God, while making allowance for a mentality that is more active than contemplative. The aim is therefore to provide, not a metaphysical statement that does not engage the will or does not appear to do so, but a key notion capable of winning over souls rooted in willing and acting rather than in knowing and contemplating; the metaphysical limitation is here a consequence of the priority accorded to what is effective for the governing and saving of souls. That being so, one is justified in saying that Semitic religious thought is by force of circumstances a kind of dynamic thought with moral overtones, and not a static thought in the style of Greek or Hindu wisdom.

From the point of view of such wisdom, the idea of emanation, in place of *creatio ex nihilo*, in no way compromises either the transcendence or the immutability of God; between the world and God there is at once discontinuity and continuity, depending on whether our conception of the Universe is based on a scheme of concentric circles or on one of radii extending outward from the center to the periphery: according to the first mode of vision, which proceeds from the created to the Uncreated, there is no common measure between the contingent and the Absolute; according to the second mode of vision, which proceeds from the Principle to its manifestation, there is but one Real, which includes everything and excludes only nothingness, precisely because the latter has no reality whatsoever. The world is either a production drawn from the void and totally other than God, or else it is a manifestation "freely necessary" and "necessarily free" of Divinity or of Its Infinitude, liberty as well as necessity being divine perfections.

As for the contention that the creationist concept is superior to the so-called "emanationist" or "pantheistic" concepts because it is Biblical and Christ-given, and that the Platonic doctrine cannot be right because Plato cannot be superior either to Christ or the Bible, this has the fault of bypassing the real fundamentals of the problem. First, what is rightly or wrongly called "emanationism" is not an invention of Plato's;[1] it can be found in the most diverse sacred texts; second, Christ, while being traditionally at one with the creationist thesis, nevertheless did not teach it explicitly and did not deny the apparently opposite thesis. The message of Christ, like that of the Bible, is not *a priori* a teaching of metaphysical science; it is above all a message of salvation, but one that necessarily contains, in an indirect way and under cover of an appropriate symbolism, metaphysics in its entirety. The opposition between the divine Bible and human philosophy, or between Christ and Plato, therefore has no meaning so far as the metaphysical truths in question are concerned; that the Platonic perspective should go farther than the Biblical perspective brings no discredit on the Bible, which teaches what is useful or indispensable from the point of view of the moral or spiritual good of a particular humanity, nor does it confer any human superiority on the Platonists, who may be mere thinkers just as they may be saints, according to how much they assimilate of the Truth they proclaim.

For the Platonists it is perfectly logical that the world should be the necessary manifestation of God and that it should be without origin; if the monotheistic Semites believe in a creation out of nothing and in time, it is evidently not, as some have suggested, because they think that they have the right or the privilege of accepting a

---

1. Wrongly, if one understands emanation in a physical sense; rightly, if one acknowledges that it is purely causal while at the same time implying a certain consubstantiality due to the fact that reality is one.

"supralogical" thesis that is humanly absurd; for the idea of creation appears to them on the contrary as being the only one that is reasonable and therefore the only one that is capable of logical demonstration, as is proven precisely by the method of argumentation used in theology. Starting from the axiom that God created the world out of nothing, the Semites reason thus, *grosso modo*: since God alone has Being, the world could not share it with Him; there had to be a time, therefore, when the world did not exist; it is God alone who could give it existence. On the religious plane, which as far as cosmology is concerned demands no more than the minimum necessary or useful for salvation, this idea of creation is fully sufficient, and the logical considerations which support it are perfectly plausible within the framework of their limitation; for they at least convey a key truth that allows a fuller understanding of the nature of God, as it intends to reveal itself in the monotheistic religions.

More than once we have had occasion to mention the following erroneous argument: if God creates the world in response to an inward necessity, as is affirmed by the Platonists, this must mean that He is obliged to create it, and that therefore He is not free; since this is impossible, the creation can only be a gratuitous act. One might as well say that if God is One, or if He is a Trinity, or if He is all-powerful, or if He is good, He must be obliged to be so, and His nature is thus the result of a constraint, *quod absit*! It is always a case of the same incapacity to conceive of antinomic realities, and to understand that if liberty, the absence of constraint, is a perfection, necessity, the absence of arbitrariness, is another.

If, in opposition to the Pythagorean-Platonic perspective, the concept is put forward of an Absolute which is threefold in its very essence and therefore devoid of the degrees of reality that alone can explain the hypostatic polarizations—an Absolute which creates without metaphysical necessity and which, in addition, acts without cause or motive—and if at the same time the right is claimed to a sacred illogicality in the name of an exclusive "Christian supernaturalism", then an explanation is due of what logic is and of what human reason is; for if our intelligence, in its very structure, is foreign or even opposed to divine Truth, what then is it, and why did God give it to us? Or to put it the other way round, what sort of divine Message is it that is opposed to the laws of an intelligence to which it is essentially addressed, and what does it signify that man was created "in the image of God"?[2] And what motive could induce us to accept a message that is contrary, not to our earthly materialism or to our passion, but to the very substance of our spirit? For the "wisdom after the flesh" of Saint Paul does not embrace every form of metaphysics that does not know the Gospels, nor is it logic as such, for the Apostle was logical; what it denotes is the reasonings whereby worldly men seek to prop up their passions and pride, such as the teaching of the Sophists and Epicureans and, in our day, the current philosophy of the world. "Wisdom after the flesh" is also the gratuitous philosophy that does not lead us inwards and that contains no door opening to spiritual realization; it is philosophy of the type "art for art's sake", which commits one to nothing and is vain and pernicious for that very reason.

The incomprehension by theologians of Platonic and Oriental emanationism arises from the fact that monotheism puts in parenthesis the metaphysically essential notion of divine Relativity or *Mâyâ*;[3] it is this parenthesis, or in practice this ignorance, which inhibits an understanding of the fact that there is no incompatibility whatever between the "absolute Absolute", Beyond-Being, and the "relative Absolute", creative Being, and that this distinction is even crucial. The divine *Mâyâ*, Relativity, is the necessary consequence of the very Infinitude of the Principle: it is because God is infinite that

---

2. We take the liberty of adding here, by simple association of ideas, the following consideration: according to Genesis, "God created man in His own image," and "male and female created He them." Now according to one Father of the Church, the sexes are not made in the image of God; only the features that are identical in the two sexes resemble God, for the simple reason that God is neither man nor woman. This reasoning is fallacious because, although it is evident that God is not in Himself a duality, He necessarily comprises principial Duality in his Unity, exactly as He comprises the Trinity or Quaternity; and how can one refuse to admit that the Holy Virgin has her prototype in God, not only as regards her humanity, but also as regards her femininity?

3. The fact that we have drawn attention on a number of occasions to this Vedantic notion must not prevent our insisting on it once more; we shall return to it again later. Here the reader may be reminded that the term *Mâyâ* combines the meanings of "productive power" and "universal illusion"; it is the inexhaustible play of manifestations, deployments, combinations, and reverberations, a play with which *Âtmâ* clothes itself even as the ocean clothes itself with a mantle of foam ever renewed and never the same.

He comprises the dimension of relativity, and it is because He comprises that dimension that He manifests the world. To which it should be added: it is because the world is manifestation and not Principle that relativity, which at first was only determination, limitation, and manifestation, gives rise to that particular modality constituting "evil". It is neither in the existence of evil things that evil lies nor in their existential properties nor in their faculties of sensation and action, if it be a question of animate beings, nor even in the act insofar as it is the manifestation of a power; evil resides only in whatever is privative or negative with respect to good, and its function is to manifest in the world its aspect of distance from the Principle, and to play its part in an equilibrium and a rhythm necessitated by the economy of the created universe. In this way evil, wholly evil though it be when looked at in isolation, fits within a good and is dissolved *qua* evil when one looks at it in its cosmic context and in its universal function.

The Platonists feel no need whatever to try to fill the gap that might seem to exist between the pure Absolute and the determinative and creative Absolute; it is precisely because they are aware of relativity *in divinis* and of the divine cause of that relativity that they are emanationists. In other words, the Hellenists, if they did not have a word to express it, nevertheless possessed in their own way the concept of *Mâyâ*, and it is their doctrine of emanation that proves it.

The notion of mystery and an obligatory anti-Hellenism have given rise in the Christian climate to the idea of the "natural" character of intelligence in itself; now if human intelligence is created "in the image of God", it cannot be purely and simply, and therefore exclusively, "natural", for the very substance of intelligence is opposed to its being so. The human spirit is natural in its contingent operations, but supernatural in its essence; there is no reason whatever for saying that human thought is not capable in principle of adequation to the transcendent Real; certainly, it could never in fact attain thereto by its own powers, but this is only an accidental infirmity. The very existence of the theologies is proof of this; as soon as a dogma or mystery is called into question, the theologians know very well how to defend it. Thought or logic, reviled while in the service of a foreign religion or of a wisdom derived from that immanent Revelation which is the Intellect, suddenly becomes good for something and is robed in the purple of the infallibility and prestige of the Holy Spirit.

To say that a truth is situated "beyond logic" can mean only one thing, namely, that it does not provide in its formulation the data which would allow logic to resolve an apparent antinomy; and if it does not provide those data, it is because they are too complex or too subtle to be expressed in a single formulation, and also because it would be disproportionate and useless to provide them, since the formulation in question has the virtue and aim of awakening intellection in those who are capable of it.

The part that may be played by the *intellectus agens* with respect to the *intellectus possibilis*—the first considered as bringing about the abstraction for the second—is eminently contingent, as is reasoning in general with respect to intellection. Discursive thought may or may not be necessary for a particular intuition of the real; it may eliminate an obstacle or attract the lightning flash of direct knowledge, but it cannot produce that knowledge; it possesses therefore the character of an indirect cause, though it may already carry a part of knowledge within itself, when it is adequate in its ordering and its content. The activity of the *intellectus agens* recalls a magic that works through cosmic analogies, and also alchemy, the principles of which are similar: it conjures up the underlying substance of forms by means of affinities, in the sense that the partial truth evokes its own complement or totality.

* * *

In the Christian climate one may come across two ways of supporting Semitic creationism and also Trinitarianism: the one appeals to logic and so to reason, while the other on the contrary claims for transcendence a mysterious right to absurdity; in other words, the "supernatural" appeals at once to human "good sense" and to a hypothetical divine illogicality. The fault of the first argument lies in thinking that the reasoning employed has an absolute validity, and that consequently it invalidates the Platonic and Vedantic points of view; the fault of the second lies in thinking that logic, once it is placed at the service of Platonism or other non-Christian metaphysics, proves thereby its own anti-spiritual character, coupled with the quite gratuitous assumption that the said metaphysics are products of the reasoning faculty alone.

It must be borne in mind in the first place that logic, on whatever plane it may be applied, is the capacity to draw conclusions from one or more premises; only that concerning which we have no evidence, and of which we consequently have no knowledge whatever, is above logic. The divine Essence eludes logic to the extent that It is indefinable; but as we are conscious of It, seeing that we can speak of It, It constitutes a premise, which allows us to draw at least indirect and extrinsic conclusions. Everything that presents itself to our mind is therefore a premise in some respect, and as soon as there is a premise, whether direct or indirect, precise or approximate, there is the possibility of a conclusion and so of logic. To speak of concepts that impose themselves on us while concealing themselves from our logic is a contradiction purely and simply, and in fact no doctrine has ever rejected the logical explanation of any notion, at least within the limits within which logic can operate. No religion has ever imposed on the human mind, or ever could have imposed, an idea which logic was incapable of approaching in any way; religion addresses itself to man, and man is thought.

If logic is incapable of drawing out of itself the truths of the Invisible, it is for the obvious reason that it cannot draw anything whatever out of itself, and because the least rational operation has need of evidence that is furnished to it either by the senses or by information or again by intellectual intuition; but intuition is unable to operate in the absence of factors that actualize it. If the premises provided by the senses are in principle easy to obtain in the spatial and temporal field that is accessible to us, the same is not true *a priori* of premises that pertain to suprasensorial reality; we say *a priori* because in principle the visible proves the Invisible by its complexity no less than by its simplicity, but this presupposes the actualization of pure intellection, which is difficult to obtain under the spiritual conditions of the "dark age", and even impossible to obtain outside a traditional spirituality. It would be ridiculous to maintain that Plato discovered his doctrine by force of logic, and therefore through the use of reason alone; he belonged intellectually to the Aryan world, and his doctrine is like a distant modality of Brahmanism, apart from the things he was able to learn from the Egyptians.

In view of this, it may readily be accepted that there is not and cannot be any human knowledge of the Invisible or of the Transcendent without Revelation, given that the cyclical decadence of the human race has had as its first consequence the loss of spontaneous intellection. And Revelation, if it is to be credible, must take account of a certain intellectual, rational, and passional predisposition, which explains the nature of its means, on the one hand, and its effectiveness, on the other, at least extrinsically.

Reason is the faculty of knowing indirectly in the absence of a direct vision and with the help of points of reference; one who embraces everything in a direct knowledge has no need of reason, nor *a fortiori* of points of reference, and this is the case of the angelic intelligences, although they necessarily have certain limitations but of a different order, inasmuch as, not being God, they cannot have an absolute knowledge of God; each angelic intelligence manifests one particular divine quality to the exclusion of others, and it will envisage things in relation to the particular quality it manifests. A man may know that there is a certain distance between one place and another, he may also know that a horse takes a certain time to travel that distance, and he can then work out, with the help of these points of reference or these premises, that it will take him so many hours on horseback to arrive at such and such a place. But an angel has no need of this reasoning or calculation; he embraces in a single view all the premises of the situation.

Evolutionism, let it be said in passing, provides a typical example of reasoning in the absence of sufficient evidence. Modern scientism starts from the gratuitous and crude axiom that there is no reality outside sensorial—or virtually sensorial—experience, with the highly relative exception of psychology, a very limited domain which, in any case, can be reduced philosophically to a subtle mode of the sensorial; and since it starts from this axiom, it will reason in accordance therewith, leaving out of account evidence that surpasses it. Now in the case of a reality that does surpass the sensorial and empirical order, any such reasoning must evidently be false—one might reason just as well about a sparrow while denying the existence of birds—and it will demonstrate its falsity by replacing the missing evidence with purely functional hypotheses; and these hypotheses will betray their chimerical nature by their monstrousness, as witness the concepts of the ape-man or of "hominization". All this is truly sinister if one considers that the essential truth has reference, on the one hand, to the transcendent Absolute and, on the other, to the suprasensible cosmos, or to the extrasensorial character of the greater part of the cosmos, including our souls, which appertain to this order precisely.

Two words are capable of expressing what is being spoken of here, and they are terms of ordinary speech: "God" and "beyond". The genesis of our world can be explained only by these two terms; the beyond is dependent upon God, and our world is dependent upon the beyond; our world is but a furtive and almost accidental coagulation of an immense beyond, which one day will burst forth and into which the terrestrial world will be reabsorbed when it has completed its cycle of material coagulation.

*　　*　　*

The theology of "transubstantiation"[4] provides an example of the passage from a revealed premise into the sphere of a particular logic. A logic is particular, not in its functioning, for two and two everywhere make four, but in its natural presuppositions, which among Roman Catholics have the characteristics of physical empiricism and juridicism, whence the tendency toward trenchant equations and simplistic and irreducible alternatives. When Jesus, an Oriental, expresses himself thus: "This is my body; this is my blood," that means, in Eastern parlance, that the bread and wine are equivalent to the body and blood of Jesus in the context of divine inherence and saving power, it being these, precisely, that confer on the body and blood their sufficient reason and their value; in Western parlance, however, the words of Christ can only carry the meaning of a rigorous and massive physical equation, as if any such equation comprised the smallest metaphysical or sacramental advantage.[5] It may nevertheless be acknowledged that this dogmatism is inevitable in a climate of emotional totalitarianism, and that in this climate it consequently represents the most effective solution from the point of view of safeguarding the mystery. It may also be acknowledged, all question of expediency apart, that the Lateran Council was right in the sense that the Eucharistic elements, even while remaining

4. The Orthodox Church speaks more prudently of a "transmutation".
5. If one had to interpret literally every word of the Gospels, one would have to believe that Christ is a vine or a door, or one would have to hate father and mother, or to pluck out one's eye, and so on.

what they are, quite plainly cannot be what they are in the same way that they were before, given that bread penetrated by a divine Presence or Power must thereby change its substance in a certain respect. However, this consideration leads us into the realm of the indefinite and the inexpressible and cannot wholly justify the logic of the theory of transubstantiation; in any case, the words of Christ that are regarded as necessitating this formulation do not in reality necessitate it at all, for an Oriental ellipsis is not a mathematical or physical equation; "to be equivalent in a certain respect" does not necessarily mean "to be the same thing in every respect".

The problem could also be approached in the following way: if in truth the Eucharistic species have literally become the flesh and blood of Jesus, what is the advantage of this so to speak "magical" operation, given that the value of this flesh and this blood lies in its divine content, and that this same content can itself penetrate the bread and the wine without any "transubstantiation"? For we can neither desire nor obtain anything greater than the divine Presence; if that Presence were in a tree, the tree would then be equivalent to the body of Christ, and there would be no need to ask oneself whether the wood was something other than wood, or to conclude that it was a tree without being one, or that it was a "form" that contradicted its substance, and so forth. It is not the body of Jesus that sanctifies God; it is God who sanctifies this body.[6]

Let there be no misunderstandings: we have no preconceived opinion about the idea of transubstantiation, but if anyone says that the proof of this idea is in the words of Christ, we have no choice but to reply that these words in themselves do not imply the meaning attributed to them. It can be admitted, however—setting aside any question of intrinsic truth—that the idea of transubstantiation has the value of an impelling argument, well-fitted to forestall any

---

6. The luxury of being precise in matters that concern the "Real Presence" has not precluded a forgetfulness of the difference in significance and in effect between the Eucharistic species themselves, as if there could be, in that order of greatness, differences lacking meaning or concrete relevance. The bread visibly refers to the formal order and perfection, and the wine to the supraformal and infinity; we say "visibly" because the message of the symbols results from the nature of things and because wine has always been an image of celestial nectar and of passage to the "greater mysteries".

naturalistic or psychological interpretation of the mystery in a society all too easily led into that kind of betrayal.

* * *

Trinitarian theology gives rise to a comparable hiatus between a very subtle and complex transcendent reality, described as "inexhaustible" by Saint Augustine himself, and a logic that is dogmatically coagulative and piously unilateral, that is to say, determined by the necessity of adapting the mystery to a mentality more volitive than contemplative. The theology of the Trinity does not constitute an explicit and homogeneous revelation; it results on the one hand, like the concept of transubstantiation, from a literalistic and quasi-mathematical interpretation of certain words in the Scriptures, and on the other hand from a summation of different points of view, deriving from different dimensions of the Real.

The first paradox of the Trinitarian concept is the affirmation that God is at the same time absolutely one and absolutely three. Now the number one alone manifests absoluteness; the number three is necessarily relative, unless one accepts that it is to be found in unity in an undifferentiated and potential manner only, but then the fact of considering it distinctively represents a relative point of view, exactly as in the case of the Vedantic *Sat* (Being), *Chit* (Intelligence), and *Ânanda* (Bliss). The second paradox of the Trinitarian concept is the affirmation that the divine Persons are distinct from one another, but that each is equal to the Essence, which is something that no explanation of relationships can attenuate, since no theologian can admit that in one connection the Persons are inferior to the Essence and that in another the Persons are indistinguishable. Finally, the third paradox is in the affirmation that the Persons are only relations, and that outside those relations they are the Essence, which amounts to saying that they are nothing, for a pure and simple relation is nothing concrete. One cannot have it both ways: either the relation confers on the Person a certain substance, and then it is by that substance that the Person is distinguished from the other Persons; or else the relation confers no substance, and then it is a pure abstraction about which it is useless to speak, unless one attributes it to the Essence and says that the

115

Essence comprises relations that render explicit its nature, which would lead us to the modalism of the Sabellians.[7]

There is still a fourth difficulty in Trinitarianism, however, which is its exclusiveness from a numerical point of view, if so inadequate a term be permitted. For if God incontestably comprises the Trinity which the Christian perspective discerns in Him, He also comprises other aspects which are, in a manner of speaking, numerical and which are taken into account by other traditional perspectives.[8] It is precisely this diversity that indicates in its own way the relativity, in the most exalted sense possible, of the Trinitarian conception and above all of the "divine dimension" that conditions that conception.

Christianity is founded on the idea and the reality of divine Manifestation. If it were not a religion but a sapiential doctrine, it might rest content with describing why and how the Absolute manifests itself; but being a religion, it must include everything within its fundamental idea of Manifestation; the Absolute itself must therefore be envisaged exclusively in connection therewith, and it is just this that gives rise to the Trinitarian doctrine, not only in itself but also in its theological and therefore totalitarian and exclusive form.

---

7. Rejected because of an inability to combine it with the complementary thesis. The truth is here antinomic, not unilateral: the *hypostases* are at the same time three modes of one divine Person and three relatively distinct Persons.

8. According to Hindu doctrine, the Divinity is One, envisaged as *Brahma* or *Âtmâ*; it is binary when envisaged as *Brahma nirguna* ("unqualified") and *Brahma saguna* ("qualified"), or as *Para-Brahma* ("supreme") and *Apara-Brahma* ("non-supreme"), or, in another context, as *Purusha* and *Prakriti*; it is ternary when envisaged as *Brahma nirguna, Brahma saguna,* and *Buddhi*, and it is again ternary at each of these three levels, namely, as *Sat-Chit-Ânanda* at the two unmanifested levels and as *Trimûrti* ("Triple Manifestation") at the level of manifestation. The divine Quaternity is the central idea of the American traditions, wherein Divinity essentially possesses the positive qualities of the four cardinal points, Purity or Strength belonging to the North, Life or Felicity to the South, Light or Knowledge to the East, Water or Grace to the West. The eight Guardians of the Universe in Hinduism are related to the same reality, at once metacosmic and cosmic, though doubtless in a less marked manner. The same holds for the *Dhyâni-Buddhas* and *Dhyâni-Bodhisattvas*, who in theistic language represent divine aspects, with the difference that in this case it is the number five or the number ten that expresses the polarization through *Mâyâ* of the divine Substance.

*　　*　　*

According to a first possible interpretation of the Holy Trinity, the Father is the Absolute whereas the Son and the Holy Spirit pertain to Relativity and are as it were its foundations. This interpretation is irrefutable, because if the Son were the Absolute he could not be called "Son", and he could not even have become incarnate; and if the Holy Spirit were the Absolute, it could neither proceed nor be sent nor delegated. The fact of the incarnation proves the relativity of the Son with respect to the Father, but not with respect to men, for whom the Son is the manifestation of the Absolute. It is true that the words of Christ announcing his subordination are attributed to his human nature alone, but this delimitation is arbitrary and interested, for the human nature is bound by its divine content; if it is a part of the Son, it must manifest him. The fact that this human nature exists and that its expressions manifest its subordination and, by the same token, the hypostatic subordination of the Son shows that the interpretation of the Son as the first Relativity in relation to the purely Absolute Father is not contrary to Scripture and is inherently irrefutable.

But there is another interpretation of the Trinity, horizontal this time, and conforming to another real aspect of the mystery: God is the Absolute; He is the single Essence, whereas the three Persons are the first Relativities in the sense that on a plane that is already relative they actualize the indivisible characteristics of the Essence. This interpretation is also irrefutable and Scriptural, in that there are scriptural expressions which can be explained only with its help; and it is this interpretation that justifies the affirmation that the divine Persons are equal, while being necessarily unequal in a different context. And what makes it possible to concede that they are equal to the single Essence is precisely the fact that the Essence comprises, principially, synthetically, and without differentiation, three Qualities or Powers, which are called "Persons" *a posteriori* on the plane of diversifying Relativity; from this standpoint it is evident that each "Person" is the Essence in a total and direct sense; the relative, on pain of being impossible, has its root in the Absolute, of which it is a dimension that is either intrinsic or extrinsic according to whether it is considered in its pure possibility or as a projection.

What has just been said implies that the Trinity affirms itself on three planes that exoterism confuses, and cannot do otherwise than confuse, in view of its concern for a simplifying synthesis and for what is psychologically opportune with reference to certain human tendencies or weaknesses. The first plane, as we have seen, is that of the Essence itself, where the Trinity is real since the Essence admits of no privation, but undifferentiated since the Essence admits of no diversity; from this standpoint one may say that each Person or each Quality-Principle is the other, which is just what one cannot say from the standpoint of diversifying relativity. The second plane is that of the divine Relativity, of the creative Being, of the personal God: here the three Quality-Principles are differentiated into Persons; one is not the other, and to affirm without metaphysical reservation that they are the Essence is to pass without transition, either by virtue of a purely dialectical ellipsis or through lack of discernment and out of mystical emotion, to the plane of absoluteness and non-differentiation. One may envisage also a third plane, already cosmic but nevertheless still divine from the human point of view, which is the point of view that determines theology, and this is the luminous Center of the cosmos, the "Triple Manifestation" (*Trimûrti*) of Hindu doctrine, and the "Spirit" (*Rûh*) of Islamic doctrine; here also the Trinity is present, radiating and acting. To repeat: the first metaphysical plane is that of the Essence or the Absolute; the second is that of the diversified Personality or metacosmic Relativity; and the third is that of the diversified and manifested Personality, or cosmic Relativity, which is nonetheless still divine and thus principial and central. It will have been noticed that these three planes themselves also correspond respectively to the three *hypostases*, with each plane in turn and in its own way comprising the Ternary.

* * *

Saint Augustine, with the object of demonstrating that the Son cannot be otherwise than equal to the Father, poses two questions: "Did God not want to have a Son who should be equal to Himself, or was He unable to have such a Son? If He did not want to, He is jealous; if He could not, He is incapable." It must be recognized that this reasoning, apart from having a certain symbolical value *pro domo*, involves the begging of a question, in the sense that it proceeds on the theoretical assumption that these possible obstacles to a divine "Will" or "Power" can only be deficiencies. This is arbitrary, since these deficiencies, differently motivated, become qualities. One could in fact reply to the question cited: "Yes, God is 'jealous', but of His Uniqueness; yes, He is 'incapable', but of not being He who is!" To deny the first proposition would be polytheism; to deny the second, atheism. One sees that the terms "jealous" and "incapable", chosen with a preconceived conclusion in view, are not sufficient to displace the total truth, which surpasses Trinitarian exclusivism, and that this truth is strong enough to impose itself on these terms by providing them with another and positive meaning, one conforming moreover to Biblical language. Indeed, if the Essence cannot engender a Manifestation equal to itself, it is because no manifestation can be the Essence.

As proof that the Son is equal to the Father, this saying of Christ has been quoted: "All things that the Father hath are mine." This is to lose sight of the fact that if this saying is to be understood in an absolutely literal sense, fatherhood and innascibility, and thus the quality of principle or origin or the fact of not being engendered, must appertain equally to the Son; if they do not, this is a proof that this equality—apart from its underlying and impersonal reality, which is not bound by hypostatic determination—is equality only by participation or reflection and is consequently not absolute, though this clearly does not deprive it of its own intrinsic reality. In a certain sense the reflection of the sun in a mirror is equal to the sun: "everything that the sun has it has"; all the same it is not the sun, even though it is the light of the sun and nothing else.

Every relation indicates a substance; otherwise it represents nothing positive or intrinsic; if it is equivalent to a substance, it is evidently so in a relative sense, rather in the same way that the color green is a different substance from the color red, unlike the luminosity which makes them both visible and is their common substance. A *hypostasis* is a substantial mode of the unique Substance, or it is nothing; we may paraphrase the Augustinian questions and answers quoted above in an inverse sense by saying that if the Son cannot bear to be subordinate—since he is engendered—to the Father, he must be "proud". If this argument is worthless, so also is that of Saint Augustine; if Saint Augustine's argument has the merit of supporting the real unity of Essence between the Father and the Son, ours has the merit of supporting the no less real subordination of the Son to the Father; but in both cases the poverty of the argument outweighs the merit of the intention.

Once Revelation decided that the Word made flesh should be called "Son", it took upon itself the responsibility and the consequences of that designation. If the quality of Sonship implies no kind of subordination in itself, and if this lack of subordination therefore holds good at all levels, and for as long as one distinguishes a Son from a Father, then the term is ill-chosen, and a different one ought, out of pity, to have been proposed. But since the Word intended to be called "Son", it is from the starting point of a relationship of subordination that one must envisage a transcendent dimension of equality, or of unity of Essence. Not only does this not contradict Scripture, but it also maintains all possible glory without abolishing subordination in the dimension to which it belongs.

*   *   *

The question at issue can also be expressed in the following way, though without its being possible to spare the reader from some repetition, inevitable in a subject of this kind. In order to give the Trinitarian metaphysics a dogmatic face, one is obliged, on pain of being able to say nothing about it, to make explicit the modes of its differentiation; but one is then obliged to interrupt the sequence of ideas at the decisive moment and return without transition to the initial affirmation that the Essence is one, an affirmation which, however, in no way answers the question of the meaning of the differences between the Persons. Thus it is said that the Father possesses Divinity as Principle, whereas the Son possesses it by generation; or that the Father is Light and Life and Wisdom in the manner of a source, whereas the Son is these same things in the manner of a stream; or that the Father is the generator of greatness, whereas the Son is himself greatness. From this it is concluded that the Father and the Son differ, but then one hastens to add, in order to annul the consequences implied in this conclusion, that they do not differ by Essence but only by "origin"; this seems to overlook the fact that "origin", on pain of being a pure and simple nothingness, necessarily reflects an aspect of Essence, that is, something that is *ad se* and not *ad alterum*; to say that each divine Person possesses an

Essence of its own, an Essence that reflects its origin, is not to deny the single Essence that "subsists" in what one could call the "Essence of Person", for the latter is only a mode of affirmation of the single Essence.[9]

The inherence of one substance in another and their essential identity ought to offer no difficulty whatever, for there are numerous examples of it in nature herself. Every individual has inherited from his parents the elements that make him up, which does not prevent him, while being of the same species and the same race as his forbears, from being at the same time distinct from them in a concrete way, and not merely in an abstract way as the theological notion of "relation" would have it. Similarly, a light of a certain color is neither a light of another color nor colorless light, but it is nonetheless light and nothing else, and it illuminates because it is really light and not because it is red or green. An apparent antinomy, if it is not absurd in the simple natural order, which is so narrowly logical and so easily verifiable, is obviously no more so in the supernatural and divine order.[10]

Here is a further illustration: ice is water and nothing else but water, but it is at the same time a sort of new substance—otherwise one would call it water and not ice; it is not the mere notion of congelation and nothing else. Congelation, without changing in any respect the nature of water, nevertheless adds to it a mode which makes ice at the same time both water and other than water; if ice were in no way distinct from water, because nothing had arisen to modify its substantial nature, there would be no difference between a running stream and one that had been transformed into blocks of ice. When Christ proclaims his identity with God, he cannot mean that apart from the relationship of filiation he is absolutely God;

---

9. When one defines the *hypostases* as "modes", an objection at once presents itself, which is the following alternative: if they are modes, they are therefore not Persons—as if there were here an irreducible incompatibility, whereas modes can perfectly well have a personal nature, and whereas this tri-personalism in no way prevents God from being a unique Person, to the extent that, or on the plane on which, this definition can properly be applied to Him.

10. Saint John says first: "the Word was with God", and then: "the Word was God". He thus indicates two modes of identity and consequently two substances, or more precisely a single Substance in two different aspects, the one relative and the other absolute.

and when he bears witness to his subordination, he cannot by virtue of his human nature say something that he would not say by virtue of his divine nature, for that would be to identify human nature with God. The Son by his divine nature is consequently both different from the divine Essence and identical with it; filiation is not merely a "relationship of origin" without concrete content; it determines at the same time a substantial reality, and that reality is precisely the Person, if this word is to have a meaning.[11]

If it be objected that the contradiction contained in the Trinitarian conception is the mark of an antinomism that is inevitable in the realm of the mysteries, it may be answered, firstly, that this antinomism is the consequence of a dialectical ellipsis which is in principle avoidable, and secondly, that it necessitates above all the recognition that God is as much One single Person-Substance as Three Persons in One single Substance; the exclusive point of view of Unity even takes precedence, for reasons that should be apparent enough, over the point of view of Diversity. And since the virtues of antinomism are thrust upon us when it comes to covering over the fissures in a theological formulation, it is permissible to observe that the only perfectly disinterested antinomism is the kind that admits apparently incompatible aspects of transcendent Reality, whereas pious prejudice contents itself with hurling anathemas.[12]

---

11. The following is a typical line of reasoning: the three divine Persons are equal, for if they were not, they would not have the same Essence and would not be one single God—as though there were a common measure between the hypostatic determinations and the essential Undetermined, which is the Absolute. Furthermore, it is arbitrary of Saint Thomas to attribute to the terrestrial Jesus alone the subordination that the Scriptures attribute to the Son. What the Gospels show is that the Son is at once subordinate and equal to the Father, and it is precisely this antinomy that opens up for us in an indicative manner the mystery of Relativity *in divinis*. "God became man in order that man might become God": the Absolute became Relativity in order that the relative might become absolute. This paraphrase of the Patristic formula suggests, with no more and no less success than the formula itself, a metaphysical situation that it would be difficult to express otherwise in a few words.

12. It must be recognized that more than one heresy, or so-called heresy, was worthy of interest, and could have been made use of if the dogmatic point of view were not narrow by definition. The whole problem of Trinitarianism is that it was found necessary to make divergent realities fit into a formula which had to present them bluntly as being convergent, while dogmatic opportunism nipped in the bud certain intermediate truths that are metaphysically indispensable.

When Saint Thomas says that in God the relations are the Essence itself, since they cannot be accidents in Him, he is right in the sense that the *hypostases*, produced by *Mâyâ*, have their roots in the Essence, which by definition is single; but one cannot support him when he presents an equation that passes over the difference in the degree of reality between, on the one hand, the *hypostases* as such, and, on the other hand, their common foundation in the Essence. For Saint Thomas, the relation, when compared to the Essence, does not differ from the latter except in our own reason— a feat of ingenuity which is by no means self-explanatory, and which serves no purpose once it is understood that the divine nature comprises degrees, unless the Essence alone is to be called "God";[13] but in that case there are no longer any "Persons", and the world itself, completely cut off from God, becomes unintelligible. To explain the hiatus between "Essence" and "Person", Thomism makes the nature of human reason intervene like a *deus ex machina*; this mysterious *ratio* then becomes the substitute for the universal principle of relativity, separativity, illusion.[14]

* * *

Trinitarianism in its theological elaboration, at once contradictory and totalitarian, is "accepted" by God as a "spiritual means" in the sense of the Buddhist term *upâya*, of which we have often spoken: if on the one hand it is as an *upâya* that a limitative dogma is given or accepted by Heaven, it is on the other hand because of its limitation that this *upâya* will be providentially contradicted by other *upâya*s;

13. Analogous opinions are met with among Muslims, when, for example, in order to safeguard the unity of God, which is really in no way threatened, they affirm that diversity in the divine order exists only in the human reason; but if that is true, the world also is distinct from God only in our reason. If the existence of the world does not impugn the unity of God, then neither is that unity impugned by the diversity of the divine qualities, evidently prefigured in the Essence in an undifferentiated manner.

14. Thomism is a quasi-rationalism insofar as it maintains that we derive our science from sensible things and apply them to God as best we can; but it is eminently more than that in its dogmatic content, which provides the Thomistic method with suprarational premises and thereby actualizes intellections properly so called.

hence religious divergences, which are at once a scandal and a bless-ing. It is the limitlessness of *Âtmâ* that necessitates the plurality of *upâya*s; every limit demands a repetition that completes it while apparently contradicting it.[15]

Now, whatever may be the effects of *Mâyâ in divinis*, the divine Substance remains what it is, so that God remains "always and every-where" God; but this simultaneity of antinomic aspects is repugnant to volitive alternativism, which will hasten to deny relativity *in divi-nis* with the intention of safeguarding the absoluteness of God—which is in no way under attack—especially as the devotional mentality tends to confuse the metaphysical absolute with the human sublime.

In exoteric formulations, questions of psychological expediency or viability, which are of strictly human interest, play a part that is in some respects determinative and that gives rise to a totalitarianism that is more mystical than metaphysical; Trinitarian theology pro-vides examples, and so does the unitarian theology of the Muslims. The former is not content to allow three aspects in the divine Unity, but must make these aspects enter into the very definition of Unity itself—as though Unity were no longer Unity outside the Trinity, and as though the Absolute could be defined by any number other than One. Unitarian Islamic theology, on the other hand, is not content to allow that the One is the cause of all; it feels the need to follow this up by denying secondary causes, more particularly natu-ral laws, by declaring, for example, that fire does not burn, that it is God who makes it burn, and so on, as if the one were incompatible with the other. The contrary is termed "hypocritical", because it is said that the affirmation that "there is no God save the only God" demands, if it is sincere, the denial of intermediate causes.

---

15. The Trinity "Father, Son, and Mother", which the Koran attributes to Christianity, has three meanings: first, it expresses a psychological situation *de facto*, Mary being much more present to Christian people, as far as a truly divine func-tion is concerned, than the Holy Spirit; second, it implies that the Holy Virgin is identified with the Spirit insofar as she is the Wisdom that was "set up from ever-lasting, from the beginning, or ever the earth was" (Proverbs 8:23); third, the Koranic formulation has to stress the exoteric incompatibility of Christian Trinitarianism with Islamic Unitarianism.

Whatever may be the necessity or the expediency of Trinitarian theology, from the standpoint of pure metaphysics it appears to confer the quality of absoluteness on relativities. Hinduism shows us by all sorts of examples that the divinization of a relativity can be a way or an *upâya*, a "provisional means" that is relatively illusory but nonetheless effective and as such accepted by the Divinity; but other aspects of the Real retain all their rights. This being so, it is understandable that Islam should have come to stress the metaphysical foundation of monotheism, thus re-establishing a certain equilibrium in the total manifestation of the monotheistic Idea. Only Unity as such can be a definition of the Absolute; in the realm of number, unity alone represents an element of absoluteness, as the point or the center does in space and the instant or the present in time, or as the circle or the sphere—simplicity or perfection—does in form, or as ether—subtlety or purity—does in matter. The *Vedânta* teaches that the Absolute, *Âtmâ*, comprises the Trinity *Sat-Chit-Ânanda*, "Being-Intelligence-Bliss"; it does not assert that this ternary constitutes *Âtmâ* in an absolute fashion or that *Âtmâ* has no reality apart from this ternary.

In monotheistic theology, truths which ought to retain their internal metaphysical fluidity are readily presented as exclusive coagulations: the ocean is reduced to a piece of ice, doubtless symbolical and intrinsically truthful, but all the same not exhaustive, to say the least. Dogmatism—or exoterism—is essentially a planimetry, not an integral geometry; the missing dimension is replaced by notion-symbols which, precisely because they are only solutions by replacement, cannot always avoid paradox or even contradictions; this is what affords the opportunity for certain zealots to speak of sacred illogicality and to malign the so-called "natural" intelligence.

* * *

When Christian theology seems to attribute absoluteness to the divine Persons, it is referring consciously or unconsciously to the relative absoluteness possessed by every uncreated reality with regard to creatures as such, unless its intention is to affirm elliptically the unity of the Essence which, whether one likes it or not, transcends the hypostatic Divinity as it is in itself;[16] but to assert, as one has heard it done, that the Trinitarian relationships belong, not to this relative absoluteness, but to the pure and intrinsic Absolute, or to the absoluteness of the Essence, amounts to asking us to accept that two and two make five or that an effect has no cause, which no religious message can do and which the Christian message has certainly never done. A celestial message that would radically affront intelligence as found in men of the best intentions, disposed to recognize and accept anything of a miraculous order, would be gravely tainted by imperfection; it would not in fact be a celestial message.

Let us summarize, in order to be as clear as possible. First, in the Absolute, which is the Essence, the Persons are not discernible as Persons, although they are in it in a certain non-distinctive manner, in the sense that the Essence is necessarily the archetype of each possible Person, which amounts to saying that the Essence comprises aspects without itself being differentiated; in the divine Relative, however, the Persons are present as such, and for man this Relative in practice functions as the Absolute. Second, there is but one single divine Person, having three modalities, though according to another aspect the modalities appear in their turn as Persons. Third, the three Persons are distinct from one another, but in this respect they are not identical with the Essence. Fourth, each Person is identical with the Essence, and in this respect each is in the Essence; this makes it permissible to say that in a certain manner each Person is in the other two or, speaking paradoxically and elliptically, that it is identified with them, the One Essence being each Person in the undifferentiated Absolute.

*   *   *

16. The reservations expressed by the words "as such" and "as it is in itself" are strictly necessary: in the first case because the Intellect in a certain respect surpasses the creaturely condition since it can have the notion of the uncreated, and in the second case because the hypostatic realities belong to the Essence and are detached from it only by virtue of the differentiation assigned to them by the root-relativity, the first there is.

"Our Father": this opening invocation of God in the Lord's Prayer establishes the doctrine of the Trinity in the following way: it teaches us first of all that we are "children" of God and not merely "slaves", that is, that "deified" man constitutes as it were a divine dimension, manifested in the first place by Christ and then inaugurated by him for men. For men, God is "Our Father"; for Christ He is "My Father", and He is "Our Father" through Christ and in him; we are "children" in the "Son" and through him, but not outside the *Logos*. Christianity realizes the perspective of the Fatherhood of God, and so of human sonship: man is saved by his sonship with regard to God and so by virtue of the divine attribute which in fact we designate by the term "Paternity"; the crowns of the elect, it is said, are made of uncreated light, which indicates the deification of man in Christ. The Holy Spirit is like divine blood, which unifies the Son and the Father, and which unites man to God insofar as man places himself in the Son; and the Virgin is an aspect of Christ: she personifies the passive and receptive qualities of the divine Substance—she is the "soul" if Christ is the "spirit"—and this means that man cannot be integrated into Christ without first being integrated into the Virgin, for there is no "vertical" illumination without the corresponding "horizontal" perfection.

This entire mystical constellation is to be found prefigured in God Himself: there can be no manifested Son without the principial "pre-existence" of the Son in God; and this confrontation *in divinis* also presupposes the "pre-existence" of the Holy Spirit, for duality demands a link that betokens its essential unity. This is the doctrine of the necessary adoption of man by the *Logos*: there is no way to God without such an adoption nor consequently without the theophany that makes it possible.

* * *

It is contradictory to maintain that it is the Absolute as such which produced the tissue of contingencies that is the Bible; the existence of the Scriptures, and above all the existence of the world, proves the element of relativity in God. If there is anything that is relative in God, then relativity is divine; hence the Universe is divine,[17] not just the physico-psychic universe of animal existence, as pantheists imagine, but the total Universe with its Root at once transcendent and immanent. If one refuses to admit relativity in God, then relativity is fundamentally evil, the world is fundamentally evil, and one falls into Manichaeism.

Relativity has essentially two dimensions: distance and difference. It is by virtue of the "vertical" dimension of distance that Being becomes crystallized *in divinis* on this side, so to speak, of Beyond-Being and that, in consequence of this hypostatic polarization, the world becomes separated from God; and it is again by virtue of this dimension that the intellective Substance engenders the animic Substance, which in turn engenders the material Substance. It is by virtue of the "horizontal" dimension of difference that All-Powerfulness is distinguished from All-Goodness, or that on earth a rose is distinguished from a water lily. The whole Universe is a tissue of these two dimensions: all phenomena can be explained by their infinitely varied combinations; what unites them is Existence and, in the last analysis, a Reality at once absolute and infinite, the only Reality there is.

* * *

As the Taoists have said, "error alone is transmitted, not truth": "error," that is to say, form, which is limitative by definition and therefore exclusive, and then contingencies of temperament. This is *upâya*, the net which first imprisons and then saves; it is the half-truth that is a key to the total Truth. "Why callest thou me good?" Jesus himself asked; this is the very definition of an *upâya* in its formal aspect; a saving form, certainly, but nonetheless a form, therefore a limitation, and for some a two-edged sword.

On the subject of relativity being rooted in the divine order itself, we might also express the matter in the following way—at the risk of

---

17. This highly conditional truth gave rise, by deviation and massive coagulation, to the cosmolatry of the ancient Mediterranean peoples.

repeating ourselves, but in any case without having to fear an excess of clarity. One of two things: either we set the creature and the Creator face to face in their relationship of reciprocity or causality, in which case both terms are situated in *Mâyâ*, whatever may be the requirements of a simplifying and devotional totalitarianism; or else we envisage God in His pure essentiality or absoluteness, and then He is the Subject-Principle of which the Universe is the objectification or radiation.[18] Basically this radiation is nothing less than an aspect of the supreme Subject, for "all things are *Âtmâ*"; *Mâyâ* is the endlessly subdivided veil of the infinite Self, which alone is the pure Absolute.[19]

*   *   *

If one insists on maintaining that there are truths which are inherently supralogical, it ought to be made clear that this does not mean that they are intrinsically absurd *de jure*, but simply that they are by their nature inexpressible. But even when formulated in this way the above assertion remains contestable, for if we speak of a truth it is because we are conscious of it, and as soon as we are conscious of it we can *ipso facto* express it in one way or another, and without clashing with common sense, if we are willing or able to take the trouble to express ourselves otherwise than by ellipses or antinomies. To repeat once more, the logical absurdity of certain spiritual pronouncements is merely dialectical and elliptical; every formulation that is illogical for motives of profundity can be reduced to logical formulations of a subtle and complex character; doubtless there will always remain the gap of the inexpressible, but the inexpressible does not necessarily affirm itself in an illogical manner; silence is not an illogicality. The fact that logic is limited on account of

18. This was well understood by Eckhart, Silesius, and others. A truth is never in itself either Eastern or Western; it belongs to anyone able to grasp it.

19. For there is a relative Absolute, namely, whatever is absolute in relation to a lesser reality. For the creature as such, the Creator is the Absolute, but from the point of view of the Absolute in itself, the Creator is the first of relativities. "All things were made by him, and without him was not anything made that was made" (John 1:3).

some personal characteristic or some particular ignorance in no way implies that what surpasses it is illogical or has any metaphysical right to be so; on the contrary, logic manifests in its own way the very essence of Truth. There are in God aspects that are independent of all limitative logic, and it is from them that the cosmic play and the musical aspects of things arise; but there is nothing in God that opposes the principles of non-contradiction and sufficient reason, which are rooted in the divine Intellect. God is not limited by what we call "good", but He is essentially its Principle; consequently He is Goodness itself. The knowledge that God cannot be limited by the relativity of our goodness in no way permits the conclusion that God is evil, *quod absit*; as in the case of any positive quality, one must not confuse, where logic is concerned, the positive essence with the existential limitation, or the substance with the accident. If logically correct conclusions can be false, it is not because logic is worthless; it is either because it is accidentally equipped with insufficient data, or because its mechanism is directed by some passion and for this reason chooses false starting points.

It is clear enough that we must not demand of logic what it cannot provide for us; where logic is no longer applicable, symbolism steps in; many things that logic cannot express in a satisfactory way can be suggested effectively by symbolism. Logic is concerned with the "mathematical" and not with the "musical" aspect of things, but this in no way signifies that logic is to be despised; in a word, colors are not the same things as shapes, and a drawing is not a melody. If in the case of some dogma or some mystery one were in principle and *de jure* in a supposed domain of meaningless supralogic—a hypothesis that permits any kind of supernaturalization on the part of denominational bias or sentimentalist absurdity—then Revelation itself would be a mistake because it would be of no use to us; or else it was a mistake to give us intelligence.

Strictly speaking, one can say that antinomies between religions are situated "beyond logic"—since the logic of each dogmatism is impeccable, though in practice inoperative outside its own framework—but this is pure convenience, for one can always demonstrate, if there is reason to do so and if circumstances allow, that these antinomies are but complementary opposites arising from an identical substance.

The inexpressible is what can be approached more or less closely in a thousand different ways without ever being able to be touched at its center. A suggestive image is that of a spiral, with a centripetal movement progressing indefinitely toward a center which is never reached, but which can be grasped—speaking now of the reality symbolized—by an intellection which, like its content, is itself ineffable.

11

An Enigma of the Gospel

The dialectic of sacred Scriptures can be synthetic to the point of over-saturation, whence an aspect of "incoherence", which is the penalty of an implicit richness. According to a Hindu text, "the gods are fond of obscure language"; this is not to say that the celestial powers are opposed to clear expression when it is warranted, for truth always has its rights; but it is necessary that everything remain in the place which its nature assigns to it. The mysteries of divine Possibility, thorny for the common run of mortals, are not made for the public square; this does not mean, however, that there is an impenetrable barrier between ordinary theology and integral metaphysics, in spite of differences in nature and mission. The great difficulty for sacred language is to have to, or wish to, suggest profound and complex truths in the form of historical accounts and moral injunctions; nonetheless, "the origin and the end hold hands",[1] and the same applies to the "outward" and the "inward".

*　　*　　*

In speaking of the Last Supper, the Gospel relates an enigmatic and even disturbing incident: Christ gives Judas a sop of bread to eat and tells him, "That thou doest, do quickly"; and at that moment, Satan enters into Judas, who then leaves the room. This gives the impression that Christ took upon himself the responsibility for the betrayal, *quod absit.*

The explanation of the enigma is as follows: nothing can happen counter to the Will of God; the fact that something happens means

---

1. German proverb: *Anfang und Ende reichen sich die Hände.*

that God has "willed" it. Now God cannot expressly will a particular evil, but He must tolerate in a certain fashion evil as such, since this is included in the limitlessness—in part paradoxical—of the divine All-Possibility. For this reason, God cannot not allow some particular evil, but it should be said that He "permits" it and not that He "wills" it; and He permits it, not inasmuch as it is an evil, but inasmuch as it is an indirect and inevitable contribution to a good. Christ willed, certainly not the betrayal in itself, but Redemption.[2]

It remains to be understood why Christ acted as we have said, for his acceptance of the evil could have been silent; now it could have been so in principle, but not in fact, and that is the root of the problem. It was necessary to show the world that the devil has no power over God, that he can oppose God only in appearance and thanks to a divine will, that nothing can be done outside the Will of the Sovereign Good, that if the powers of evil oppose—or believe they can oppose—Divinity, this can only be in virtue of a divine decision; whence the injunction, "That thou doest, do quickly." Thus, the devil does not even have the power to betray without a divine causation, metaphysically speaking; in the Gospel account, this power escapes him; therefore he could not triumph. And if, in this account, the devil enters into Judas, this is because he obtained the freedom to do so—a subtle entanglement of causes, but ontologically plausible. What is "ill-sounding" in the salvific drama of Christianity is that Redemption seems to depend upon a traitor; it was necessary to deprive the adversary of this satisfaction.

Be that as it may, the fact that Christianity had need of Judas implies—and this seems the height of paradox—that this traitor could not be a fundamentally bad man, as the popular belief would have it; and in fact he was not, as is proven by his repentance and despair.[3] Neither were the other two accused, Caiaphas and Pilate, as black as they are painted; for Caiaphas the extenuating circumstance was his orthodoxy, and for Pilate his good will. We would even go so far as to say that their necessary cooperation in the

---

2. Let us recall here that Saint Augustine, speaking of the sin of Adam and Eve, exclaimed: *felix culpa!* since, he thought, this sin was the cause of Redemption.

3. If Judas had been what is thought, he would on the contrary have been proud of his crime. At the very moment of the betrayal, Jesus called him "friend"; in this expression there was perhaps a glimmer of divine pardon.

Redemption implies that in the final analysis all three were forgiven; only this conclusion, so it seems to us, can protect Christianity from the possible charge of depending upon criminal causes and of being founded upon them, so to speak, at least materially. And we think here of this prayer of Christ: "Father, forgive them, for they know not what they do"; now it is impossible to assume in good logic that a prayer of Christ would not have been granted.

It would have been a kind of victory if the Church had instituted a feast of the three great Pardons, but it could not—for moral reasons—"allow itself this luxury", because it would have given a free rein to all evildoers; *de facto*, not *de jure*, of course. It is for this reason that Christ had to say, speaking of Judas, that "it had been good for that man if he had not been born"; this does not mean that Judas is in the eternal hell that Christian theology imagines, but it may mean that Judas, while not being damned, must remain in purgatory until the end of the world.

Caiaphas could be blamed for not having been sensitive to the divine nature of Christ nor to the profound intentions of his preaching, but besides his Mosaic orthodoxy, he had also as an extenuating circumstance the fact that Christ was never concerned with making himself comprehensible. In addition, Christ was not interested in the "commandments of men", even if they were plausible; what mattered to him was solely the sincerity of our love for God. This is not exactly the perspective of Moses, and the Pharisees cannot be blamed for not adhering to it at their level, any more than one can blame the authorities of Brahmanism for not having converted to the Buddha's perspective.

It could be argued that the Jews have had to suffer as heirs of Judas and Caiaphas, but it could as well be argued that the Christians as heirs of Pilate[4]—through the Renaissance—have had, and still have, to suffer by undergoing the consequences of the "humanist", but finally inhuman, world which they created at the time of the Borgias and which they continue to create in our day;[5]

---

4. Pilate was the representative of Tiberius, of whom Charlemagne as well as Constantine were the heirs; it is worth noting that, for the Muslim, the Christian is *rûmî*, "Roman".

5. It could be objected that the Eastern Church was not responsible for the Renaissance, which is true, but the Orthodox countries were dragged into its orbit

incontestably, the Renaissance was a betrayal, although it also comprised some positive elements, but these were not able to compensate for its sweeping errors.

In order to understand Christ's attitude towards "the scribes and the Pharisees", one has to keep in mind the following: at that time, Judaism was undergoing a phase of "ossification" comparable to that of Brahmanism at the time of the Buddha, and this was providential in both cases. The history of mankind is a *lîlâ*, a "divine play": possibilities have to manifest and exhaust themselves each in its turn. Be that as it may, Caiaphas and his partisans can be blamed for not wanting to acknowledge the decadence of their surroundings, which was incontestable, or else Christ would not have stigmatized it; and it is certainly not for the first time in the history of Israel that a prophet hurls thunderbolts at a corrupted and hypocritical clergy.

Like al-Hallaj—that "Christic" manifestation in the midst of Islam—Christ manifested his celestial nature without being concerned with making it intelligible; he incarnated his destiny, and he wished to be what he had to be in the economy of religious and mystical possibilities. A founder of religion personifies a spiritual perspective and a path of salvation; he expresses himself in a direct and quasi-absolute fashion and need not offer the commentaries which theologians and wise men will later provide.

"And the light shineth in darkness, and the darkness comprehended it not." This concerns not only Jews and pagans, but also Christians, as history proves.[6] Christ, like Moses, put God above man; the Renaissance, like Tiberius, put man in the place of God; whereas Christ had said: "Thy kingdom come."

by Peter the Great. In fact, Eastern Europe is part of the modern world, mentally as well as materially; Greece was speedily "brought to heel" after the departure of the Turks.

6. Let us remark that there are orthodox Jews who, while rejecting Christianity, and in flagrant opposition to the Talmud, admit that Jesus was a misunderstood prophet, of an Eliatic and Essenian type.

12

The Seat of Wisdom

The Blessed Virgin is inseparable from the incarnate Word, as the Lotus is inseparable from the Buddha and as the Heart is the pre-destined seat of immanent Wisdom. In Buddhism there is an entire mysticism of the Lotus, which communicates a celestial image of unsurpassable beauty and eloquence, a beauty analogous to the monstrance containing the Real Presence and analogous above all to that incarnation of divine Femininity which is the Virgin Mary. The Virgin, *Rosa Mystica*, is like a personification of the celestial Lotus; in a certain respect, she personifies the sense of the sacred, which is the indispensable introduction to the reception of the Sacrament.

* * *

One of the names which the Litany of Loreto gives to the Blessed Virgin is *Sedes Sapientiae*, "Throne of Wisdom"; and indeed, as was noted by Saint Peter Damian (11th century), the Blessed Virgin "is herself that wondrous throne referred to in the Book of Kings", namely, the Throne of Solomon the Prophet-King, who, according to the Bible and rabbinical traditions, was the wise man *par excellence*.[1] If Mary is *Sedes Sapientiae*, this is first of all because she is the

---

1. If the Bible condemned his conduct, it was because of a difference of level—the Bible's point of view being *a priori* legalistic and thus exoteric—and not because of an intrinsic wrong on his part. In Solomon there is manifested the mystery of "wine" and "intoxication", as is indicated, on the one hand, by his Song of Songs and, on the other, by the actions for which he is blamed in the Bible; but Solomon could have said, with his father David: "I have remembered thy Name, O Lord, in the night, and have kept thy Law" (Psalms 119:55).

Mother of Christ, who, being the Word, is the "Wisdom of God"; but it is also, quite obviously, because of her own nature, which results from her quality as "Spouse of the Holy Spirit" and "Co-Redemptress";[2] that is to say, Mary is herself an aspect of the Holy Spirit, its feminine counterpart, if one will, or its aspect of femininity, whence the feminization of the divine *Pneuma* by the Gnostics. Being the Throne of Wisdom—the "Throne quickened by the Almighty" according to a Byzantine hymn—Mary is *ipso facto* identified with the divine *Sophia,* as is attested by the Marian interpretation of some of the eulogies of Wisdom in the Bible.[3] Mary could not have been the locus of the Incarnation did she not bear in her very nature the Wisdom to be incarnated.

The wisdom of Solomon—it is well to recall here—is at once encyclopedic, cosmological, metaphysical, and also simply practical; in this last respect, it is political as well as moral and eschatological. That it is at the same time much more[4] emerges not only from cer-

---

2. Not losing sight of the fact that the body and blood of Christ are those of the Virgin-Mother, there being no human father.

3. "The Lord possessed me in the beginning of His way, before His works of old. I was set up from everlasting, from the beginning, or ever the earth was. When there were no depths, I was brought forth; when there were no fountains abounding with water" (Proverbs 8:22-24 and the following verses).

4. This is what the majority of modern critics tend to dispute; if, however, the wisdom of Solomon had been only practical and encyclopedic, the following sentences would be quite inexplicable: "Neither compared I unto her [unto Wisdom] any precious stone; because all gold in respect of her is as a little sand, and silver shall be counted as clay before her. I loved her above health and beauty, and chose to have her instead of light: for the light that cometh from her never goeth out. . . All such things as are either secret or manifest, them I know. For wisdom, which is the worker of all things, taught me; for in her is an understanding spirit, holy, one only, manifold, subtle, lively, clear, undefiled, plain, not subject to hurt, loving the thing that is good, quick, which cannot be letted, ready to do good . . . having all power, overseeing all things, and going through all understanding, pure, and most subtle spirits. . . . For she is the breath of the power of God, and a pure influence flowing from the glory of the Almighty; therefore can no defiled thing fall into her. For she is the brightness of the everlasting light. . . . And being but one, she can do all things: and remaining in herself, she maketh all things new: and in all ages entering into holy souls, she maketh them friends of God, and prophets. . . . Being compared with the light, she is found before it. For after this cometh night: but vice shall not prevail against wisdom" (Wisd. of Sol. 7:9-30). If the Wisdom of the Bible were only practical and encyclopedic, there would assuredly be no reason to identify it with the Blessed Virgin, or to identify her with the Throne of Solomon.

tain passages of Proverbs and the Book of Wisdom, but also from the Song of Songs, a book particularly revered by the Cabalists.

As for the Wisdom of the "divine Mary", it is less diverse, because it does not embrace certain contingent orders; it could never be either encyclopedic or of an "Aristotelian" tendency, if one may put it thus. The Blessed Virgin knows, and wishes to know, only that which concerns the nature of God and the condition of man; her science is of necessity metaphysical, mystical, and eschatological, and it thereby contains in virtuality every possible science, as the one and colorless light contains the varied and colored hues of the rainbow.

One observation that should be made at this point is the following: if Mary is seated upon the Throne of Solomon and is even identified with that Throne[5]—with the authority it represents—this is not only by divine right but by human right as well, in the sense that, being descended from David, she is heiress and queen in the same way that Christ, in like respect, is heir and king. One cannot but think of this when one sees Romanesque Virgins, crowned and seated with the Child on a royal Throne, those Virgins which all too often display considerable artistic crudeness and only a few of which are masterpieces,[6] but which then convey with all the greater hieratic eloquence the majesty and gentleness of Virginal Wisdom: majesty and gentleness, but also rigor; the *Magnificat* bears witness to this when it affirms, with the accents of a martial Psalm, that *vincit omnia Veritas*.

According to the First Book of Kings (10:18-20), Solomon "made a great throne of ivory, and overlaid it with the best gold. The throne had six steps, and heads of bulls behind,[7] and there were

5. Theologians—let it be said in passing—do not seem to realize the immense "rehabilitation" that this association with the living *Sedes Sapientiae*, and thereby with the Word, implies for Solomon, an association which is either profound or else utterly meaningless.

6. The Germanic peoples knew nothing of the plastic arts; the Greeks and Romans practiced only classical naturalism; Christian art, at least in the Latin world, had great difficulty arising from this twofold vacuum. In the Byzantine world, the art of icons was able to escape from such pitfalls.

7. Jewish translations and the Vulgate of Saint Jerome state that "the top of the throne was round behind"; they do not speak of "heads of bulls", as do some Christian translations, whose authors base themselves upon certain semantic factors and the fact that the Second Book of Chronicles (9:18) mentions a "golden

stays on either side on the place of the seat, and two lions stood beside the stays. And twelve lions stood there on the one side and on the other upon the six steps: there was not the like made in any kingdom."[8] First of all, some observations on the symbolism of the animals: the lions represent, beyond any question, the radiant and victorious power of Truth, whereas the bulls may represent, correlatively, weighty and defensive power: on the one hand, prospective power and, on the other, retrospective power, or imagination that creates and memory that conserves—invincibility and inviolability, or again, alchemically speaking, sun and moon. But there is also the symbolism of the materials: ivory is substance and gold is radiation, or else ivory, a material associated with life, is the "naked body" of Truth, whereas gold is the "raiment", which on the one hand veils the mystery and, on the other, communicates the glory.

The six steps of the throne refer to the very "texture" of Wisdom, one might say; six is the number of Solomon's seal. It is the number of total unfolding: the creation was completed in six days, and the fundamental metaphysical or mystical perspectives, the *darshana*s, are—and must be—six in number, according to Hindu tradition. This mystery of totality results from the combination of the numbers two and three, which, the first being even and the second odd, initially summarize every numerical possibility,[9] in the Pythagorean and not the quantitative sense. Spiritually speaking, the number two expresses the complementarity of "active perfection" and "passive perfection", as Taoists would say; in its turn the number three indicates in this context the hierarchy of spiritual modes or degrees, namely, "fear", "love", and "knowledge", each of these viewpoints containing, precisely, an active or dynamic aspect and a passive or static one.

---

lamb", in order—as they see it—to avoid an association of ideas with the pagan cult of the bull. It should be noted that the Jewish historian Josephus (reign of Vespasian) says: "In the place where this prince [Solomon] was seated, there were seen arms in relief, which appeared to be receiving him, and at the place where he could support himself, the figure of a bullock was placed as if to support him."

8. This last phrase, applied to the Virgin, indicates her incomparability, her "avataric" uniqueness in the universe of the Semites.

9. This is what space demonstrates: it has three dimensions, but the introduction of a subjective principle of alternative or opposition gives it six directions; this structure retraces the totality of the Universe.

The cosmic and human significances of the six directions of space—and the subjectification of space is certainly not arbitrary—reveal the contents of Wisdom, its dimensions or "stations", so to speak. The North is divine Purity and human renunciation, *vacare Deo*; the South is Life, Love, Goodness, and, in human terms, trust in God or hope; the East is Strength, Victory, and, on the human side, spiritual combat; the West is Peace, Beatitude, Beauty, and, in human terms, spiritual contentment, holy quietude. The Zenith is Truth, Loftiness, Transcendence, and thus also discernment and knowledge; the Nadir is the Heart, Depth, Immanence, and thus also union and holiness. This complexity brings us back to the cosmological and encyclopedic dimensions of Solomon's wisdom; it permits us to have a glimpse of the ramifications of the diverse orders of possibilities that unfold between the Nadir and the Zenith, that is to say, between the Alpha and the Omega of universal Possibility.

*　*　*

The foregoing considerations enable us to extend our analysis of the Solomonian number even further, at the risk of becoming involved in a digression that would raise fresh problems; but this does not matter, since further precisions may be useful. The axes North-South, East-West, and Zenith-Nadir correspond respectively to the complementarities Negative-Positive, Active-Passive, and Objective-Subjective, which summarize the principal cosmic relationships; this is the fundamental symbolism of the three dimensions of space: length, breadth, and height. When looking toward the East, whence comes light, the East will be "in front", the West "behind", the South "on the right", and the North "on the left", whereas the Zenith and the Nadir remain immutable; these last two refer also to the pair Principle-Manifestation, the first term being for us "objective", by reason of its Transcendence, and the second term "subjective", because in the face of the Absolute the world is ourselves, and we are the world. But the Nadir may also represent "depth" or "inwardness" and thus the divine Self, in which case the Zenith will assume an aspect of "projection", of limitless *Mâyâ*, of unfolding and indefinite Possibility; in the same way, the root of a tree is manifested and unfolds in and by the crown.

Space is defined likewise, and even *a priori*, by two principal elements, the point—subjectively the center—and extension, which respectively express the two poles "absolute" and "infinite"; time for its part also comprises such elements, namely, the instant—subjectively the present—and duration, with the same significance.[10] In the number six, the implicit number three corresponds to the center or present, and the number two to extension and duration; the center-present is expressed by the ternary, and not by unity, because unity is here envisaged in respect to its potentialities and thus in relation to its possibility of unfolding; the actualization of that unfolding is expressed precisely by the number two.[11] All this is a way of presenting the "Pythagorean" aspect of the number six and consequently the role of this number in integral Wisdom.

* * *

"Fear", "love", and "knowledge", or rigor, gentleness, and substance; then "active" and "passive" perfections, or dynamic and static ones: herein, as we have seen, lies the elementary spiritual message of the principial number six. This scheme expresses not only the modalities of human ascent, but also, and even primarily, the modalities of divine Descent; it is by the six steps of the Throne that saving Grace comes down towards man, just as it is by these six steps that man ascends towards Grace. Wisdom is in practice the "art" of emerging from seducing and fettering illusion, of emerging first through the intelligence and then through the will; it consists first in knowledge of the "Sovereign Good" and then, by way of consequence, in the adaptation of the will to this knowledge, the two things being inseparable from Grace.

10. From a quite different point of view, it can be pointed out that the number three refers more particularly to space, which has three dimensions, whereas the number two is concerned rather with time, whose "dimensions" are the past and the future—without speaking here of the cyclic quaternary which is contained in duration and which is no more than a development of duality.

11. The number three evokes in fact not absoluteness itself, as does the number one, but the potentiality or virtuality which the Absolute necessarily comprises.

Divine *Mâyâ*—Femininity *in divinis*—is not only that which projects and creates; it is also that which attracts and liberates. The Blessed Virgin as *Sedes Sapientiae* personifies this merciful Wisdom, which descends towards us and which we too, whether we know it or not, bear in our very essence; and it is precisely by virtue of this potentiality or virtuality that Wisdom comes down upon us. The immanent seat of Wisdom is the heart of man.

13

The Mystery of the Two Natures

It is a strange fact in the history of Christianity that Pope Honorius I, though an impeccable pontiff, was expelled from the Church by the Sixth Ecumenical Council for the sole reason of having hesitated concerning the question of the "two wills" of Christ. A century and a half after this pope's death, the Seventh Ecumenical Council considered it useful or necessary to ratify the excommunication of Honorius I and to include his name in the anathema of all known heresies.

This ostracism is logically surprising when one is aware of the complexity of the issue at stake. For some, Christ has two wills since he is "true man and true God"; for others, these two wills are but one since—as Honorius himself said—Christ's human will cannot operate in contradiction to his divine will. One could say *grosso modo* that Christ possesses two wills in principle and one in fact; or again, one could use the image of two overlapping circles and express oneself thus: if it goes without saying that Christ possesses *a priori* two distinct wills, given his two incommensurable natures, there nonetheless is a region in his person where the two wills blend, as is seen precisely in the geometric symbolism of two intersecting circles.

What can be said concerning the two wills applies above all and with all the more reason to the two natures: if it is true that Christ is at the same time both man and God, two things are then incontrovertible, namely, the duality and the unity of his nature. We are not saying that the monophysites, who admit only the unity of Christ's nature, are right as against the Orthodox and Catholics, but neither do we say that they are intrinsically wrong from their point of view; and the same holds, as a result, for the monothelites, who simply apply the monophysite principle to a particular aspect of the nature of the God-Man. The justification of the monophysites appears, quite paradoxically, in the Catholic doctrine of transubstantiation: it seems to us that it would be appropriate to apply to the Eucharistic elements what is affirmed dogmatically of Christ, namely, that he is "true man and true God"; if this is so, one could equally admit that the Eucharist is "true bread and true Body" or "true wine and true Blood" without compromising its divinity. To say that the bread is but an appearance is to apply to the Eucharist the doctrine—judged heretical—of the monophysites, for whom Christ is, precisely, only apparently a man since he is really God; now just as the quality of "true man" in Catholic and Orthodox doctrine does not preclude Christ from being "true God", so should the quality of "true bread" not preclude the host from being "true Body" in the minds of theologians, all the more so as both things— the created and the Uncreated—are incommensurable, which means that the physical reality of the elements does not exclude their divine content, any more than the real corporeality of Christ prevents the presence of the divine nature.

It must be said again that monophysitism and therefore also transubstantiationism are not intrinsically wrong—the opposite would in fact be astonishing—and for the following reason: to acknowledge that Christ's humanity is a vehicle of the divine nature amounts to saying that if, in one respect, the human side is really human, it is so in a way that is nonetheless different from the humanity of ordinary men; the divine Presence transfigures or transubstantiates in a certain way, and *a priori*, the human nature; Christ's body is already here below what heavenly bodies are, with the sole difference that it is nevertheless affected by some of the accidents of earthly life. The same is true for the Eucharist: if in one respect it is "real bread" and "real wine", in another—which does not abolish the first—it is in fact substantially more than ordinary matter; metaphysically, this does not oblige one to pretend that this matter is "only an appearance", but theologically, from the point of view of uni-dimensional—we might say "planimetric"—alternatives, the negation of real matter is probably the only means for a certain mentality of affirming effectively and enduringly the transcendence of the Eucharist. Nonetheless, this doctrine is bound to be a "two-edged sword", the dangers of which can be neutralized only by esoteric truth, or "theosophy" in the ancient and true sense of the word.

Theologians seem to think that bread and wine, as natural substances, are unworthy of the divine Presence, and this sentiment brings to mind a thesis of Saint Gregory of Nyssa, which is not irrelevant here. Hellenists[1] deemed the Incarnation to be unworthy of God owing to the frailty and impurity of earthly bodies; in his "Great Catechesis", Saint Gregory answers that sin alone, not fleshly materiality, is unworthy of God. The Greeks might have responded that corporeal miseries, being traces of original sin and the fall, partake in the indignity of sin and unquestionably manifest it; and the Bishop of Nyssa could have retorted that a proof of the compatibility between the human body and a divine inherence is provided by the inherence of the Intellect, which is of a heavenly order and whose transcendence the Greeks are the first to acknowledge. The decisive argument is that these two orders, the created and the Uncreated, share no common measure and that nothing that is merely natural—whatever its distant cause may be—can oppose itself to the Presence of God.

* * *

The uninformed reader who finds in the Koran that Jesus was "one of those brought nigh" (*muqarrabûn*) and "one of the righteous" (*sâlihûn*)—*Sûrah* "The Family of Imran" [3]:45, 46—has the following reaction: that Christ is "one of those brought nigh" is evident from every point of view, for if the greatest Prophets are not "close" to God, who then could be? And that Christ was "one of the righteous" is evident *a fortiori* and by several orders of magnitude, mathematically speaking. In reality, both seeming pleonasms are merely ellipses meant to illustrate a doctrinal position directed against the Christian thesis of the twofold nature of Christ; generally speaking, when the Koran appears to make statements that are all too obvious, and disappointing in their context, it is engaging in implicit

---

1. We are referring here to the partisans of Hellenism, that is to say, of the Hellenist tradition, which we cannot term "pagan" since we are envisaging it with respect to its spiritual values, though the word "Hellenist" more often designates, on the one hand, the Hellenized Jews of antiquity and, on the other, scholars versed in Greek language and literature.

polemics; in other words, it is aiming at a particular opinion, which it does not enunciate and which needs to be known in order for one to understand the passage. What Islam intends to affirm, in its way and according to its perspective, is that Jesus is "true man and true God": instead of saying "man", the Koran says "righteous" so as to define immediately the nature of this man; and since its intention is to specify that no man is God, it suggests what in Christian terms is called the "divine nature" of Christ by using the expression "brought nigh", which denotes the most elevated station Islam can attribute to a human being.

Be that as it may, the twofold nature of Christ is sufficiently specified in the following verse: "Jesus the Messiah, son of Mary, is the Messenger of God and His Word, which He (God) placed in Mary, and (Jesus is) of His Spirit (the Spirit of God)" (*Sûrah* "Women" [4]: 171). In admitting the Immaculate Conception and the Virgin Birth, Islam accepts in its way the divine nature of Jesus:[2] "in its way", that is, with the obvious reservation that it always intends to dissociate the divine from the human, and therefore that the Christic phenomenon is for it no more than a particular marvel of Omnipotence.

* * *

We have said above that the ostracism by the two Councils of Honorius I in particular and of the monophysites-monothelites in general is logically surprising; now to say "logically" is to imply a reservation, for it is no surprise from an exoteric point of view that a too fragmentary or in some respects inopportune formulation should be considered a crime;[3] this shows that one is dealing with a

2. According to a *hadîth*, Jesus and Mary were the only human beings the devil did not touch at birth with his claw, and who therefore did not utter a cry.

3. Let it be said in passing that the anathematization of Honorius I proves, moreover, not that he was heretical, but that he was considered as such and that, as a result, the Church admits that a pope can lapse into heresy—except, of course, when promulgating a dogmatic or moral definition *ex cathedra*; one might reject this by proposing that Honorius I did no more than sin against discipline; but in that case, the anathemas heaped upon him canonically would be inexplicable. Be that as it may, there is nothing in principle to prevent a pope from ruining the

domain that must be distinguished from that of pure, hence disinterested, knowledge, which admits the interplay of aspects and points of view without ever getting locked in artificial or inflammatory alternatives. It is important, however, not to confuse theological elaborations, which are fluid and productive of scissions, with dogmas themselves, which are fixed; such elaborations—though also providential on their level—take on the appearance of dogmatic systems in their turn, but far more contingently so than those within which they are situated as modalities; these are minor *upâyas*, if one will, that is, "saving mirages" or "spiritual means", designed to render more accessible that major *upâya* which is religion. Now it is essential to keep in mind the idea of "lesser truth" or "relative error" contained in this Buddhist notion; it means that there is, on the part of Heaven, "tolerance through Mercy" and not "complete approbation". For man is a form, and he needs forms; but since he also—and even above all—needs the Essence, which religion or wisdom is supposed to communicate to him, he really needs a "form of the Essence" or a "manifestation of the Void" (*shûnyamûrti*). If in one respect form is a prolongation of Essence, in another it contradicts it, which accounts on the one hand for the ambiguity of the exoteric *upâya*, and on the other hand for two aspects of esoterism, one of which extends and intensifies the dogmatic *upâya*, whereas the other is independent of it to the point of being able to contradict it. To the objection that esoterism also belongs to the formal order, one must respond that esoterism is aware of this and that it tends to transcend the accidentality of its own form, whereas exoterism is totally and heavily identified with its form.

What results from this, in an altogether self-evident way, is that the dividing line between orthodoxy and apparent, and therefore merely extrinsic, heresy depends on psychological or moral contingencies of an ethnic or cultural provenance; while the fundamental

Church without in the least having to make an *ex cathedra* pronouncement; the greatest theologians admit the possibility of a pope lapsing into heresy, and the whole problem for them then becomes whether the heretical pope is deposed *ipso facto* or must be deposed canonically. However, the possibility at issue here—of which Honorius I is not at all an example—can occur in so severe a degree only under utterly abnormal circumstances, which the twentieth century in fact affords; there would still be the question whether the pope who might be incriminated was a legitimate pope with regard to the conditions of his election.

upâya, quite clearly, transmits total truth through its symbolism, the same cannot be said of that minor *upâya* which is theology; its relativity—with respect to total truth—is moreover proven, in the Christian sphere, by the notion of "theological progress", which contains an admission at once candid and appalling.[4] It is true that every theology can lead incidentally to the profoundest insights, but it cannot, in its general and official doctrine, draw the conclusions such insights entail.

It is a radical error to believe that the greatest spokesmen of theology, even if they are canonized saints, hold *ipso facto* all the keys to supreme wisdom;[5] they are instruments of Providence and are not called upon to go beyond certain limits; on the contrary, their role is to formulate what these limits are, according to a perspective willed directly or indirectly by Heaven. By "indirectly" we mean those cases where Heaven tolerates a limitation required—or made desirable—by a particular human predisposition, perhaps not well-defined *a priori*, but nonetheless proving to be predominant; this explains the majority of the differences or divergences—in most cases unilateral[6]—between the Western and Eastern Churches. Some of these differentiations may seem a gratuitous luxury, but they are nonetheless unavoidable and finally opportune, collective

4. One of two things: either there is theological progress, in which case theology is of little importance; or theology is important, in which case there can be no theological progress.

5. Thus the "wisdom of the saints", which some seek to set in opposition to metaphysics, is but an abuse of language; the "wisdom" of Ecclesiasticus is not, after all, of the same order as that of the Upanishads. It should be noted in this connection that if the Semitic Scriptures, even the most fundamental, do not have the tenor of the *Vedânta*, this is because, unlike the *Vedânta*, they are not directed exclusively to an intellectual elite, but have a function that obliges them to take account of possibilities found in the collective soul and to forestall the most diverse of reactions. To this it must be added that a sacred book, like the Gospel for example, which seems to speak to sinners, at least at the outset, really addresses any man insofar as he sins; this confers upon the notion of sin the widest significance possible—that of a centrifugal motion, whether compressive or dispersing—even when there is properly speaking no objective transgression. Sacred language, even if directed at first to specific men, is finally directed to man as such.

6. For the spirit of innovation is to be found with the Latins, a fact resulting moreover from the paradoxical coincidence between prophetism and caesarism in the papacy.

mentalities being what they are. Even so, this opportuneness has nothing absolute about it and cannot prevent a kind of poison, concealed in this or that theological particularism, from manifesting itself in the course of history, belatedly and upon contact with false ideas whose possibility theologians were unable to foresee.

In considering the most general factors of the issue, we shall say that Semitic dogmatisms, as well as Hindu *darshana*s like Ramanujan Vishnuism, pertain to the chivalrous and heroic spirit,[7] which necessarily tends toward voluntarism and individualism, and thus toward a moralizing anthropomorphism. It is in view of such a temperament, and because of it, that exclusivist[8] dogmas are crystallized and their corresponding theologies elaborated, which clearly implies that this temperament or this manner of seeing and feeling is acceptable to God as the "raw material" of the *upâya*; nonetheless, since each religion is by definition a totality—as is proven by its imperative and unconditional character—and since God could never impose absolute limits, the religious phenomenon by definition comprises the esoteric phenomenon, which is transmitted in principle and as a matter of preference, in different degrees, by vocations that favor contemplation, including sacred art.

---

7. The fact that Ramanuja was a *brâhmana* and not a *kshatriya* is no grounds for objection, since all castes—inasmuch as they are particular predispositions—are reflected or repeated in each single caste, so that a *brâhmana* of a *kshatriya* type is individually equivalent to a *kshatriya* of a *brâhmana* type. Furthermore, every human collectivity produces a human type with no affinity for speculative thought; it is all the more paradoxical and significant that this is the type or mentality— which a Hindu would call a *shûdra* outlook—that determines all the so-called "new theology" and constitutes its sole originality and sole mystery.

8. Such an adjective is not a pleonasm, for a metaphysical axiom itself can also have a dogmatic character, practically speaking, but without therefore having to exclude formulations diverging from it. On the other hand, there are metaphysical axioms whose conditional character is recognized *a priori*, depending on the degree of relativity of the idea expressed: hence, archetypes contained in the creative Intellect are more real than their cosmic manifestation while being illusory with respect to the divine Essence; such and such Hindu Divinities are dogmatically inviolable, but they vanish before *Paramâtmâ* or, rather, are reabsorbed therein, so that it may be possible to deny without heresy their existence, provided of course that by the same token one deny all beings that are even more relative.

A certain underlying warrior or knightly mentality[9] accounts for many theological oscillations and their ensuing disputes—the nature of Christ and the structure of the Trinity having been the notable questions at issue in the Christian world—just as it accounts for such forms of narrow-mindedness as the incomprehension and intolerance of ancient theologians toward the metaphysics and mysteries of Hellenism. It is moreover this same mentality that produced the divergence, in the very heart of the Greek tradition, between Aristotle and Plato, Plato having personified in essence the *brâhmana* spirit inherent in the Orphic and Pythagorean tradition,[10] whereas the Stagirite formulated a metaphysics that was in certain respects centrifugal and perilously open to the world of phenomena, actions, experiences, and adventures.[11]

After this parenthesis, which the general context of the case of Honorius I permits or even demands, let us return to our doctrinal subject.

* * *

The problem of the two natures of Christ can be reduced, in the last analysis, to the relationship between the relative and the Absolute: if Christ is the Absolute entered into relativity, it follows, not only that the relative should return thereby to absoluteness, but also and

---

9. One cannot lose sight of the fact that, in all climates, the same causes produce the same effects—in highly diverse proportions—and that India is no exception; the quarrels of sectarian Vishnuism are a case in point.

10. It goes without saying that the classical period—with its grave intellectual and artistic deviation—and its recurrence at the time of the Renaissance are patent examples of warrior or knightly, and hence *kshatriya*, Luciferianism; however, we do not have in mind here deviations as such since, on the contrary, we are speaking of normal manifestations, which are acceptable to Heaven; otherwise there could be no question of voluntarist and emotional *upâyas*.

11. But let us not make Aristotelianism responsible for the modern world, which is due to a convergence of various factors, such as the abuses—and subsequent reactions—provoked by the unrealistic idealism of Catholicism, and also by the diverging and irreconcilable demands of the Latin and Germanic mentalities, all of which lead, precisely, to scientism and the profane mentality.

above all that the relative should be prefigured in the Absolute; this is the meaning of the uncreated Word, which manifests itself in the human order, not only in the form of Christ or the *Avatâra*, but also and *a priori* in the form of the immanent Intellect, and this brings us back to the complementarity between Revelation and Intellection. The Absolute manifested in the human world is at once Truth and Presence, or one or the other of these two elements, but without being able to exclude its complement. The element "Presence" takes precedence in Christianity, hence the sacraments and the emphasis on the volitive aspect of man; in other climates, and above all in universal *gnosis*, which retains its rights everywhere, it is the element "Truth" that determines the means of the path, in diverse ways and on diverse levels.

In order to be as clear as possible, it is necessary to insist on the following principle: there is no possible relationship between the Absolute as such and relativity; for such a relationship to exist there must be something relative in the Absolute and something absolute in the relative. In other words: if one admits that the world is distinct from God, one must also admit that this distinction is prefigured in God Himself, which means that His unity of Essence—which is never in question—comprises degrees; not to admit this polarization *in divinis* is to leave the existence of the world without a cause, or it is to admit that there are two distinct realities and thus two "Gods", namely, God and the world. For one of two things: either the world is explained starting from God, in which case there is in God prefiguration and creative act, and thus relativity; or else there is in God no relativity, in which case the world is unexplainable and is placed on a level with God. We once again emphasize that divine Relativity, the cause of the world, fulfills the role of the Absolute in relation to the world; in this sense, theologians are right to uphold in certain cases the absoluteness of all that is divine; absoluteness, for them, is thus synonymous with Divinity.

At the risk of repeating ourselves, we could express this as follows: whoever admits the presence of the Absolute in the world, in the form of Christ for example, must admit equally the presence of the relative in God—in the form of the Word, precisely; whoever denies that there can be any relativity in God must consider the Creator, the Revealer, or the Redeemer as being situated beneath God, in the manner of the demiurge; for the Absolute as such neither creates, nor reveals, nor saves. In refusing to admit the relativity of the *hypostases*, there is an element of confusion between the absolute and the sublime: since the Divinity deserves or demands worship, there are some who want the Divinity to be "absolutely absolute" in every possible respect, if we may express ourselves, provisionally and incidentally, in such a manner. Now God is deserving of the worship of *latria*, not inasmuch as He comprises no relativity—for in this respect He is humanly inaccessible—but inasmuch as He is absolute with respect to the relativity of the world, while comprising an aspect of relativity in view of this very contact.

One might object that the thesis of reciprocity between the Absolute and the relative does not take into account the incommensurability, and hence the asymmetry, between the two terms; this is both true and false. If one wished to place emphasis on the incommensurable nature of God, one could not do so simply by denying relativity within the divine Principle; one could do so adequately only by separating the creative Principle from the intrinsic Absolute, which takes us back to the alternative between *Paramâtmâ* and *Mâyâ*, and then to the absorption of the second term by the first, precisely as a result of their incommensurability. This reduction of the real to the One without a second is exactly what those who deny relativity *in divinis* do not want, all the more as they hold fiercely to the unconditional and in some way massive reality of the world; in wanting an "absolutely absolute" God situated above an unconditionally real world, they seek to keep "both feet on the ground" without sacrificing anything of transcendence. In reality, however, the Universe is no more than an inward and, as it were, dreamlike dimension of God: it reflects the divine qualities in a mode that entails contrast, movement, and privation, thereby realizing the possibility for God to be other than God, a possibility contained in the divine Infinitude itself.

14

Christic and Virginal Mysteries

God became man that man might become God. The first mystery is the Incarnation; the second is the Redemption.

However, just as the Word, in assuming flesh, was already in a sense crucified, so too man, in returning to God, must participate in both mysteries: the ego is crucified to the world, but the grace of salvation is made incarnate in the heart; sanctity is the birth and life of Christ in us.

This mystery of the Incarnation has two aspects: the Word, on the one hand, and its human receptacle, on the other: Christ and the Virgin-Mother. To be able to realize in itself this mystery, the soul must be like the Virgin; for just as the sun can be reflected in water only when it is calm, so the soul can receive Christ only in virginal purity, in original simplicity, and not in sin, which is turmoil and disequilibrium.

By "mystery" we do not mean something incomprehensible in principle—unless it be on the purely rational level—but something which opens on to the Infinite, or which is envisaged in this respect, so that intelligibility becomes limitless and humanly inexhaustible. A mystery is always "something of God".

*   *   *

Ave Maria gratia plena, Dominus tecum: benedicta tu in mulieribus, et benedictus fructus ventris tui, Jesus.[1]

1. "The devotion of the Rosary . . . is, when correctly grasped, as ancient as the Church. It is the appropriate devotion of Christians. It serves to revive and maintain the spirit and life of Christianity. The novelty of the Name can offend only those who do not know its real sense: and Saint Dominic, who is regarded as the

Maria is the purity, beauty, goodness, and humility of the cosmic Substance; the microcosmic reflection of this Substance is the soul in a state of grace. The soul in a state of baptismal grace corresponds to the Virgin Mary; the blessing of the Virgin is on him who purifies his soul for God. This purity—the Marian state—is the essential condition, not only for reception of the sacraments, but also for the spiritual actualization of the Real Presence of the Word. By the word *ave*, the soul expresses the idea that, in conforming to the perfection of Substance, it places itself at the same time into harmony with it, while imploring the help of the Virgin Mary, who personifies this perfection.

Gratia plena: primordial Substance, by reason of its purity, its goodness, and its beauty, is filled with the divine Presence. It is pure because it contains nothing other than God; it is good because it compensates and absorbs all forms of cosmic disequilibrium, for it is totality and therefore equilibrium; it is beautiful because it is totally submissive to God. It is thus that the soul, the microcosmic reflection of Substance—corrupted by the fall—must again become pure, good, and beautiful.

Dominus tecum: this Substance is not only filled with the divine Presence in an ontological or existential manner, in the sense that it is imbued with it by definition, that is, by its very nature, but it is also constantly communicating with the Word as such. Thus, if *gratia plena* means that the divine Mystery is immanent in the Substance as such, *Dominus tecum* signifies that God, in His metacosmic transcendence, is revealed to the Substance, just as the eye, which is filled with light, sees in addition the sun itself. The soul filled with grace will see God.

Benedicta tu in mulieribus: compared with all secondary substances, the total Substance alone is perfect and totally under divine Grace. All substances are derived from it by a disruption of equilibrium; in the same way all fallen souls are derived from the primordial soul through the fall. The soul in a state of grace—the soul pure, good, and beautiful—rejoins primordial perfection; it is thereby "blessed" among all microcosmic substances.

Author of this devotion, is in effect only its Restorer" (*La solide Dévotion du Rosaire*, by an unknown Dominican of the beginning of the 18th century).

Et benedictus fructus ventris tui, Jesus: what in principle is *Dominus tecum* becomes, in manifestation, *fructus ventris tui, Jesus*; that is, the Word, which communicates with the ever-virgin substance of the total Creation, is reflected in an inverse sense within this Creation: it will appear as the fruit, the result, not as the root, the cause. And again: the soul submissive to God by its purity, its goodness, and its beauty seems to give birth to God, according to appearances; but God, being thus born in it, will transmute and absorb it, as Christ transmutes and absorbs his mystical body, the Church, which from being militant and suffering becomes triumphant. But in reality, the Word is not born in the Substance, for the Word is immutable; it is the Substance that dies in the Word. Again, when God seems to germinate in the soul, it is in reality the soul that dies in God. *Benedictus*: the Word which becomes incarnate is itself Benediction; nevertheless, since according to appearances it is manifested as Substance, as soul, it is called blessed; for it is then envisaged, not with respect to its transcendence—which would render Substance unreal—but with respect to its appearance, its Incarnation: *fructus*.

Jesus: it is the Word that determines Substance and reveals itself to it. Macrocosmically, it is the Word that manifests itself in the Universe as the divine Spirit; microcosmically, it is the Real Presence, affirming itself at the center of the soul, spreading outwards, and finally transmuting and absorbing it.[2]

* * *

The virginal perfections are purity, beauty, goodness, and humility; it is these qualities which the soul in quest of God must realize.

Purity: the soul is empty of all desire. Every natural movement that asserts itself in the soul is then considered in respect of its passional quality, its aspect of concupiscence, of seduction. This perfection is cold, hard, and transparent like diamond. It is immortality that excludes all corruption.

---

2. This expression should not be taken quite literally, any more than other expressions of union that will follow; what is essential here is to be aware of "deification", whatever significance one may give to this term.

Beauty: the beauty of the Virgin expresses divine Peace. It is in the perfect equilibrium of its possibilities that the universal Substance realizes its beauty. In this perfection, the soul gives up all dissipation in order to repose in its own substantial, primordial, ontological perfection. We said above that the soul must be like a perfectly calm expanse of water; every natural movement of the soul will then appear as agitation, dissipation, distortion, and so as ugliness.

Goodness: the mercy of the cosmic Substance consists in this, that, virgin in relation to its products, it comprises an inexhaustible power of equilibrium, of setting aright, of healing, of absorbing evil, and of manifesting good; being maternal towards beings who address themselves to it, it in no way refuses them its assistance. Likewise, the soul must divert its love from the hardened ego and direct it towards the neighbor and the whole of creation; the distinction between "I" and "other" is as if abolished; the "I" has become "other" and the "other" become "I". The passional distinction between "I" and "thou" is a state of death, comparable to the separation between the soul and God.

Humility: the Virgin, despite her supreme sanctity, remains woman and aspires to no other role; the humble soul is conscious of its own rank and effaces itself before what surpasses it. It is thus that the *Materia Prima* of the Universe remains on its own level and never seeks to appropriate to itself the transcendence of the Principle.

The mysteries—joyful, sorrowful, and glorious—of Mary are so many aspects of cosmic reality on the one hand and of the mystical life on the other.

Like Mary, and like universal Substance, the sanctified soul is "virgin", "spouse", and "mother".

* * *

The nature of Christ appears in four mysteries: incarnation, love, sacrifice, divinity; and in these the human soul must participate in diverse ways.

The incarnation: this is manifested, as principle, in every positive divine act, such as creation, or within creation in various divine affirmations, such as the Scriptures. In the soul, it is the birth of the Divine—grace—but also *gnosis,* which transforms man and gives him salvation; likewise, it is the divine act of prayer of the heart, the Name of God made incarnate in the soul as an invincible force. Christ, as pure divine affirmation, enters the world—and the soul—with the force of lightning, of the drawn sword; all natural imagery of the soul appears then as a passivity or an indulgence toward the world, a forgetfulness of God out of weakness and negligence. The incarnation is, in the soul, the victorious—and ceaselessly renewed—presence of divine Miracle.

Love: God is love, infinite life. The ego, on the contrary, is a state of death, comparable, in its congenital egoism, to a stone, and also, in its vain pettiness, to sterile and shifting sand. The hardened heart must be liquefied; its indifference toward God must turn into fervor, and it will thereby become indifferent with regard to the ego and the world. The gift of tears is one manifestation of this liquefaction; spiritual intoxication is another.

Sacrifice: on the cross, the annihilation of Christ attains its culminating point in the state of abandonment between Heaven and earth. It is thus that the ego must be annihilated, in a perfect void, before the exclusive Reality of God.

Divinity: what corresponds to this in the soul is pure spirituality, that is, permanent union with God. It is the remembrance of God, which must become the true center of our being in place of the illusory ego, which dissipates itself in the appearances of this world below. The human person becomes perfectly "itself" only beyond itself, in profound and inexpressible Union.

*   *   *

The Lord's Prayer is the most excellent prayer of all, since it has Christ for its author; it is therefore more excellent, as a prayer, than the *Ave,* and that is why it is the first prayer of the Rosary. But the *Ave* is more excellent than the Lord's Prayer in that it contains the Name of Christ, mysteriously identified with Christ himself, since "God and His Name are one". Christ is more than the Prayer he taught, and the *Ave,* which contains Christ through his Name, is thus more than this Prayer; this is why the recitations of the *Ave* are much more numerous than those of the *Pater*, and why the *Ave* constitutes, with the Name of the Lord that it contains, the very substance of the Rosary. What we have just stated amounts to saying that the prayer of the "servant" addressed to the "Lord" corresponds to the "Lesser Mysteries"—and we recall that these concern the realization of the primordial or Edenic state, and thus the fullness of the human state—whereas the Name of God itself corresponds to the "Greater Mysteries", the finality of which is beyond all individual states.

From the microcosmic point of view, as we have seen, "Mary" is the soul in a state of "sanctifying grace", qualified to receive the "Real Presence"; "Jesus" is the divine Seed, the "Real Presence", which must bring about the transmutation of the soul, namely, its universalization or its reintegration in the Eternal. "Mary"—like the "Lotus"—is "surface" or "horizontal"; "Jesus"—like the "Jewel"[3]—is "center" and, in dynamic relationship, "vertical". "Jesus" is God in us, God who penetrates us and transfigures us.

Among the meditations of the Rosary, the "joyful Mysteries" concern, from the point of view adopted here and in connection with ejaculatory prayers, the "Real Presence" of the Divine in the human; as for the "sorrowful Mysteries", they describe the redemptive "imprisonment" of the Divine in the human, the inevitable profanation of the "Real Presence" by human limitations; finally, the "glorious Mysteries" relate to the victory of the Divine over the human, the freeing of the soul by the Spirit.

---

3. We are here alluding to the well-known Buddhist formula: *Om mani padme hum.* There is an analogy worth noticing between this formula and the name "Jesus of *Nazareth*": the literal meaning of Nazareth is "flower", and *mani padme* means "jewel in the lotus".

15

The Cross

If the Incarnation has the significance of a "descent" of God, Christ is thus equated with the whole of creation. He contains it, as it were; he is a second creation, which purifies and redeems the first. He assumes, with the cross, the evil of Existence; to be able to assume this evil, it was necessary that God should become Existence. The cross is everywhere because creation is of necessity separated from God; Existence affirms itself and blossoms out through enjoyment, but enjoyment becomes sin to the extent that God is not its object, although all enjoyment contains a metaphysical excuse in the fact that it is directed to God by its existential nature; every sin is broken at the foot of the cross. But man is not made solely of blind desire; he has received intelligence that he may know God; he must become conscious of the divine end in everything, and at the same time he must "take up the cross" and "offer the other cheek", that is, he must rise even above the internal logic of the prison of existence; his logic, which is "foolishness" in the eyes of the world, must transcend the plane of this prison: it must be "vertical" or celestial, not "horizontal" or terrestrial.

Existence or "manifestation" has two aspects: the tree and the cross; the joyous tree, which bears the serpent, and the sorrowful cross, which bears the Word made flesh. For the impious, Existence is a world of passion that man justifies by a philosophy "after the flesh"; for the elect, it is a world of trial transpierced by grace, faith, *gnosis.*

Jesus is not only the new Adam, but also the new Creation. The old is totality and circumference; the new, unicity and center.

* * *

We can no more escape the cross than we can escape Existence. At the root of all that exists, there is the cross. The ego is a downward path drawing man away from God; the cross is a halting of that path. If Existence is "something of God", it is also something "which is not God", and it is this which the ego embodies. The cross brings the latter back to the former and in so doing permits us to overcome Existence.

What makes the problem of Existence so complex is that God shows through everywhere, since nothing could exist outside of Him; what matters is never to be separated from this distant perception of the Divine. And that is why enjoyment in the shadow of the cross is conceivable and even inevitable; to exist is to enjoy, even though it be at the foot of the cross. That is where man must keep himself, since such is the profound nature of things; man can violate this nature only in appearance. Suffering and death are none other than the cross reappearing in the cosmic flesh; Existence is a rose signed with a cross.

* * *

Social morals distinguish between the rightness of one man and the wrongness of another; but the mystical morals of Christ, strictly speaking, admit no one to be right, or rather they are situated on a plane where no one is entirely right, since every man is a sinner, and "there is none good but one, that is, God."[1] The Law of Moses has a man stoned for wronging society, an adulterer for example, but for Christ there is only God who can be wronged, and this excludes all forms of vengeance; every man is guilty before the Eternal. Every sin is that of Adam and Eve, and every human being is Adam or Eve;[2] the first act of justice will therefore be to forgive our neighbor.

---

1. "For I know nothing by myself; yet am I not hereby justified: but he that judgeth me is the Lord" (1 Cor. 4:4).

2. Saint Gregory the Great says in a letter, quoted by the Venerable Bede in his *Ecclesiastical History of the English Church and People*, that "every sin proceeds from three causes, namely, suggestion, pleasure, and consent. Suggestion comes from the devil, pleasure from the body, and consent from the will. The serpent suggested the first sin, and Eve, as flesh, found in it a carnal pleasure, whereas Adam, as mind, consented to it; but only the most subtle intelligence can discern between suggestion and pleasure, and between pleasure and consent".

The fault of "the other" is at root our own; it is only a manifestation of the latent fault which constitutes our common substance.

But Christ, whose Kingdom is "not of this world", leaves open a door for human justice insofar as it is inevitable: "Render therefore unto Caesar the things which are Caesar's." To deny this justice on every plane would amount to setting up injustice; however, it is necessary to overcome hatred by bringing evil back to its very root, to that "offence" that must needs come, and above all by discovering it in our nature, which is that of every ego; the ego is an optical illusion that makes a mote out of a beam, and conversely, according to whether it is a question of "ourselves" or "another". It is necessary to find, through the Truth, that serenity which understands all, "forgives all", and reduces all to equilibrium; it is necessary to overcome evil with peace, which is beyond evil and is thus not its contrary; true peace has no contrary.

"He that is without sin among you, let him first cast a stone": we are all of a same sinful substance, a same matter susceptible to this abscess that is evil, and we are, in consequence, all joint partners in evil, in a way that is doubtless indirect but nonetheless real; it is as if everyone carried in himself a particle of responsibility for all sin. Sin then appears as a cosmic accident, exactly like the ego on a larger scale; strictly speaking, he is without sin who is without ego and who, thereby, is like the wind, of which no man can "tell whence it cometh, and whither it goeth". If God alone has the right to punish, it is because He is beyond the ego; hatred means to arrogate to oneself the place of God, to forget one's human sharing of a common misery, to attribute to one's own "I" a kind of absoluteness, detaching it from that substance of which individuals are only so many contractions or knots. It is true that God sometimes delegates his right of punishment to man insofar as he rises above the "I", or must and can so rise; but to be the instrument of God is to be without hatred toward man. In hatred, man forgets "original sin" and thereby burdens himself, in a certain sense, with the sin of the other; it is because we make ourselves God whenever we hate that we must love our enemies. To hate another is to forget that God alone is perfect and that God alone is Judge. In good logic one can hate only "in God" and "for God"; we must hate the ego, not the "immortal soul", and hate him who hates God, inasmuch as he hates God and not otherwise, which amounts to saying that we should hate his hatred of God and not his soul.[3]

* * *

"To take up the cross" is to keep oneself close to the existential cross, which is to say: there is in Existence the pole "sin" and the pole "cross", the blind launching into enjoyment and the conscious stopping, the "broad way" and the "narrow way". To "take up the cross" is, essentially, not to "swim with the tide"; it is to "discern spirits", to keep oneself incorruptible in that apparent nothingness which is the Truth. To "take up the cross" means therefore to endure this nothingness, this threshold of God; and since the world is pride, egoism, passion, and false knowledge, it means to be humble and charitable, to "die" and become "as a little child". This nothingness is suffering to the extent that we are pride and that it thereby makes us suffer; the fire of purgatory is nothing else: it is our substance that burns, not because God wishes to hurt us, but because it is what it is—because it is "of this world"—and in proportion to its being so.

* * *

The cross is the divine fissure through which Mercy flows from the Infinite. The center of the cross, where the two dimensions intersect, is the mystery of forsakenness: it is the "spiritual moment" when the soul loses itself, when it "is no more" and when it "is not yet". Like the whole Passion of Christ, this cry is not only a mystery of grief, in which man must share by renunciation, but also, on the contrary, an "opening" that God alone can effect, and which He did effect because He is God; and that is why "my yoke is easy, and my

---

3. Likewise, when Christ says that it is necessary to "hate" one's "father and mother", that means that it is necessary to reject whatever in them is "against God", that is, the attachment that serves as an obstacle in respect of "the one thing needful". Such "hatred" implies for those whom it concerns a virtual liberation; it is thus, on the plane of eschatological realities, an act of love.

burden is light". The victory that devolves upon man has already been won by Jesus; for man nothing remains but to open himself to this victory, which thus becomes his own.

*   *   *

What is "abstraction" in the case of the logician becomes as it were corporeal in the case of the Word made flesh. The spear of the centurion Longinus has just pierced Christ's side; a drop of divine blood, flowing down the spear, touches the man's hand. At that moment, the world collapses for him like a house of glass; the darkness of existence is torn away; his soul becomes like a weeping wound. He is as if drunk, but with a drunkenness that is cold and pure; his whole life is henceforth like an echo repeating a thousand times that single instant at the foot of the cross. He has just been reborn, not because he has "understood" the Truth, but because the Truth has seized him existentially and torn him, with a "concrete" gesture, from this world. The Word made flesh is the Truth that has in a way become matter, but at the same time a matter transfigured and new-minted, a matter that is burning light, transforming and delivering.

APPENDIX

A Sampling of Letters and
Other Unpublished Materials

Intrinsic esoterism is essentially discernment between *Âtmâ* and *Mâyâ*, and permanent concentration on *Âtmâ*.

In Christianity, pure esoterism answers these questions: in which respect does Christ represent *Âtmâ* or *Mâyâ*, and in which respect does the Holy Virgin represent *Mâyâ* or *Âtmâ*? And also: how does the Holy Trinity represent *Âtmâ*?

Christianity is the perspective of divine Manifestation. This perspective finds its synthetical expression in the following Patristic saying: "God became man so that man might become God"—in the appropriate sense of *unio mystica*.

This means in Vedantic terminology: *Âtmâ* became *Mâyâ* so that *Mâyâ* might become *Âtmâ*. This is the universal, hence esoteric, meaning of the saying.

Concerning the Blessed Virgin, it could be said on the contrary: *Mâyâ* (Mary) became *Âtmâ* (through the Immaculate Conception) so that *Âtmâ* (the Word) might become *Mâyâ* (through Christ's human nature). In Tibetan terms: Mary the Immaculate is *Padme*, and Jesus the Incarnate is *Mani*—"the Jewel in the Lotus".

The Persons of the Holy Trinity are different aspects of *Âtmâ* in connection with *Mâyâ*. In one sense, the Persons correspond respectively to *Âtmâ* (Beyond-Being), *Îshvara* (Being), and *Buddhi* (Universal Intellect); in a more relative sense, the Father is Being in its Substance, and the Son is Being as conceiving the World.

In the first case, the Son is *Âtmâ* at the summit of *Mâyâ*, and the Holy Spirit is *Âtmâ* at the summit of *Jagat* or *Samsâra* (Existence, Manifestation); in the second case, the Father also belongs to *Mâyâ*—one does not envisage a Beyond-Being (Eckhart's "Godhead" above the personal "God")—and the Son appears as the inner Radiation of the Father. But let us not forget that the Persons are eminently present in pure *Âtmâ*; otherwise they could not actualize themselves within *Mâyâ*. In this sense, the hypostatic Persons are above Relativity; they are intrinsic aspects of the Absolute: *Sat, Chit, Ânanda*.

If Jesus manifests the Word, Mary manifests the Holy Spirit; otherwise he, the Spirit, would not have entered into her. In a quite different sense, if "Jesus" and "Mary" are conceived as divine Names, Jesus refers to the Absolute, to the divine Power, and Mary refers to the Infinite, also to divine Mercy. This explains the possibility of the invocation of their Names (Ἰησοῦ Μαριὰμ or *Jesu Maria*); by invoking them, man invokes God, and at the same time assimilates their respective mysteries.

Discernment between *Âtmâ* and *Mâyâ*, and permanent concentration on *Âtmâ*; concentration is invocation. The basis of invocation is that we should "pray without ceasing", and that "the kingdom of God is within you"; and "in the beginning was the Word".

* * *

If one does not find a spiritual guide, one can—within the framework of the Orthodox Church—ask the Blessed Virgin for help, in a solemn prayer and in front of a traditional icon.

Then one can practice the Jesus Prayer (Κύριε Ἰησοῦ Χριστέ ἐλέησον ἡμᾶς or *Domine Jesu Christe, miserere nobis*) and the first sentence of the Lord's Prayer (Πάτερ ἡμῶν ὁ ἐν τοῖς οὐρανοῖς or *Pater noster qui es in Caelis*), and also the Hail Mary (Χαῖρε Μαριὰμ κεχαριτομένη ὁ κύριος μετὰ σοῦ or *Ave Maria gratia plena, Dominus tecum*), or simply the Name of Jesus (Κύριε Ἰησοῦ Χριστέ or *Domine Jesu Christe*).

If you have any difficulty with the practice of invocation, you can always write to me. And I shall pray for you, as you requested.

* * *

The Holy Spirit is God insofar as He manifests Himself, either objectively or subjectively.

Sins against the Holy Spirit exclude those dispositions of soul through which the remission of sins takes place. They are six in number:

1. Presumption (overestimating oneself, in principle or in fact);
2. Despair (doubting God's Mercy);
3. Attack against the known truth;
4. Envy of another's gifts of grace;
5. Obstinacy (in evil, intellectual or moral);
6. Final Impenitence (in the face of death).

Faqr is the quality that excludes these sins. There is no valid *dhikr* without *faqr*.

A sin wrongs God, or ourselves, or our neighbor; in the last case it is grievous, not only insofar as the evil committed is so, but also insofar as the neighbor represents God.

*   *   *

Now that you have learned of the doctrine—metaphysical, cosmo-logical, eschatological—you wish to put it into practice in the measure possible, and to do so upon the formal basis of Christianity; in other words, you are aspiring to follow a Christian esoteric way. You know that pure metaphysics is 1. essential, 2. primordial, and 3. universal: being essential, it is independent of all religious or confessional formulations; being primordial, it is the truth that existed prior to all dogmatic formulations; being universal, it encompasses all intrinsically orthodox symbolism and can therefore be combined with every religious language. Next comes method, which is quintessentially prayer, not only in the most far-reaching sense, but also in the profoundest; examples of this in the Christian climate are the practice of the Hesychasts and the life of the "Russian Pilgrim". And all of this requires, imperatively, the funda-mental virtues on the one hand and on the other, extrinsically speaking, a corresponding mode of behavior, namely, one that is in conformity with the doctrine and the way.

Metaphysics is not a religion, but it brings profound and uni-versal meaning to the ideas and phenomena of any religion: thus it teaches *a priori* the distinction between the Absolute and the rela-tive, *Âtmâ* and *Mâyâ*, the Principle and Manifestation; now the phenomenon of Christ—or the metaphysical truth that determines it—means that "God became man that man might become God", according to a famous Patristic saying, which however is not to be taken literally, since man as such could never "become God"; but this is not the place to specify what this reservation entails, which in any case I have explained in my books. "God became man": *Âtmâ* became *Mâyâ*; owing to this, Christ is a bridge between *Mâyâ* and *Âtmâ*, and as a result—this is the mystery of the *Avatâra*—his Name contains a saving power; and likewise the Name of the Blessed Virgin, for she too is an avataric phenomenon, in the sense that she embodies the feminine aspect of the *Logos*.

Ejaculatory prayer is altogether fundamental; it has a function that is in fact Eucharistic; and yet man also has need of individual and ordinary prayer: it is necessary to speak to God and ask for His help; this can be done through a celestial intermediary, in particular the Blessed Virgin.

Before entering upon a way of prayer—before committing oneself to invoke God three times a day and, insofar as one can, in every available moment—one must promise Heaven to persevere in this way until death; such a promise is equivalent to monastic vows. As for the classic vows of "poverty", "chastity", and "obedience", they have, besides a literal meaning that applies to monks, a spiritual scope that applies to all men.

You mention in your letter the man who is convinced he saw Christ; not having heard his story, I cannot express an opinion. But it is essential for you to know this: a vision never confers spiritual authority; no one is a master owing to a spiritual vision. Unquestionably, the vision of a personification of the *Logos* is in itself a very rare and very lofty experience; but circumstances compel us to be neutral with respect to this particular incident.

When one devotes oneself to a spiritual practice, it is necessary to have the right intention; one must not have intentions that are beneath the purpose of the practice. God accepts that we invoke Him for several motives, and for these alone: first of all He permits us to invoke Him to save our soul, and this is the intention of fear; next He permits us to invoke Him because we enjoy the celestial climate, so to speak, and this is the intention of love; "I love because I love", as Saint Bernard said; finally He accepts the intention of *gnosis*, which is based on metaphysical evidence of the Real or the Absolute. But God will never accept the aim of obtaining sensible graces, or of having experiences, or of making an experiment, or of realizing a particular virtue or some other distinction, or of becoming this or that. And when a man experiences a spiritual state or a grace, or when he has a vision or audition, he must never desire that it happen again, and above all he must not base his spiritual life on such a phenomenon nor fancy that it has granted him some kind of superiority. All that matters is that we practice what brings us closer to God, while heeding the conditions that this practice requires; we do not have God's measures, and it is not for us to ask ourselves what we are. Life is a dream, and to think of God is to awaken; it is to find Heaven already, here below.

* * *

It can be said that Christian esoterism is "dead" in fact, but not in principle—*de facto,* but not *de jure.* It is "dead" because no one knows how to find it and not because it is absent; by contrast, in Oriental traditions everyone knows where esoterism is. On this subject, one can read my "Outline of the Christic Message"; the "Russian Pilgrim" ought to be read as well.

Pure and integral esoterism derives from *jnâna,* and that is what most Western seekers have in mind; it is self-evident that *jnâna* can be found in Christianity, but not in an institutional form. It is enough to be a *jnânin* while practicing the Christian religion, and this will give us a Christian *jnâna. Spiritus autem ubi vult spirat.* Christianity, however, no longer offers a visible spiritual homeland, and this has been the case for centuries; the world that is the material vessel of the Christian religion—the modern world—is a world of extreme ugliness, whatever its causes. It is clear that the Christian esoterist will have to take into account the need for a visible ambiance that is in conformity with the sacred, with contemplation, with prayer. "Beauty is the splendor of the true."

The elements constituting all esoterism are Discernment between the Real and the illusory (integral metaphysical Doctrine), quasi-permanent Concentration on the Real (invocatory Method), and Initiation (Baptism in Christianity); in addition, and extrinsically, there is a sense of the relativity of forms and an acknowledgment of foreign traditional forms, that is, other religions; and clearly the modern world and its superstitions of "civilization" and "progress" must be rejected. In the category of extrinsic elements, it is also appropriate to mention the interpretation of symbolisms, thus above all hermeneutics, without overlooking arts and crafts that have an initiatic basis; but none of these elements is indispensable from the point of view of spiritual realization, whatever their importance on their respective planes. To be a Christian esoterist does not necessarily mean that one must interpret every symbol or know all the texts containing metaphysical insights; but it does mean that one knows metaphysics as such (*Advaita Vedânta*) and that one practices the invocation of the Name of Jesus, or the Names of Jesus and Mary, or that one practices invocation with the help of the first sentence of the Lord's Prayer, or with the help of the "Jesus Prayer" of the Hesychasts, without forgetting the extrinsic conditions I have mentioned above.

I wrote somewhere that for Christians holiness is the door to esoterism; this means—but I ought to have specified it—that in Christianity, which is an avataric religion, the Eucharistic assimilation of the holiness of Christ is the door toward higher paths, namely, those that are not limited by official theology. Esoterism, by definition, comprises elements that go beyond this theology; thus invocation can in principle replace communion, for the divine Names are identified with the Eucharistic species, something that lies outside the scope of ordinary theology. In principle, a single act of communion could suffice for the whole of one's life; this explains how some saints, such as Saint Mary Magdalene or Saint Mary of Egypt, lived for years in solitude without taking communion.

In the absence of a master who grants the right to practice invocation, a Christian aspirant who is qualified from the point of view of both intelligence and character can request this right from the Blessed Virgin—not on his own initiative, but with the permission of an instructor—by joining to his request a solemn vow, namely, the promise to practice the invocation for his entire life and to observe the required conditions. In this case, the Blessed Virgin, or Christ, is the master; but there is also the instructor, that is, the man who communicates to the aspirant all the necessary information concerning doctrine and method. Of course this solution is not ideal, but there is no other in the world as it is today. "It is better to divulge the mysteries than to forget them," say the Cabalists.

Exoterism is subjective in that it is based on a "way of seeing things"; esoterism is objective in the sense that it is based on the "nature of things". Plenary esoterism is essentiality, universality, primordiality, perennialism. Exoterism tends to complicate and to externalize everything; esoterism, on the contrary, tends to simplify and bring everything inward. "The kingdom of God is within you."

* * *

Esoterism comprises *grosso modo* two degrees, one accentuating method and the other doctrine; in the first the methodic element largely determines the doctrinal element, and in the second it is the inverse that takes place. The first mode of esoterism brings about the interiorization—or spiritualization—of the Law, and this is Christianity as distinct from Mosaism; the second brings about the interiorization—and thus also the universalization—of doctrine, and this is pure metaphysics or *gnosis* as distinct from theologies. In the West, the historical gropings of theology on the one hand and the very notion of "theological development" on the other prove that theology is a relatively "outward" form of thought—whence the word "exoterism", this phenomenon having existed since antiquity—a form of thought that is *ipso facto* unsuited to the explicit and direct articulation of truths transcending the understanding of the average man, or let us say the man of passional mentality, who is thereby individualistic and voluntaristic; furthermore, dogmatic "totalitarianism" and its resulting intellectual stiffness prevent theology—in Islam as well as in Christianity—from conceiving degrees of Reality, hence the complex play of Relativity, and oblige it to compensate for this incapacity by symbolic solutions and detours, which are in no way concrete, but which nonetheless satisfy a certain need for explanation, the accent being less on metaphysical truth than on moral and mystical efficacy.

Theology is not so much an adequate and exhaustive explanation of the *hypostases* as a veil drawn over their mystery; a veil of charity as much as a veil of rigor. Analogically speaking—and one needs to have recourse to analogies in order to be clear, and not because one makes an affectation of them—Christianity is a sort of Vishnuite "monism", and not a Shivaite "non-dualism"; one cannot make a "religion" out of *Advaita Vedânta.* Christianity "is" not an *advaita* (non-dualism), but it "contains" it implicitly and virtually, whence the possibility of Christic *gnosis.*

Certainly, the line of demarcation between theology and *gnosis* is fluctuating; there is no impermeable barrier between them; yet a line does exist, and it has its openings as well as its closings; in any case it would be vain to deny, out of either piety or reverential sentiment, the limitations that intervene in certain theological definitions, and especially in Trinitarian doctrine.

Esoterically, the key to the Trinitarian mystery is that the Absolute by definition is the Good, and that the Good, also by definition, comprises both radiation and refraction, or projection and polarization; refraction actualizes in differentiated mode the potentialities of the Good, and radiation gives rise to levels—more and more contingent—of this actualization: whence—in the divine order—the *hypostases,* which one can envisage in the double respect of degrees and modes. To the principle of radiation or projection—inherent in the Absolute, the "Father"—corresponds the "Holy Spirit", and to the principle of polarization or refraction corresponds the "Son"; this complementarity can also be represented respectively by "Mary" and "Jesus", hence the feminization of the *pneuma* by certain Gnostics. The "Son" is to the "Father" what the circle is to the center, and the "Holy Spirit" is to the "Father" what the radius is to this same center; since the radius, which "emanates" from the center, does not stop at the circle but passes through it, one can say that from the circumference outwards it is "delegated" by the circle, just as the "Spirit" emanates from the "Father" and is delegated by the "Son"; the nature of the *filioque,* both justifiable and problematical, is clarified by the aid of this image.

To say that "the Father is nothing without the Son" can mean only that the Absolute would not be the Absolute without its potentiality of hypostatic and cosmogonic "exteriorization" and thus also of "repetition"; between the Absolute and its projection, both intrinsic and extrinsic—depending on the ontological degree— there is both inequality and equality, something that theology expresses by the notion of "subsistent relations", "relation" referring logically to inequality and "subsistence" to equality; for the theologians a "theological" explanation abolishes its contrary, for dogmatic thought is static and does not admit of movement, of the interplay of points of view or aspects, or of degrees of Reality. It offers keys, but it also creates veils; these veils are indeed appeasing and protective, but they are veils that dogmatic thought cannot remove.

The essence of metaphysics, and therefore of integral esoterism, is the distinction (*viveka*) between *Âtmâ* and *Mâyâ*; now—analogically speaking—average and official theology admits only *Âtmâ*; while *de facto* allowing for certain appearances of *Mâyâ* in *Âtmâ*—namely, the *hypostases*—it manages in the same breath to affirm that they are *Âtmâ* and denies that they are *Mâyâ*. Theology is quite willing to admit *Mâyâ* as world or creation, while denying that it is *Mâyâ* as a lesser reality or non-reality, and therefore in practice it attributes to the world the reality of *Âtmâ*, while not seeing—this goes without saying—that the reality of the world "is" the reality of *Âtmâ*; likewise theology does not see that the world can be real only because, in a certain manner, it can only "be" *Âtmâ*, and this is also the position of Ramanujan Vishnuism. I should add that discernment of the Absolute, by the very nature of its object, calls for contemplative union with it—something that demands the whole man—since the means obviously have to correspond with the end; for there are indirect means that lead toward union just as there are indirect concepts of the Absolute; but they do not constitute esoterism, at least not by themselves and to the exclusion of their profound meaning.

To say that Christ was born of a Virgin, that he had both a divine and a human nature, that he raised the dead, that he himself was resurrected, and that he ascended into heaven is clearly not exoterism; it is simply historical facts, just as are the conquests of Alexander, for example; a Buddhist who knows of them must accept them; but to say that these facts prove that only Jesus Christ saves is exoterism. It is obvious that esoterism does not consist in denying the facts on which the exoteric religion is founded; it lies in their interpretation, which refers them back to their universal prototypes and to their principles, from which they derive their saving power, or their connection with this power.

Having said this, I need do no more than recall once again that esoteric formulations, if they do not specifically require the crutches of theology—and this does not mean that theology offers nothing else—certainly find their supports in the Scriptures and in sacramental and liturgical Symbolism; consequently they are, by full right, parallel to the formulations of the "official dogmatics of the Church". And if the indirect and rigid character of theological thought favors a certain compensatory tendency to digression—by way of reaction precisely, though conversely dogmatism prevents this tendency—it is on the contrary the characteristic of esoteric thought to reduce difficulties to their underlying solutions and therefore to the simplicity of that which is. Without doubt, sapience cannot describe the ineffable, and this is not its intention; but it seeks to furnish points of reference that permit us to open ourselves, as far as is possible, to the ineffable, and according to the will of God.

Yet a further precision may be necessary—but in truth one would never end if one wished to forestall all possible objections. The *hypostases* are not "relative" inasmuch as they are "contained" in the Essence—which, according to a certain early perspective, coincides with the "Father": they are relative inasmuch as they "emanate" from Him; if they were not "contained" in Him, they could not "emanate". The *hypostases* are relative with regard to the Essence, and absolute with regard to the world, which amounts to saying—paradoxically but necessarily—that they are "relatively absolute"; they are such at the ontological level of "emanation", but not at the level of essentiality, where they coincide with the Absolute purely and simply. We are here at the limit of what can be expressed; it is no one's fault if, in every enunciation of this kind, there remain questions without an answer, and perhaps without any possible answer, at least at the dialectical level with which we are here concerned, and which alone is in question. The science of the heart is not subject to discussion.

* * *

I H S

1. The **I** indicates the natural state of man, his actual state.

The **H** indicates the connection between man and God; this sign is prolonged horizontally, which signifies a relationship (a religion); the "junction" is completed in and through Christ.

The **S** indicates the new, resurrected man, the man who has received divine life.

2. The **I** signifies descent, Incarnation, or Revelation.

The **H** indicates the connection, the relationship between man and God.

The **S** symbolizes the resurrected man.

The first interpretation starts with man, and the second starts with God, who descends toward man in order to save him and to allow him to share in the divine life.

*   *   *

The experience of which you speak in your letter to me contains nothing that ought to disquiet you; such experiences are normal in an esoteric climate, and they also have no relationship with dogmatisms or with syncretism; the link between our Path and the Blessed Virgin proves it. Heaven is well aware that we are of Christian origin on the one hand and of Vedantic formation on the other, which opens certain doors and gives us certain rights.

I have always loved the Curé d'Ars, but without losing sight of the following factors: this saint's path was a penitential *bhakti*, which by definition appeals to the will and to feeling, but not to the intelligence; that is to say, metaphysical arguments play no role in this path, whereas in the esoterism of *gnosis*, on the contrary, ideas are keys of primary importance; it is owing to this efficacy of metaphysical concepts that someone could say: "It is not I that have left the world; it is the world that has left me." This is what a disciple of the Shaykh al-Alawi told me.

In Christian mysticism—Catholic above all—one begins by "leaving the world"; in esoteric sapience, one begins by understanding what it is: "There is no lustral water like unto Knowledge"; nothing disarms seductive *Mâyâ* so well as the knowledge we have of it, around us as well as within us. The beginning of all *gnosis* and of all liberation is in fact the understanding of the relationship between *Âtmâ* and *Mâyâ*; but this doctrine—and the corresponding alchemy—remain outside the bhaktic perspectives, above all those that are voluntarist and penitential. These perspectives, which are at the same time fundamentally suspicious of all that could seem to them to be quietism, also underestimate the sacramental grace of the divine Name; they place the entire burden on man's side and wish to overlook—with some exceptions—that God can put Himself in place of our weakness.

Nevertheless, sanctity is sanctity, and Paradise is Paradise, no matter which path is taken to arrive there; the metaphysician or *jnânin* will necessarily love the saints, whoever they might be, on account of the marvel of sanctity. Obviously it is not impossible for some saint, above us in Heaven, to love us; there is nothing extraordinary in this saint's being a Catholic, while—from the point of view of form—we are in Islam, since, I repeat, we are Christian in origin. The blessed in Heaven know well why we are in Islam; they know our intellectual and spiritual motives, and they understand our quest. Ever since Islam existed, the Blessed Virgin could not be unaware of what Islam is; the proof of this is that in Ephesus—a Catholic religious told us this in Ephesus itself—Mary works as many healing miracles for the Muslims as for the Christians, without ever trying to convert the former.

So the Curé d'Ars has helped you. Other friends have had analogous experiences with other saints, in the first place with the Blessed Virgin, obviously; but given her super-eminent rank, she is situated beyond confessional denominations—not in relation to Christians, but in herself and in relation to non-Christians who have recourse to her. A question: the Curé d'Ars, to whom you addressed yourself, came to your aid; but are you certain that the benefic presence you felt afterwards did not come from the Blessed Virgin? For the Curé d'Ars always placed himself under Mary's mantle, so to speak. I am not altogether sure that an ordinary saint could grant an earthly person a permanent presence, whereas the Blessed Virgin can, and even does so readily for those who place their trust in her, as the Curé d'Ars did, precisely. Let us not ask too much from whom grace comes; it comes from Heaven.

* * *

You write me that you have reached a deadlock in the Orthodox tradition and do not know how to proceed. This comes from the fact that you are not sharply enough aware of what truly matters; and since you look to the authority of pure metaphysics and esoterism—otherwise you would not be writing to me—this gives me a reason to elucidate the essential points.

For us, there are three things that count—all the rest is a matter of form: first, discernment between the Real and the unreal, the Absolute and the relative, *Âtmâ* and *Mâyâ*, the Eternal and the transitory, God and the world; second, the constant—in principle unceasing—consciousness of the Real, the Fundamental, the Divine; and third, the conformity of our inner life and our actions, our conduct, to the Real and to our effective relationship with It. In other words: metaphysical Truth; then continuous Invocation; and lastly, beauty of soul, hence Virtue. The main emphasis here is on the Invocation; the Desert Fathers and Saint Mary of Egypt did nothing else. In the Orthodox Church the "Jesus Prayer" is used for this purpose; however, the Name of Jesus can suffice. The Name of Jesus ultimately signifies the highest Reality—for here the essential is the Divine and nothing else—whereas the Jesus Prayer is addressed more particularly to the Mercy that is inherent in the Divine. This Mercy is also expressed by the Name of Mary.

In light of the above, what the priests or laymen one meets in the Orthodox Church do or do not do, understand or do not understand, is a matter of indifference. Even Orthodox theology is finally not relevant to our needs, since for us what counts is the metaphysical Truth, whose most direct expression is in fact the *Vedânta*; then the Invocation, thus our effective relationship with that Truth; then the nobleness of our inner life, our freedom from worldliness, egoism, presumptuousness, and pettiness. For whoever has a sense of the Truth has also a sense of the Sacred, and whoever has a sense of the Sacred bears in a certain manner the Sacred in his soul. As Plato said, "Beauty is the splendor of the True."

The whole of Christian doctrine and spirituality lies, in fact, in the saying of Saint Irenaeus: "God became man that man might become God." There are various versions of this saying, but the essential is in any case in the form I have cited, which should not, of course, be taken literally. In Vedantic terms: "*Âtmâ* has become *Mâyâ* that *Mâyâ* may become *Âtmâ*", or "may return to *Âtmâ*"; for it is not the mode or degree of the union that matters, but the fact of union, whether it is a question of the "beatific vision" or something else. The way to this is the quasi-Eucharistic invocation of Jesus; the other sacraments are supplementary means of grace, but—as

Meister Eckhart said—in the last analysis we carry them within us; whether or not they are *de facto* accessible to us is another matter. In any case, that man as such cannot become God every metaphysician knows.

Many years ago I attended a service in the Athens Cathedral and know how endlessly long the Orthodox liturgy can be; this has strictly speaking nothing to do with the spiritual Way, and one who practices prayer—or invocation—as a method need certainly not reproach himself if he attends only the most essential services; after all, the Desert Fathers went for years without going to church, and the spiritual life of the "Russian Pilgrim" was likewise not dependent upon attendance at church. Esoterism, as far as we are concerned, is indeed much less bound to the outward world of forms than exoterism is. One should, however, have no feeling of inner opposition to the Church, for one ought not to expect from it what it cannot give. The Church, in fact, offers only an altogether general framework, which is not fully binding in every respect; and it represents only a very particular *bhakti*, which is inevitably sentimental and limited, and not a thoroughly comprehensive spirituality. With Islam it is of course *a priori* the same, *mutatis mutandis*, and likewise with Judaism.

You ask me whether there are criteria by which one can recognize whether one is on a wrong path. Certainly there are such criteria, but here the question arises as to whether the wrong path is an objective or a subjective one. Meister Eckhart—whom you mentioned in your letter—taught that there are as many Ways to God as there are men; this only means, however, that an objectively valid Way, for him who subjectively actualizes it aright, is at the same time a unique Way, for the simple reason that each human being is in a sense distinct from every other human being and therefore stands alone before God.

*   *   *

The *Ave* has two parts: the one concerning Substance and the other concerning the Real Presence of God. The first part is from the beginning to the word *mulieribus*, or to the word *tui*; the second part is from the word *et* to the Name of *Jesus*, or consists uniquely in this

Name. There is thus an intermediate part—*et benedictus fructus ventris tui*—which can be attached either to the first part concerning Substance, *Maria*, or to the second part concerning Presence, *Jesus.* It results from this that the formula may be recited starting from the word *et*, for the aspect of Substance is still found formulated there, but uniquely in immediate connection with the divine Presence and as a function of it. Finally, the Name of *Jesus* may be recited alone, the purity of the soul being the implicit condition of the pronunciation of this Name.

In reciting the *Ave*, it is necessary to concentrate first on the perfecting of the soul, then on the Presence of God. One may concentrate on the perfection of the soul by realizing it according to one or another of its three modes: purity, goodness, beauty.

Purity: the soul is empty of all desire. Every natural movement occurring within it is here considered in relation to its quality of passion, in its aspect of concupiscence and seduction. This perfection is cold, hard, and transparent, like the diamond.

Goodness: the soul diverts its love for the hardened ego in order to direct it toward God and thereby toward its neighbor, the entire Creation. The ego is in a state of death; love alone is life. The hardened heart must melt; from being indifferent toward God and its neighbor, it becomes fervent; but it thereby becomes indifferent to the ego and the world. The distinction between the "ego" and the "other" is dead, likewise the separation of the soul from God. In this perfection every natural movement of the soul will appear as a hardening, an indifference toward divine Love, a death.

Beauty: the beauty of the Virgin is none other than peace. It is in the perfect equilibrium of its possibilities that universal Substance realizes its beauty. In this perfection the soul leaves behind every dissipation in order to rest in its own substantial, existential, primordial, ontological perfection. The soul must be like a perfectly calm stretch of water; every natural movement of the soul will appear as an agitation, a dissipation, a disturbance, therefore an ugliness.

In reciting the *Ave*, one realizes in the soul one or another of these three perfections of the Virgin, but always one at a time: for example, in the morning, at midday, and in the evening. The three modes can be apportioned to these three times.

In pronouncing the divine Name of *Jesus*, one concentrates, without ratiocination, on this Name in its luminous obscurity. In reciting the entire formula, one does not concentrate on the words, but on the virginal or Marian perfection of the soul—which one realizes immediately and in a concrete, almost corporeal manner—and then on the divine Name, in which one retires in order to disappear. The words of the formula act by themselves on the soul, provided that their respective meanings are known; they act, conferring their illumination, in the measure in which the soul espouses the implacable purity, the fervent goodness, and the calm beauty of the Virgin.

But there is also another method of reciting the *Ave*, which is complementary to the foregoing; it is the method in which the accent is placed on the perfections of Christ: invincibility, uniqueness, Divinity. When one concentrates on one or another of these perfections—never on two at once—one no longer seeks actively to realize the Marian perfections; one strives solely to become engulfed in the perfections of Christ by concentrating on them in the second half of the *Ave*, as regards the first half of the *Ave*, the soul remains there pure and passive, without any ratiocination whatever. Just as in the realization of the Marian or virginal perfections, the Name of *Jesus* was accompanied, not by a meditation, but solely by an active concentration, so the part referring to the Virgin, when the effort is being directed toward realization of the Christic or lordly perfections, is accompanied only by a pure concentration, passive this time, but predisposing the soul to active concentration on the Christic perfections.

Invincibility: nothing in the world or in the soul can resist the divine power of the Name of *Jesus*. Christ enters the fallen world—and the soul—with the force of a flash of lightning or a drawn sword. Every natural movement of the soul appears here as a complacency or a passivity with regard to the world, as a forgetting of God through weakness. The soul must, by its perseverance and vigilance, actively associate itself with the divine and victorious act of Christ—with the invincible affirmation of the Divine in the created.

Uniqueness: the Word is unique. The Name of *Jesus* is a unique result of its mysterious identity with the Word. The soul is nothing; God alone is. It is a state of perfect humility in which the ego is annihilated through knowledge of its metaphysical nothingness before the uniqueness—the All-Reality—of God. Every natural movement of the soul is considered here as a form of pride, in the mystical sense of this word, that is, as an attempt to set oneself up as a reality before the sole Reality of God, or again as the error of wishing to add something to the Unique, which would then no longer be unique. Luciferianism is the wish to deprive God of His glory of uniqueness. No perfection is in us; every perfection is in Him.

Divinity: Christ is really God. In Him, through His Name, Deification is effected. We are powerless, and He lends us His Divinity in order to save us. Our deepest reality is His Presence in us. Every natural movement of the soul appears here as a separation between Him and us. The ordinary ego is a decadence; it is the Name of *Jesus*—He Himself—that henceforth will be our center. On the one hand He penetrates us with His deifying Grace, and on the other hand He absorbs us in it; we lose our individual life in order to find His Life, which is in Him. In this perfection, nothing can be considered as outside of God; everything is in God. The human person becomes "itself" only beyond individuality in the pure and divine Subject.

* * *

At the center of the Christian formula of invocation is the Name of Jesus, of which Saint Bernardino of Siena says the following: "Put the Name of Jesus in your houses and in your chambers, and keep it in your hearts. The best inscription of the Name of Jesus is the one in the heart, then the spoken word, and lastly the painted symbol. All that God has created for the good of the world is hidden in the Name of Jesus—the whole Bible, from Genesis to the last book. The reason for this is that the Name is Origin without origin. The Name of Jesus is as worthy of praise as God Himself." To the Name of Jesus may be added the Name of Mary, for quite evident reasons. "My yoke is easy, and my burden is light."

For the invocation to be pleasing to God, one must possess the following virtues or sincerely aspire to them: knowledge of oneself, then patience and magnanimity towards one's neighbor; surrender to the Will of God and trust in His Goodness; for hidden in the holy Name is God's desire to save us. Never may one invoke God with the intention to "realize" something; what we attain is God's affair.

In relation to God one must never wish to force anything; the invocation must be natural and calm. No secret ambition—that would be the worst thing possible! One may however invoke in a solemn manner, as if one were before an altar, or else—and this is so to speak the other pole—in a quite carefree, childlike manner, as a bird sings; this one can do, for example, while walking, whether indoors or outdoors in nature. There is no "goal of the Christian Way"; and the goal of our invocation lies in God's Hands. We invoke God—by whatever Name—because God is God, precisely, and because we wish to attain to God; in existence there is indeed no other choice. It should also not be forgotten that our starting-point is metaphysical Truth—the discrimination between *Âtmâ* and *Mâyâ*—and not a sentimental credo. Moreover, all that is true belongs principally to Christ even if it is not in the Bible, and even if theology is not conscious of this or that point, or if, for this or that reason, it cannot express it.

What is realized through the Eucharist does not depend on us. In taking Communion one should have the intention of absorbing God's saving—*a priori* desirous-of-saving—Presence and His Grace, and thereby of beginning a new life.

Christ's mediatorship means that God can become form—that through a form He can hold out His Hand to us. This is the mystery of the *Avatâra.* On the other hand, God can also act upon us from our innermost being: "The kingdom of God is within you." And again: "The wind bloweth where it listeth." This is connected with the mystery of the Holy Spirit. The mediatorship of Christ has no limits; it depends on what we are and to what we are consequently called; again, it is God's affair, not ours.

Free, personal prayer should not be neglected; it must always be introduced by the Lord's Prayer. The chief content of a prayer is a petition; one cannot, however, ask for something without giving thanks for something, any more than one can trust in God's Mercy without surrendering to His Will. One must express to God any cares or difficulties one may have and through this bring about a living relationship with Him, so that in this shifting world here below one is never alone; one may also turn to the Blessed Virgin and confide everything to her. Heaven is gracious.

God is gracious, but not soft; He is benevolent towards the heart that respects His Rigor. And "there is no right superior to that of Truth". The worldly-disposed heart is often compared to a stone; that is why one speaks of the "melting of the heart". In the invocation, the heart "drinks" the divine Name so that the Name may drink the heart. The heart must be receptive to the divine Presence; then God will be receptive to the calling of the heart.

*   *   *

In initiatic terms, the Annunciation is the entry of God into man, such as takes place in the Sacraments, which confer the Holy Spirit or Christ; God has become true man that man might become true God. The Visitation is the conformity of the soul to the "Real Presence", the consciousness that man has of "carrying" the Divinity, the devotional and joyous concentration of the whole being on the "divine Seed". The Nativity of Christ is the invocation of the saving Name—that which actualizes the spiritual virtuality implied in the "Presence". Next comes the Presentation of Christ in the Temple: man, purified and sanctified by this Presence of God, does not cease from considering himself a mere man and remains ever aware, despite the ecstasies of Grace, of his limitations as a creature, and also of the limitations that the divine support—the Name—contains in its "materiality".[1] And the Finding of the Child Jesus in the Temple: after the "dryness" in which the divine Name has left the soul, the Name is revealed as the mysterious source of all wisdom.

As for the "Sorrowful Mysteries", the Agony in Gethsemane is the forgetting of the "Real Presence", the neglecting of the "divine Seed", torpor and inadvertence, as seen moreover in the sleep of the disciples. The Scourging: this refers to actions that are incompatible with the divine Presence; it is "dissipation". The Crowning with Thorns: this is human vanity, its tendency to attribute to itself glories belonging to God alone; it is the error of deriving some vanity from Grace. Before proceeding further, a possible objection must be met, namely, that this interpretation—which strikes us as self-evident since it is in the nature of things—does not involve the participation of the contemplative in Christ's sufferings; but such a reproach is not justified, since the defects listed call for virtues, which by definition imply mortifications and which thus retrace the sufferings of the Word made flesh. Hence the crown of thorns—

---

1. The God-Man is the Divinity, but the Divinity is not the God-Man.

inflicted on Christ as a result in a sense of human vanity—becomes for the contemplative abnegation, forgetting of self, the attribution of all glory to God. It is therefore necessary on the one hand to realize in oneself the Passion of Christ and on the other hand to avoid inflicting it on him; in other words, whoever spares Christ (microcosmic, inward) the Passion must take it upon himself (in the same sense), and whoever does not take it upon himself inflicts it on Christ. The Carrying of the Cross also has a microcosmic meaning: Jesus, vessel of redemptive Grace, takes upon himself the weight of our ignorance, of our individualism; it is the divine Name that absorbs—and annihilates in its Infinitude—human miseries and in this fashion purifies man's heart for the sake of the beatific vision. And the Crucifixion: it is desire or passion that "crucifies" the "Real Presence" and immobilizes its "life".

As for the "Glorious Mysteries", the Resurrection is consciousness that the Divine alone is real, a consciousness that flowers by virtue of the Name of God. The Ascension: the soul becomes aware of its essential identity with the Divine. Pentecost: the Divine penetrates into the thoughts and actions of the "deified" man. The Assumption of the Blessed Virgin: the soul becomes extinct in God. The Coronation of the Blessed Virgin: the soul awakens in God, in the "divine Aspect" of which it had been but a shadow; the Virgin crowned by the Word—with an "uncreated" crown—is thus the soul reintegrated into its essential Infinitude, into its Reality, from which it had been separated only in an illusory mode, as if in a dream; and, let us add, this is why the Virgin is "created before creation": the soul must "become that which it is" and this is "That which is".

EDITOR'S NOTES

Numbers in bold indicate page numbers in the text for which the following definitions, descriptions, citations, and explanations are provided.

Chapter 1: Outline of the Christic Message

1: *A Patristic voice* could refer, among others, to Irenaeus (*c.* 130-*c.* 200), who taught that "the Son of God became the Son of man so that man, by entering into communion with the Word and thus receiving divine sonship, might become a son of God" (*Against Heresies*, 3:19); or to Athanasius (*c.* 296-373), who wrote, "The Son of God became man in order that we might become God" (*On the Incarnation*, 54:3); the essential teaching is common to many Church Fathers.

"Brahma *is real; the world is appearance;* the soul is not other than *Brahma*": this summation of *Advaita Vedânta* is traditionally ascribed to Shankara (788-820), whom the author regarded as the greatest of Hindu metaphysicians.

2: *Letter that killeth*: "The letter killeth, but the spirit giveth life" (2 Cor. 3:6).

"God is a Spirit: and they that worship Him must worship Him *in spirit and in truth*" (John 4:24).

"*Pray without ceasing*" (1 Thess. 5:17).

3: "*The kingdom of God is within you*" (Luke 17:21).

Hesychasts are monks of the Eastern Christian tradition whose aim is to attain to a state of *hesychia* or inner stillness through practice of the Jesus Prayer (see editor's note for Ch. 2, p. 26) or other "prayer of the heart".

"*For the hardness of your heart he* [Moses] *wrote you this precept*" (Mark 10:5).

Note 3: *Bernardino of Siena* (1380-1444) is known as "the apostle of the Holy Name" because of his devotion to the Name of Jesus.

4: That the *Good* wishes *to communicate Itself*, or is "self-diffusive", is implicit in the teaching of *Plato* (427-347 B.C.) that the Creator is "good, and what is good has no particle of envy in it; being therefore without envy He wished all things to be as like Himself as possible" (*Timaeus*, 29e); this doctrine recurs throughout the Western tradition and can be found in the teaching, among many others, of *Augustine* (354-430), Dionysius the Areopagite (*c.* 500), and Bonaventure (*c.* 1217-74).

Although never defined as dogma, popular recognition of the Blessed Virgin as *Co-Redemptress* dates from ancient times and can be found in both the Eastern and the Western Churches; echoing the belief of many Christians, Saint Louis Marie de Montfort writes, "Let us boldly say with Saint Bernard that we need a mediator with the Mediator himself and that the *divine Mary* is the one most able to fulfill this office of love" (*True Devotion to the Blessed Virgin*).

"I am *the Way, the Truth and the Life*" (John 14:6).

5: "*My yoke is easy, and my burden is light*" (Matt. 11:30).

"*In the beginning was the Word, and the Word was with God, and the Word was God*" (John 1:1).

"*All things were made by him*; and without him was not any thing made that was made" (John 1:3).

"*And the light shineth in darkness; and the darkness comprehended it not*" (John 1:5).

6: "*It must needs be that offenses come*, but woe to that man by whom the offence cometh" (Matt. 18:7).

In Zoroastrianism, *Ohrmazd* (or Ahura Mazda) is the Supreme Lord of the universe, and *Ahriman* (or Angra Mainyu) is an evil spirit corresponding to Satan in the Christian tradition.

Chapter 2: The Particular Nature and Universality of the Christian Tradition

8: Note 2: *Origen* (185-253) was the most prolific and influential of the early Church Fathers, writing many hundreds of books, including the *Contra*

Celsum, that is, "Against Celsus", a defense of Christianity against the pagan philosopher Celsus.

9: Note 4: *Augustine* (354-430), Bishop of the North African city of Hippo and the greatest of the Western Fathers, wrote a critical commentary on his own early works late in life, *Retractationes*, "Reconsiderations", though the perspective expressed in the passage here quoted was not among the teachings revised or "retracted".

The French abbot Jallabert published his *Catholicism before Jesus Christ* in 1874.

10: Note 4: *Eleusis, Lemnos, and Samothrace* were important centers for the ancient Greek mystery religions

Note 5: *"The divergence of the scholars is a blessing"* (*Ikhtilâf al-'ulamâ'i rahmah*) is a traditional saying attributed to Malik b. Anas (716-95), the founder of the Maliki school of Islamic jurisprudence, and preserved in the *al-Jami' al-Saghir* ("The Small Collection") of Jalal al-Din al-Suyuti (1445-1505).

Note 6: *Christ* says, "Among those that are born of women there is not a greater prophet than *John the Baptist*: but he that is least in the kingdom of God is greater than he" (Luke 7:28; *cf.* Matt. 11:11).

13: *"Give not that which is holy unto the dogs, neither cast ye your pearls before swine, lest they trample them under their feet, and turn again and rend you"* (Matt. 7:6).

14: *"And the light shineth in darkness; and the darkness comprehended it not"* (John 1:5).

"Before Abraham was, I am" (John 8:58).

Mansur *al-Hallaj* (858-922), the first Sufi martyr, was dismembered and crucified for his mystical pronouncement, "I am Truth".

16: *"It must needs be that offenses come;* but woe to that man by whom the offence cometh" (Matt. 18:7; *cf.* Luke 17:1).

17: *Basil* the Great (*c.* 330-79), one of the Cappadocian Fathers, wrote his work *On the Holy Spirit* in response to the heretical Pneumatomachi, who denied the Spirit's Divinity.

Dionysius the Areopagite (dated *c.* 500 by many scholars) was a disciple of Saint Paul (Acts 17:34) and author of several important mystical works, including *The Celestial Hierarchy*, from which this passage is quoted.

Note 11: *Paul Vulliaud* (1875-1950).

Vulliaud uses the French phrase *loi de l'arcane*, which has been rendered here by its traditional Latin equivalent, *lex arcani*, "law or rule of the secret".

18: Note 11: *Sozomen* (Salmaninius Hermias Sozomenus) was a Church historian of the early fifth century whose writing covers the period 323 to 425 and thus includes the Council of Nicaea (325), the first of the Ecumenical Councils.

Quintus Septimius Florens *Tertullian* (*c.* 160-*c.* 225) was an early Christian apologist and ascetical writer whose treatise against the heretic *Praxeas* constituted one of the first formulations of Trinitarian dogma.

Theodoret (*c.* 393-*c.* 466) was a bishop of Cyrrhus and an active participant in the Christological debates of his time.

Tentzelius (1455-1522)—Johannes Tetzel Reuchlin—was a Renaissance classicist and scholar of the Cabala.

In his *De Disciplina Arcani* (1685), "Concerning the Discipline of the Secret", *Emmanuel Schelstrate* (1649-92) taught that the relative absence of explicit doctrines in the earliest Church on such subjects as the sacraments was the result of a deliberate rule of silence imposed by Christ and his Apostles.

19: Note 11: *"He that hath ears, let him hear"* (Matt. 11:15).

"Seek, and ye shall find; knock, and it shall be opened unto you" (Luke 11:9).

John Chrysostom (*c.* 347-407), Patriarch of Constantinople, was a gifted orator—hence the epithet *chrysostomos*, the "golden mouthed"—and the inspired author of the most often used liturgy in the Eastern Orthodox Church.

20: *Justification by Faith*: "A man is justified *by faith* without the deeds of the law" (Rom. 3:28).

Yoke is easy and burden light: "For my *yoke is easy, and* my *burden* is *light*" (Matt. 11:30).

Note 11: *Diocletian,* Roman Emperor from 284 to 305, promoted the last great wave of persecution against the early Church.

Innocent I (d. 417) was Pope from 402.

F. T. Bègue-*Clavel* published *Picturesque History of Free Masonry and Ancient and Modern Secret Societies* in 1843.

21: Note 12: *Chaitanya* (1486-1533) was a Vaishnavite Hindu spiritual leader and teacher, regarded by his followers as an *avatâra,* or incarnation, of Krishna.

Krishna, along with Rama, is one of the two most important *avatâra*s of the Hindu God Vishnu.

Amida (Japanese) or *Amitabha* (Sanskrit) is the name of the Buddha of "infinite light" who, as a *Bodhisattva* named Dharmakara, vowed not to enter *Nirvâna* until he had brought all who invoked his Name into the paradise of his Pure Land.

Japanese Buddhist Sects was published by *E. Steinilber-Oberlin and Kuni Matsuo* in 1930.

22: Note 12: *Daisetz Teitaro Suzuki* (1870-1966) published three volumes of *Essays in Zen Buddhism* between 1927 and 1933.

Note 13: *Ramakrishna* (1834-86), a devotee of the Hindu Goddess Kali, was one of the greatest Hindu saints of modern times.

23: For the *Hesychast tradition,* see editor's note for Ch. 1, p. 3.

Faith can move mountains: "If ye have faith as a grain of mustard seed, ye shall say unto this mountain, Remove hence to yonder place; and it shall remove: and nothing shall be impossible unto you" (Matt. 17:20).

Note 13: *Vladimir Lossky* (1903-58) published *The Mystical Theology of the Eastern Church* in 1944.

24: Note 15: According to *Meister Eckhart* (*c.* 1260-1327), a German Dominican metaphysical writer, all food is Holy Communion for those who are pure in heart (see editor's notes for Ch. 3, p. 36, Note 9, Ch. 5, p. 59, Note 6, and Ch. 10, p. 129, Note 18).

25: *Benedict* of Nursia (*c.* 480-*c.* 550), known as the "patriarch of Western monasticism", composed a short *Rule* for his monks, which drew upon the spiritual practice of the Desert Fathers and an earlier rule of Saint John Cassian.

The *Desert Fathers* were Christian ascetics and hermits of the third, fourth, and fifth centuries who withdrew to the wilderness in Egypt, Syria, Palestine, and Arabia to lead lives of interior prayer.

26: The *Prayer of Jesus*, or Jesus Prayer, is the most common Hesychast orison and consists of the words, or some variation: "Lord Jesus Christ, Son of God, have mercy upon us."

27: *Holy silence* is one of several possible translations of the Greek *hesychia*.

Palamite doctrine, that is, the teaching of Gregory Palamas.

Note 17: *Gregory Palamas* (*c.* 1296-1359), a monk of Mount Athos, is best known for his defense of the psycho-somatic contemplative techniques employed by the Hesychast Fathers.

Note 18: *Om mani padme hum* is a Tibetan *mantra* meaning "O Thou Jewel in the Lotus, hail".

28: "*The sun shall be turned into darkness, and the moon into blood, before the great and the terrible day of the Lord come*"; "*whosoever shall call on the name of the Lord shall be delivered*" (Joel 2:31, 32).

"Unto the church of God which is at Corinth, to them that are sanctified in Christ Jesus, called to be saints, with *all that in every place call upon the name of Jesus Christ our Lord*, both theirs and ours: Grace be unto you" (1 Cor. 1:2).

Unceasing prayer: "Pray without ceasing" (1 Thess. 5:17).

John Damascene, or John of Damascus (*c.* 675-*c.* 749), was a Greek theologian and "doctor of the church", best known for his *Fount of Wisdom*.

Note 20: "*I cried unto the Lord with my voice, and He heard me out of His holy hill*" (Ps. 3:4); "*Then called I upon the Name of the Lord; O Lord, I beseech Thee, deliver my soul"* (Ps. 116:4); *"The Lord is nigh unto all them that call upon Him, to all that call upon Him in truth"* (Ps. 145:18); *"Open thy mouth wide, and I will fill it"* (Ps. 81:10); "Bless the Lord, O my soul . . . *who satisfieth thy mouth with good things, so that thy youth is renewed like the eagle's"* (Ps. 103:1, 5); *"Fear not: for I have redeemed thee, I have called thee by thy name; thou art mine"* (Isa. 43:1); *"Seek ye the Lord while He may be found, call ye upon Him while He is near"* (Isa. 55:6); *"I called upon God, and the spirit of wisdom came to me"* (Wisd. of Sol. 7:7).

Note 21: *Dervishes*—Persian for "the poor ones"—are members of a Sufi brotherhood.

29: Note 22: Sergius *Bulgakov* (1871-1944) published *The Orthodox Church* in 1935.

Bernard of Clairvaux (1090-1153) was a Cistercian monk and author of numerous homilies on the Song of Songs.

Chapter 3: "Our Father Who Art in Heaven"

31: Note 1: The *Talmud* comprises various collections of Jewish oral tradition and commentary.

32: *Rama* and *Krishna* are two of the ten *avatâras*, or incarnations, of the Hindu God Vishnu.

"Hail, thou that art highly favored [*full of grace*], *the Lord is with thee*: blessed art thou among women" (Luke 1:28); "For He hath regarded the low estate of His handmaiden: for, behold, from *henceforth all generations shall call me blessed"* (Luke 1:48).

The third of the Ecumenical Councils, meeting in Ephesus (431), declared that the Blessed Virgin Mary is rightly called the *Theotokos* or *Mother of God*; the *Immaculate Conception* is the Roman Catholic dogma that, from the first moment of her conception, Mary was free from all stain of original sin.

Note 4: In the author's original French, the word here rendered *Protestantism* is *Évangélisme* or "Evangelicalism", a term used in a European context to refer either to Lutheranism or to the union of the Lutheran and Reformed churches, or again to Protestant bodies in general.

33: The *definition of the God-Man*, including the relationship between Christ's Person and natures, is the subject of Chapter 13 of the present volume, "The Mystery of the Two Natures"; *Trinitarian theology* is discussed in greater depth in Chapter 10, "Evidence and Mystery".

34: *"The kingdom of God is within you"* (Luke 17:21).

35: *"But thou, when thou prayest, enter into thy closet, and when thou hast shut thy door, pray to thy Father, which is in secret"* (Matt. 6:6).

For *Hesychasts*, see editor's note for Ch. 1, p. 3.

Note 8: "But when ye pray, *use not vain repetitions* as the heathen do" (Matt. 6:7).

36: "No man speaking *by the Holy Spirit* calleth Jesus accursed" (1 Cor. 12:3).

Made in the image of God: "And God said, Let us make man in our image, after our likeness" (Gen. 1:26).

Note 9: *Meister Eckhart* (*c.* 1260-1327) was regarded by the author as the greatest of Christian metaphysicians and esoterists (see editor's notes for Ch. 2, p. 24, Note 15, Ch. 5, p. 59, Note 6, and Ch. 10, p. 129, Note 18).

Chapter 4: Some Observations

39: "I am the *Light of the world*" (John 9:5).

Origen (*c.* 185-*c.* 254), among other Church Fathers, speaks of Christ as the *Wisdom of the Father*.

"And *the light shineth in darkness*; and the darkness comprehended it not" (John 1:5).

40: In reciting the Nicene Creed, Orthodox Christians confess that the Holy Spirit "proceeds from the Father" alone (*cf.* John 15:26), but in the Roman Catholic Church the term *Filioque* is added to the Latin text of the Creed, signifying that the Spirit proceeds from the Father "and the Son".

Note 3: The *Decalogue* consists of the "Ten Commandments" given by God to Moses (*cf.* Ex. 20:3-17); in the Cabala, or Jewish mystical tradition, the

Sephiroth (literally "numbers" in Hebrew) are the ten emanations of *Ein Sof*, the Supreme Godhead.

41: λειτουργία (*leitourgia*), or "liturgy", is literally the "work" (*ergon*) of the "people" (*laos*).

Note 4: For *Augustine* (354-430), see editor's note for Ch. 2, p. 9, Note 4.

41-42: On *Calvary*, Christ addresses his mother in reference to John: "Woman, behold thy *son!*" (John 19:26); at the sea of *Tiberias*, Christ says of John that he will "tarry *till I come*" (John 21:22).

42: "*Feed my sheep*" (John 21:16, 17).

"Thou art Peter, and upon this rock I will build my church; and *the gates of hell shall not prevail against it*" (Matt. 16:18).

In the Greek East, the Bishop of Rome is accorded a primacy of honor among his fellow bishops as *primus inter pares*, that is, "the first among equals"; he is not understood to be the *pontifex maximus* or "supreme pontiff" of the Church, as he is among Roman Catholics.

The three *Evangelical counsels* of poverty, chastity, and obedience, also known as the "counsels of perfection", gave rise to the traditional vows of the monk.

Note 7: The many works of *Tertullian* (see editor's note for Ch. 2, p. 18, Note 11) include a short treatise "On Baptism".

Dionysius the Areopagite (see editor's note for Ch. 2, p. 17) writes of the sacraments in his *Ecclesiastical Hierarchy*.

43: Note 9: "God is a Spirit: and they that worship Him must worship Him *in spirit and in truth*" (John 4:24).

Louis IX (1214-70) was King of France from 1226.

"*The letter killeth, but the spirit giveth life*" (2 Cor. 3:6).

Note 10: The Eucharistic theology of *Clement of Alexandria* (*c.* 150-*c.* 215), head of the famous Catechetical School of Alexandria, is to be found in his *Stromateis* or "Miscellaneous Studies".

44: Referring to love of God and love of neighbor, Christ said, "On these two commandments hang *all the law and the prophets*" (Matt. 22:40).

The *Golden Legend*, a compendium of saints' lives and short treatises about Christian festivals, was compiled by Jacob of Voragine (*c.* 1230-*c.* 1298).

Ave Maria, or "Hail, Mary", are the first two words of the Angelical Salutation (*cf.* Luke 1:28 and see editor's note for Ch. 14, p. 155).

Ignatius (*c.* 35-*c.* 107), the successor of Saint Peter as Bishop of Antioch, was an early Christian martyr.

45: Note 11: *Catherine dei Ricci* (1522-90) was an Italian visionary.

Christe eleison is a Greek phrase meaning "Christ, have mercy".

John *Cassian* (*c.* 360-435), who was much influenced as a young man by his contact with the Desert Fathers of Egypt, later founded monasteries near Marseilles, transmitting the ascetical and mystical teachings of the East to the Western Church (see also editor's notes for Ch. 2, p. 25).

In the traditional Latin Mass, the celebrant recites the words *Panem celestem accipiam et nomen Domini invocabo* ("I will receive the Bread of Heaven and call upon the Name of the Lord") and *Calicem salutaris accipiam et nomen Domini invocabo* ("I will receive the Chalice of Salvation and call upon the Name of the Lord") as he prepares to receive the Eucharist.

The *Small Schema* and the *Great Schema* (*schêma* means "habit" in Greek) are successive grades of monastic life in the Christian East, each involving solemn vows.

"*The word of God* is quick, and powerful, and sharper than any two-edged sword, piercing even to the dividing asunder of soul and spirit, and of the joints and marrow, and is a discerner of the thoughts and intents of the heart" (Heb. 4:12).

Mary *Consolata* (1903-46) was an Italian Capuchin nun, whose "prayer of the heart", received from Christ himself, consisted of the words, "Jesus, Mary, I love you! Save souls!", and whose life and teaching is recorded in the book here noted, published by Lorenzo Sales, I.M.C., in 1955.

46: Note 12: See "The Spiritual Virtues" in *Spiritual Perspectives and Human Facts* (Pates Manor, Bedfont, Middlesex: Perennial Books, 1987), first published in 1954.

47: *Benedict* of Nursia (see editor's note for Ch. 2, p. 25) gave special emphasis to the virtues of obedience and humility in his famous *Rule*; *Bernard* of Clairvaux (see editor's note for Ch. 2, p. 29, Note 22) entitled one of his most important treatises "The Steps of Humility and Pride".

Note 13: "The Son of Man came not *to be served but to serve*, and to give his life a ransom for many" (Matt. 20:28).

"*Whosoever therefore shall humble himself as this little child, the same is greatest in the kingdom of heaven*" (Matt. 18:4).

"[The scribes and the Pharisees] love *the uppermost rooms at feasts*" (Matt. 23:6, Mark 12:39; *cf.* Luke 11:43).

Thomas Aquinas (*c.* 1225-74), known in tradition as the "Angelic Doctor" and the most important Roman Catholic theologian in history, discussed the virtue of humility in his "Treatise on the Virtues" in the *Summa Theologica*.

Note 14: "*Why callest thou me good? There is none good but one, that is, God*" (Matt. 19:17, Mark 10:18; *cf.* Luke 18:19).

48: According to *Augustine*, "All the divine precepts are referred back to *love*, of which the Apostle [Paul] says, 'Now the end of the commandment is love, out of a pure heart, and a good conscience and a faith unfeigned' (1 Tim. 1:5). Thus every commandment harks back to love" (*Enchiridion*, 32).

"*And the light shineth in darkness; and the darkness comprehended it not*" (John 1:5).

"*Judge not, that ye be not judged*" (Matt. 7:1).

The second article of the Apostles' Creed includes the following words about Christ: "He ascended into Heaven, and sitteth on the right hand of God the Father Almighty: from thence He shall come to *judge the quick and the dead.*"

49: "There is one lawgiver, who is able to save and to destroy: *Who art thou that judgest another*" (James 4:12; *cf.* Rom. 14:4).

Wisdom of serpents: "I send you forth as sheep in the midst of wolves: be ye therefore wise as serpents, and harmless as doves" (Matt. 10:16).

"There are diversities of gifts, but the same Spirit. . . . For to one is given by the Spirit the word of wisdom . . . to another *discerning of spirits*" (1 Cor. 12: 4, 8, 10).

Note 15: The *Torah* is the written foundation of Jewish law, consisting of the Pentateuch or first five books of the Old Testament and revealed to Moses on Sinai.

51: Note 19: René *Descartes* (1596-1650) propounded a method based upon a systematic doubting of everything except one's own self-consciousness, as summed up in the phrase *cogito ergo sum* ("I think; therefore I am"); Immanuel *Kant* (1724-1804), founder of the "critical" philosophy, insisted that man's knowledge is limited to the domain of sensible objects and that the idea of God is no more than a postulate of reason having no objective certainty.

52: *One thing needful*: "One thing is needful" (Luke 10:42).

Chapter 5: Delineations of Original Sin

56: *Kingdom of God within you*: "The kingdom of God is within you" (Luke 17:21).

"Thou shalt love the Lord thy God *with all thy heart, and with all thy soul, and with all thy strength, and with all thy mind*" (Luke 10:27); "this is the first and great commandment," says Christ (Matt. 22:37; *cf.* Mark 12:30, Deut. 6:5).

"So then because thou art lukewarm, and neither cold nor hot, I will spew thee out of my mouth" (Rev. 3:16).

Note 1: For the *Immaculate Conception*, see editor's note for Ch. 3, p. 32.

Note 2: For *Shankara*, see editor's note for Ch. 1, p. 1.

Note 3: "Therefore to him that *knoweth to do good, and doeth it not*, to him it is sin" (James 4:17).

57: For the teaching "Brahma *is real; the world is illusory* [or 'appearance'); *the soul is not other than* Brahma", see editor's note for Ch. 1, p. 1.

58: "After this manner therefore pray ye: *Our Father who art in heaven*, hallowed be thy name" (Matt. 6:9; *cf.* Luke 11:2).

The building of the *Tower of Babel* and the confounding of human language are told of in Gen. 11:4-9.

The *Titans* were the oldest race of Greek gods, who, under the leadership of Cronus, resisted the power of Zeus and the other Olympians; *Prometheus* stole fire from the Olympian gods; Daedalus fashioned wings for himself and his son, *Icarus*, but the young boy flew too close to the sun, melting the wax in the wings and plunging to his death.

The *forbidden tree* afforded "knowledge of *good* and *evil*" (Gen. 2:17).

According to the Koran, God, having "taught Adam all the names" of the *creatures*, commanded him, "O Adam! Inform them of *their names*", and the *angels* were in turn commanded, "*Prostrate* yourselves before Adam" (*Sûrah* "The Cow" [2]:31, 33, 34).

"And *Enoch* walked with God, and he was not, for God took him" (Gen. 5:24; *cf.* Heb. 11:5).

59: Note 6: The teaching of *Meister Eckhart* (see editor's notes for Ch. 2, p. 24, Note 15, Ch. 3, p. 36, Note 9, and Ch. 10, p. 129, Note 18) that "*there is something in the soul* [anima] *which is uncreated and uncreatable*; if the whole soul were such, it would be uncreated and uncreatable, *and this is the Intellect* [Intellectus]" was among the articles for which he was charged with heresy, and which he himself subsequently revoked "insofar as they could generate in the minds of the faithful a heretical opinion" (The Bull *In agro dominico* [1329]).

Chapter 6: The Dialogue between Hellenists and Christians

63: Regarding the *inconsistency* involved in Christian *borrowing from the Greeks*, the author writes elsewhere: "Christianity being a *bhakti*, it would in principle have been consistent and wise to renounce integral metaphysics and to hold fast to a fideism inspired solely by the Scriptures: thus, to record piously what they say of God, of the Father, of the Son, of the Holy Ghost, without seeking to build a system, and to remain humbly and lovingly content with mystery; theology, necessary *de facto*, could have done without certain speculations inspired by Aristotle. But in fact such total faithfulness to itself—or more precisely to the genius of *bhakti*—was scarcely possible for a state religion. Furthermore, it was not possible because speculation is in the nature of man, and because the proximity of philosophers was a temptation to imitate them, all the more so since man is reluctant to acknowledge in others qualities which he does not himself possess—and this, without euphemism, is called jealousy; then, because a number of converts were themselves Greeks or Hellenists, acquainted with philosophy; and finally, because the pagan environment required vigilant apologetics, without forgetting the Christian heresies which needed to be neutralized. But here a new difficulty arises: the heresy did not always consist in something that was contrary to the truth; too often it was simply something that was contrary to *bhakti*; theology therefore developed in response to a twofold necessity or a twofold temptation: to take over the dialectic—even if foreign to the Christian genius—of real or apparent adversaries and, with the help of this dialectic, to attack its very essence; in a word, to lay claim to all the rights of *gnosis* or pure intellection, while having recourse to mystery when this claim comes up against a limit, as is inevitable since it is a question here of *bhakti* and dogmatism" (*Christianity/Islam: Essays on Esoteric Ecumenicism* [Bloomington, Indiana: World Wisdom, 1985], pp. 142-43).

"We preach Christ crucified, unto the Jews a stumbling-block, and unto the Greeks *foolishness*" (1 Cor. 1:23).

Wisdom according to the flesh: "In simplicity and godly sincerity, not with fleshly wisdom, but by the grace of God, we have had our conversation in the world" (2 Cor. 1:12).

64: The *school of Alexandria*, whose teachers included Clement (*c.* 150-*c.* 215) and Origen (*c.* 185-*c.* 254), was marked by a strong Platonic tendency and by a mystical and allegorical interpretation of Scripture, while that of *Antioch* was noted for its Aristotelian and historical emphasis.

66: *Socrates* (*c.* 470-399 B.C.) was the teacher of *Plato* (*c.* 427-*c.* 347 B.C.), and Plato was the teacher of *Aristotle* (384-322 B.C.).

Aryan refers to the teachings and traditions of ancient Indo-Iranian culture; *Mazdean* is the same as Zoroastrian; *Brahmanic* signifies the doctrine of Hindu Brahmins or priests.

67: Note 3: *Pythagoras* (*fl.* 540 B.C.) taught a metaphysics that was based upon the qualitative essence of numbers.

68: The earliest of the *pre-Socratic* philosophers, the *Ionians* or Milesians, included Thales and Anaximenes (see note 4 below), as well as Anaximander (*c.* 611-*c.* 547 B.C.), who taught that all things are composed of *apeiron*, the "indefinite".

Note 4: *Thales* (*c.* 636-*c.* 546), *Anaximenes* (*fl.* 550 B.C.), *Diogenes* (*c.* 412-*c.* 323 B.C.), *Heraclitus* (*fl.* 500 B.C.).

69: The ancient Greek *Sophists* were teachers of rhetoric, much criticized by Socrates for their specious arguments and seeming indifference to truth.

Aristotle is known as the *Stagirite* because he was born in the Ionian city of Stagira in Chalcidice.

Protagoras of Abdera (*c.* 481-*c.* 411 B.C.) was a leading Sophist, known for his maxim that "man is the measure of all things".

Democritus (*c.* 460-*c.* 370 B.C.) believed that everything can be reduced to atoms moving in the void.

Epicurus (*c.* 341-271 B.C.) propounded an empiricist theory of knowledge and a hedonistic, or "epicurean", ethics, based on the conviction that the gods have no influence on human life.

72: "No man can say that Jesus is Lord, *but by the Holy Spirit*" (1 Cor. 12:3).

73: "Heaven and earth shall pass away, but *my words shall not pass away*" (Matt. 24:35, Mark 13:31, Luke 21:33).

"*Before Abraham was*, I am" (John 8:58).

Chapter 7: The Complexity of Dogmatism

75: Note 2: *Wisdom of Christ*: "We preach Christ crucified . . . unto them which are called, both Jews and Greeks, Christ the power of God, and the wisdom of God" (1 Cor. 1:24).

"We speak wisdom among them that are perfect: yet not the *wisdom of this world*, nor of the princes of this world, that come to nought" (1 Cor. 2:6).

"I beseech you, that I may not be bold when I am present with that confidence, wherewith I think to be bold against some, which think of us as if we walked *according to the flesh*" (2 Cor. 10:2); "Though we have known Christ *according to the flesh*, yet now henceforth know we him no more" (2 Cor. 5:16).

76: For the word *Protestantism*, see editor's note for Ch. 3, p. 32, Note 4.

78: Note 4: The *Law of Manu* (*Mânava-Dharma-Shâstra* or *Manu-smriti*) is a collection of precepts concerning every important aspect of social and religious life in traditional Hinduism.

The *Paradise* of the Buddha *Amitabha* is the Pure Land to which he vowed to bring all who invoke his Name.

Chapter 8: Christian Divergences

81: For the word *Protestantism* throughout this chapter, see editor's note for Ch. 3, p. 32, Note 4.

Dante Alighieri (1265-1321), author of *The Divine Comedy*, composed his *De Monarchia* or *"Treatise on Monarchy"* in honor of Emperor Henry VII.

82: Note 2: The author's longest and most detailed study of Protestantism (*Évangélisme*) was published as "The Question of Evangelicalism" in his book *Christianity/Islam: Essays on Esoteric Ecumenism* (Bloomington, Indiana: World Wisdom, 1985), pp. 15-53.

83: *Augustine* (see editor's note for Ch. 2, p. 9, Note 4) taught that before the fall man was "able not to sin" (*posse non peccare*), but that fallen man "is not able not to sin" (*non posse non peccare*).

According to Martin *Luther* (1483-1546), man is wholly under the power of evil and can do nothing but sin, justification itself being a kind of legal fiction whereby the righteousness of Christ is imputed to the Christian.

85: "It is profitable for thee that one of thy *members* should perish, and not that thy whole body should be cast into hell" (Matt. 5:29, 30).

Ulrich *Zwingli* (1484-1531) believed that the Eucharist was merely a memorial service and that Christ was not really present in the bread and wine.

According to the Catholic doctrine of *transubstantiation*, the essence of the elements is changed, though they still appear in their "accidents" to be bread and wine; Luther preferred a doctrine of *consubstantiation*, according to which the body and blood of Christ co-exist with the essence or substance of the bread and wine.

86: In the view of John *Calvin* (1509-64), the faithful communicant receives the virtue or power of the Body and Blood.

For *Bernard* of Clairvaux, see editor's note for Ch. 2, p. 29, Note 22.

"*In my Father's house are many mansions*" (John 14:2).

"Gloria in altissimis Deo *et in terra pax hominibus bonae voluntatis*" is the Vulgate text of Luke 2:14, "Glory to God in the highest, and on earth peace, good will toward men".

Paul attests that "he that eateth and drinketh unworthily eateth and drinketh damnation to himself, not discerning the Lord's body" (1 Cor. 11:29).

87: Note 7: It was taught by Abu l-Hasan al-Ashari (873-935) and the *Asharite* school of Islam that anthropomorphic descriptions of God in the Koran should not be interpreted as metaphors, but accepted *bi-lâ kayf*, that is, "without asking any questions", and that God creates all human acts, thereby determining them, but that men acquire these acts and are thus responsible for them.

88: The term *impanation*, literally a "turning into bread", is sometimes applied to Eucharistic doctrines which seek to safeguard a belief in the Real Presence with the idea that the Son of God "becomes bread" in the sacrament even as he "became flesh" (*cf.* John 1:14) in Jesus.

The consecrating words of Christ are "Take, eat; this is my body" and "Drink ye all of it; for this is my blood of the new testament" (Matt. 26:26-28; *cf.* Mark 14:22, 24; Luke 22:19-20; 1 Cor. 11:24-25).

89: The teachings of *John Damascene* (*c.* 675-*c.* 749) on the Eucharist are included in his influential treatise *On the Orthodox Faith* (see the author's note 10 concerning Damascene's *Exposé précis de la Foi orthodoxe*).

91: "In vain they do worship me, teaching for doctrines the *commandments of men*" (Matt. 15:9; Mark 7:7).

For *High Church Anglicanism*, the French reads "*l'Anglicanisme du type* High Church".

The *Seventh* Ecumenical *Council* was held at Nicaea in 787.

Note 13: As a test of authentic tradition, Vincent of Lérins (d. before 450) proposed the three-fold Latin formula *quod ubique, quod semper, quod ab omnibus creditum est*, that is, "what has been believed *everywhere, always, by all*".

91-2: As for the proper relationship between the Pope and the other *patriarchs, who are his brothers*, the author has this to say elsewhere: "Regarding the question of ecclesiology, the most ancient Christian texts sometimes uphold the Latin thesis and sometimes the Greek; the ideal, or rather the normal situation, would therefore be an Orthodox Church recognizing a pope who was not totally autocratic, but in spiritual communion with all of the bishops or patriarchs; this would be a pope without *filioque*, but having nonetheless the right, in theology, liturgy, and other domains, to certain particularities that are opportune or even necessary in a Latin and Germanic setting" (*Form and Substance in the Religions* [Bloomington, Indiana: World Wisdom, 2002], p. 203).

Note 14: One reason for the schism between Orthodoxy and Roman Catholicism was the unilateral decision of the West to interpolate the word *filioque* into the Latin text of the Nicene Creed, thus expressing a double procession of the Holy Spirit from the Father "and the Son".

Note 16: In the French text of the Gospel cited by the author in this note, the passage from Matthew 23:10 reads, "Ne vous faites pas non plus appeler Docteurs: car vous n'avez qu'un Docteur, le Christ", thus making the phrase *Doctors of the Church* (Docteurs de l'Eglise) rather more problematic than it may seem in English translation.

93: "God is a Spirit: and they that worship Him must worship Him *in spirit and in truth*" (John 4:24).

94: Donato *Bramante* (1444-1514), a Renaissance painter and architect, developed the original plan for Saint Peter's Basilica in Rome and designed the Vatican's Belvedere Courtyard; *Michelangelo* (1475-1564) painted the celebrated frescoes on the ceiling of the Sistine Chapel in the Vatican Palace.

Czar *Peter the Great* (1672-1725), who was enamored of European culture and science, brought his efforts to "modernize" Russia into the very heart of the Church—for example, by replacing traditional Byzantine and Kievan plainchant with Western polyphonic music imported from Italy.

95: *Gamaliel,* a teacher of Saint Paul (Acts 22:3), advised his fellow members of the Sanhedrin not to put Peter and the other Apostles to death, on the grounds that "if this counsel or this work be of men, it will come to nought: but if it be of God, ye cannot overthrow it" (Acts 5:38-39).

96: The Roman Catholic *Council of Trent* (1545-63), convened in response to the Reformation and embodying the ideals of the *Counter-Reformation,* aimed to eliminate abuses in the Church and to put forward a comprehensive system of Catholic doctrine and practice.

"But thou, when thou prayest, enter into thy closet, and when thou hast shut thy door, pray to thy Father which is in secret" (Matt. 6:6).

"One is your Master, even Christ; and *all ye are brethren"* (Matt. 23:8).

Note 24: For *Hesychasts,* see editor's note for Ch. 1, p. 3.

97: In speaking to Christ about the *Samaritan* practice of worshipping God "in this mountain", that is, on *Mount Gerizim* (*cf.* Joshua 8:33)—a practice that conflicted with the Jews' worship of God "in Jerusalem"—a "woman of Samaria" prompted *the injunction of Christ* concerning true worship "*in spirit and in truth"* (*cf.* John 4:20-24).

Like other Cistercian authorities, *Bernard* (see editor's note for Ch. 2, p. 29, Note 22) insisted that churches of his Order should be plain in character and that vestments and ornaments should not be made of precious materials.

Teaching, like Luther, that man cannot attain salvation by his own efforts, but must place absolute faith in the help of Heaven—manifest, in this case, by the Buddha Amida—the Japanese Buddhist priest *Shinran* (1173-1262) was noted for advocating the marriage of monks, since he wished to minimize the distance between the clergy and laity.

Note 25: The *Fedeli d'Amore* (Italian for "the faithful of love") were a group of Medieval poets, including Dante, who transposed the courtly ideal of love for the earthly beloved—in Dante's case, Beatrice—into a means of deepening one's love for God.

The kingdom of God which is within you: "The kingdom of God is within you" (Luke 17:21).

98: *"For where two or three are gathered together in my Name, there I am in the midst of them"* (Matt. 18:20).

Note 27: For full bibliographical information concerning *Christianity/Islam: Essays on Esoteric Ecumenicism,* see editor's note for the present chapter, p. 82, note 2.

Chapter 9: Keys to the Bible

101: That *the Holy Spirit teaches all truth* is a fundamental idea, not only for *Meister Eckhart* (see editor's notes for Ch. 2, p. 24, Note 15, Ch. 3, p. 36, Note 9, Ch. 5, p. 59, Note 6, and Ch. 10, p. 129, Note 18), but for many Christian authorities, beginning as early as Ambrose (*c.* 339-97), whom Thomas Aquinas credits with having first propounded the maxim.

The *Convivio* or "Banquet" of *Dante* Alighieri (1265-1321) is an unfinished series of poetical odes, with extensive prose commentary, on various philosophical and scientific topics, composed during the years 1304-1307 and serving in part as the foundation for his *Divine Comedy.*

103: For the *Torah,* see editor's note for Ch. 4, p. 49, Note 15.

The *Mishnah* is a collection of Jewish oral tradition, including commentary on the Torah and an application of its principles, which is said to have been given to Moses, but which was only made known to the spiritual and temporal authorities of the tradition, the *Sanhedrin,* by Moses' successor, the prophet *Joshua.*

"The kingdom of God is within you" (Luke 17:21).

104: "Ask, and it shall be given you; seek, and ye shall find; *knock, and it shall be opened unto you"* (Matt. 7:7; Luke 11:9).

Chapter 10: Evidence and Mystery

106: *Plato* (see editor's note for Ch. 6, p. 66) taught that the visible things of this world are but shadows or copies of invisible and eternal forms, which themselves reflect the supreme reality of the Good.

108: *Wisdom after the flesh*: "Not many wise men after the flesh, not many mighty, not many noble, are called" (1 Cor. 1:26).

The ancient Greek *Sophists*, placing their rhetorical skills at the service of a materialist philosophy, taught their students how to gain political power by making the worse cause seem the better; according to the *Epicureans*, man is a strictly physical being, whose highest good consists in the cultivation of secure and lasting pleasure (see also editor's notes for Ch. 6, p. 69).

Note 2: "*God created man in His own image*, in the image of God created He him; *male and female created He them*" (Gen. 1:27).

Maximos the Confessor (*c.* 580-662) was *one Father of the Church* who taught that "instead of being men and women, clearly divided by sexual distinctions, we are properly and truly only human beings", made in the image of a God who transcends all such divisions, who unites us to Himself "through the abolition of the distinction between male and female" (*Ambigua*, Ch. 2).

110: To explain the process of knowing, Thomas Aquinas (see editor's note for Ch. 4, p. 47) and other medieval scholastic writers distinguished between two faculties of the soul: the *intellectus agens*, or agent Intellect, which is responsible for abstracting intelligible forms from the data of sense, and the *intellectus possibilis*, that is, the possible or potential Intellect, which is actuated or informed by these forms and thus led to the act of understanding.

111: The *dark age* is the *Kali Yuga* of Hindu chronology, the last and most corrupt of the ages.

Aryan is used by the author to refer to the intellectual and spiritual world of the noblest castes—*ârya* means "noble" in Sanskrit—in ancient Persia and India.

In this context, *Brahmanism* is the doctrine of Hindu Brahmins or priests.

113: At the Fourth *Lateran Council* (1215) the word "transubstantiation" was used for the first time in an official Roman Catholic definition of the Eucharist.

Note 4: In the Eucharistic prayer of the Liturgy, the Orthodox priest calls upon God to effect this *transmutation* with the words: "Make this bread the precious Body of Thy Christ, and that which is in this cup the precious Blood of Thy Christ, changing (*metaballôn*) them by Thy Holy Spirit."

115: In the last book of his great work *On the Trinity, Augustine* (see editor's note for Ch. 2, p. 9, Note 4) confesses, "There is nothing that I dare to profess myself to have said worthy of the ineffableness of that highest Trinity."

According to Thomas Aquinas, the divine *Persons* are distinguished from each other only by the acts which define their *relations*, namely, paternity, filiation, spiration, and procession.

116: *Modalism* or Sabellianism was an ancient Trinitarian heresy, which claimed that each Person is merely a temporary mode or mask of an essentially unitarian Deity.

Note 8: The *eight Guardians of the Universe in Hinduism*, each of whom rules one of the eight spatial zones, are Indra (East), Varuna (West), Kubera (North), Yama (South), Agni (Southeast), Niruthi (Southwest), Isana (Northeast), and Vayu (Northwest).

119: "*All things that the Father hath are mine*" (John 16:15).

121: Note 10: "In the beginning was the Word, and *the Word was with God, and the Word was God*" (John 1:1).

122: Note 11: *Saint Thomas* teaches that when Christ says, "My Father is greater than I" (John 14:28), and when he asks, "Why callest thou me good? There is none good but one, that is, God" (Matt. 19:17), "he hereby gave us to understand that he himself in his human nature did not attain to the height of divine goodness" (*Summa Theologica*, Q. 20, Art. 1, Pt. III).

God became man in order that man might become God is the formulation of Irenaeus (*c.* 130-*c.* 200) and Athanasius (*c.* 296-373), among other Church Fathers (see editor's note for Ch. 1, p. 1).

123: According to *Saint Thomas*, "It is clear that in God relation and essence do not differ from each other, but are one and the same" (*Summa Theologica*, Q. 28, Art. 2, Pt. I).

124: The first part of the *Shahâdah*, or "Testimony" of faith in Islam, consists of the words *there is no God save the only God.*

128: *Manichaeism* is a dualistic, and syncretistic, religion based on the sectarian Gnostic idea that spirits from a transcendent realm of light have become imprisoned in the darkness of matter and can be liberated from their bondage only by agents sent by the "Father of Light", who in different versions include Zoroaster, the Buddha, the prophets of Israel, Jesus, and the founder of the sect itself, Mani (*c.* 216-76).

"Why callest thou me good? There is none good but one, that is, God" (Matt. 19:17, Mark 10:18, Luke 18:19).

129: Note 18: The author often recommended the works of Meister *Eckhart* (see editor's notes for Ch. 2, p. 24, Note 15, Ch. 3, p. 36, Note 9, and Ch. 5, p. 59, Note 6) and Angelus *Silesius* (1624-77), a Catholic priest and mystical poet, as excellent examples of Christian esoterism.

Chapter 11: An Enigma of the Gospel

133: That *the gods are fond of obscure language* is a fundamental doctrine among traditional Hindu authorities, including Shankara (see editor's note for Ch. 1, p. 1), who teaches, with regard to *Brahma nirguna*, that "that which cannot be expressed is expressed through false attribution and subsequent denial".

"That thou doest, do quickly" (John 13:27).

134: *Caiaphas*, a high priest of the Jews, presided at the trial of Christ (Matt. 26:57); *Pilate*, a Roman procurator, delivered Christ to be crucified (Matt. 27:22-24).

Note 2: The words of an ancient liturgical hymn for Holy Saturday—"O truly necessary sin of Adam, which by the death of Christ is done away! O happy fault (*felix culpa*), which merited such and so great a Redeemer!"— are traditionally ascribed to Augustine (see editor's note for Ch. 2, p. 9, Note 4).

Note 3: "And Jesus said unto him, *Friend*, wherefore art thou come?" (Matt. 26:50).

135: *"Father, forgive them, for they know not what they do"* (Luke 23:34).

"It had been good for that man had he not been born" (Matt. 26:24; *cf.* Mark 14:21).

"In vain they do worship me, teaching for doctrines the *commandments of men*" (Matt. 15:9).

Brahmanism here refers to the religious and social system of orthodox Hinduism as prescribed in the Vedas.

Cesare *Borgia* (1475-1507), an illegitimate son of Pope Alexander VI, was a military leader and cardinal; Lucrezia *Borgia* (1480-1519), his sister, was a duchess of Ferrara and patroness of the arts.

Note 4: *Tiberius* Caesar (42 B.C.-A.D. 37) was Roman Emperor at the time of Christ's death; *Constantine* the Great (d. 337) was the first Christian emperor; *Charlemagne* (742-814) was the first emperor of the Holy Roman Empire.

136: "*The scribes and the Pharisees* sit in Moses' seat: all therefore whatsoever they bid you observe, that observe and do; but do not ye after their works: for they say, and do not" (Matt. 23:2).

For Mansur *al-Hallaj*, see editor's note for Ch. 2, p. 14.

"*And the light shineth in darkness, and the darkness comprehended it not*" (John 1:5).

"*Thy kingdom come*, thy will be done on earth as it is in heaven" (Matt. 6:10; Luke 11:2).

Note 5: For *Peter the Great*, see editor's note for Ch. 8, p. 94.

Note 6: For the *Talmud*, see editor's note for Ch. 3, p. 31, Note 1.

The return of Elijah, or Elias—whether in person or by virtue of his *Eliatic* function being performed by another—is held by Jews to be a necessary prelude to the deliverance of Israel (Mal. 4:5; *cf.* Matt. 16:14, Mark 6:15, Luke 9:8).

The *Essenes* were a Jewish ascetic and quasi-mystical sect of the first and second centuries.

Chapter 12: The Seat of Wisdom

137: *Rosa Mystica*, that is, "Mystic Rose", is one of the traditional epithets of the Blessed Virgin.

The *Litany of Loreto* is a traditional Roman Catholic litany in honor of the Virgin, often recited at the Benediction of the Holy Sacrament and consisting of a series of invocations of Mary, each followed by the petition: "Pray for us".

Peter Damian (1007-72) was a Benedictine prior and Cardinal Bishop of Ostia.

According to 1 *Kings* 10:18, Solomon "made a great throne" (see the text below).

Note 1: The *Bible* appears to have *condemned* Solomon, for example, in 1 Kings 11:9.

Quoting a French translation of this passage, the author has used the divine "Name" *Yahweh*: "Je me rappelle dans la nuit ton Nom, *Yahvé*, afin que j'observe ta Loi."

138: Note 3: Again *Yahvé* appears in the French for *Lord*.

139: *Magnificat* is Latin for "magnify" and is used in reference to the Virgin's words in the Gospel: "And Mary said, My soul doth magnify the Lord" (Luke 1:46).

Vincit omnia Veritas—Latin for "truth conquers all"—is a traditional maxim, often quoted by the author, based upon the words of 1 Esdras 3:12: *super omnia autem vincit veritas*, "But truth conquereth over all" (*cf.* 1 Esdras 4:35, 41).

Note 7: The *Vulgate*, the Latin translation of the Bible most often used in the West, is based upon the work of *Jerome* (*c.* 342-420).

139-40: Note 7: In the Authorized Version, 2 Chronicles 9:18 speaks of a "footstool of gold", not a *golden lamb*.

140: Note 7: Flavius *Josephus* (*c.* 37-*c.* 100), author of an "Antiquities of the Jews", won the favor of *Vespasian*, who reigned from 69-79, by prophesying that he would become emperor.

Chapter 13: The Mystery of the Two Natures

145: *Honorius I* (d. 638) was Pope from 625.

The *Sixth Ecumenical Council* (Constantinople, 680) decreed that in Christ there are not only two natures, but *two* corresponding *wills*, one divine and one human.

The *Seventh Ecumenical Council* (Nicaea, 787) reaffirmed the Sixth Council's sentence: "There shall be expelled from the Holy Church of God and anathematized Honorius, who was some time Pope of Old Rome."

According to the Athanasian Creed, Christ is *"true God and true man,* of a reasonable soul and body, equal to the Father as touching his Godhead, and inferior to the Father as touching his manhood".

Monophysites believe that there is only one *physis,* or "nature", in Christ—namely, his Divinity—whereas *monothelites,* acknowledging the existence of two natures, teach that they are united in a single *thelêma,* or "will".

147: *Gregory of Nyssa (c.* 330-*c.* 395) wrote his famous "Catechetical Orations" or *Great Catechesis* as an aid for those who were responsible for the instruction of catechumens in the basic doctrines of the faith, including the nature of sin and its remedy in the Sacrament of Baptism.

150: Note 5: The Book of *Ecclesiasticus* is also traditionally known as "The Wisdom of Jesus, the Son of Sirach".

The *Upanishads,* also referred to as the *Vedânta* since they were traditionally placed at the "end" of the *Veda*s and are seen by such authorities as Shankara (see editor's note for Ch. 1, p. 1) as a summing up of Vedic teaching, are Hindu scriptures which contain metaphysical, mystical, and esoteric doctrine.

151: *Vishnuism,* or Vaishnavism, is a theistic sect of the Hindu religion whose members worship the God Vishnu as the Supreme Deity; Vishnuite theology of a specifically *Ramanujan* form comes from the philosopher Ramanuja (1017-*c.* 1157), widely regarded as the classic exponent of *Vishishta Advaita,* that is, the Hindu *darshana* or school of "qualified non-dualism", in which emphasis is placed on the personal nature of God.

152: The *Orphic* tradition stems from an ancient Greek mystery religion, into which Plato may have been initiated and about whose strict ascetical rules he writes with favor in the *Laws*; Orphism was like the *Pythagorean tradition* in teaching a doctrine of transmigration, echoes of which may be found in the "Myth of Er" in Plato's *Republic*; in offering its adherents the possibility of spiritual rebirth; and in distinguishing among them various degrees of initiatic attainment.

For the *Stagirite*, see editor's note for Ch. 6, p. 69.

Chapter 14: Christic and Virginal Mysteries

155: *Ave Maria gratia plena, Dominus tecum: benedicta tu in mulieribus, et benedictus fructus ventris tui, Jesus*: these are the words of the Angelical Salutation, or "Hail Mary", in the Latin Rosary: "Hail Mary, full of grace, the Lord is with thee; blessed art thou amongst women, and blessed is the fruit of thy womb, Jesus" (*cf.* Luke 1:28, 42).

Note 1: *Dominic* (1170-1221), founder of the Order of Friars Preachers, is sometimes held to have instituted the devotion of the Rosary.

156: Note 1: The title of the anonymous work *La solide Dévotion du Rosaire* may be rendered as "True Devotion of the Rosary".

160: *Pater* is the first word in the Latin *Pater Noster*, the "Our Father" or Lord's Prayer, which is recited once for each ten recitations of the *Ave Maria* in the traditional use of the Rosary.

The five *joyful Mysteries* are the Annunciation, the Visitation, the Nativity of Christ, the Presentation of Christ in the Temple, and the Finding of the Child Jesus in the Temple; the five *sorrowful Mysteries* are the Agony in Gethsemane, the Scourging, the Crowning with Thorns, the Carrying of the Cross, and the Crucifixion; the five *glorious Mysteries* are the Resurrection, the Ascension, the Descent of the Holy Spirit at Pentecost, the Assumption of Mary, and the Coronation of Mary (see the Appendix, pp. 185-86).

Note 3: The Tibetan Buddhist formulation *Om mani padme hum* is a *mantra* meaning "O Thou Jewel in the Lotus, hail".

Chapter 15: The Cross

161: "Go thy way, sell whatsoever thou hast, and give to the poor, and thou shalt have treasure in heaven: and come, *take up the cross*, and follow me" (Mark 10:21).

Offer the other cheek: "Unto him that smiteth thee on the one cheek offer also the other" (Luke 6:29).

"We preach Christ crucified, unto the Jews a stumbling-block, and unto the Greeks *foolishness*" (1 Cor. 1:23).

"If ye live *after the flesh*, ye shall die: but if ye through the Spirit do mortify the deeds of the body, ye shall live" (Rom. 8:13).

Jesus as *the new Adam*: "The first man Adam was made a living soul; the last Adam was made a quickening spirit" (1 Cor. 15:45).

162: "Why callest thou me good? *There is none good but one, that is, God*" (Matt. 19:17, Mark 10:18, Luke 18:19).

Note 2: *Gregory the Great* (*c.* 540-604) was Pope from 590.

Bede (*c.* 673-735), styled "the Venerable", was a monastic scholar, whose *Ecclesiastical History of the English Church and People* was completed in 731.

163: "My kingdom is *not of this world*" (John 18:36).

"*Render therefore unto Caesar the things which are Caesar's*" (Matt. 22:21; *cf.* Mark 12:17, Luke 20:25).

Offence: "It is impossible but that offences will come: but woe unto him through whom they come" (Luke 17:1).

A mote out of a beam: "Why beholdest thou the mote that is in thy brother's eye, but considerest not the beam that is in thine own eye?" (Matt. 7:3; *cf.* Luke 6:42).

Forgives all: "Beareth all things, believeth all things, hopeth all things, endureth all things" (1 Cor. 13:7).

"*He that is without sin among you, let him first cast a stone*" (John 8:7).

"The wind bloweth where it listeth, and thou hearest the sound thereof, but canst not *tell whence it cometh, and whither it goeth*: so is every one that is born of the Spirit" (John 3:8).

164: *Broad way, narrow way*: "Enter ye in at the strait gate: for wide is the gate, and broad is the way, that leadeth to destruction, and many there be which go in threat: because strait is the gate, and narrow is the way, which leadeth unto life, and few there be that find it" (Matt. 7:13-14).

Discern spirits: "There are diversities of gifts, but the same Spirit. . . . For to one is given by the Spirit the word of wisdom . . . to another *discerning of spirits*" (1 Cor. 12: 4, 8, 10).

"Whosoever shall not receive the kingdom of God *as a little child*, he shall not enter therein" (Mark 10:15; *cf.* Luke 18:17).

Note 3: "If any man come to me, and *hate* not his *father, and mother*, and wife, and children, and brethren, and sisters, yea, and his own life also, he cannot be my disciple" (Luke 14:26).

The one thing needful: "One thing is needful" (Luke 10:42).

164-65: "*My yoke is easy, and my burden is light*" (Matt. 11:30).

165: According to tradition, *Longinus* was the soldier who pierced the side of Christ with his spear (John 19:34).

Appendix: A Sampling of Letters and Other Unpublished Materials

167: For the *Patristic saying: "God became man so that man might become God"*, see editor's note for Chapter 1, p. 1.

Meister *Eckhart* (see editor's notes for Ch. 3, p. 36, Note 9, Ch. 5, p. 59, Note 6, and Ch. 10, p. 129, Note 18) distinguished between *Gott* or God, that is, the Divine insofar as it expresses itself as a person, and *Gottheit* or *Godhead*, which is the transpersonal divinity of the Absolute as such.

168: The author gives both the Greek and the Latin for the *Names* of "*Jesus*" and "*Mary*".

"*Pray without ceasing*" (1 Thess. 5:17).

"*The kingdom of God is within you*" (Luke 17:21).

"*In the beginning was the Word*, and the Word was with God, and the Word was God" (John 1:1).

The author gives both the Greek and the Latin for one of the forms of the *Jesus Prayer*, "Lord Jesus Christ, have mercy upon us", for the *first sentence of the Lord's Prayer*, "Our Father who art in Heaven", and for the *Hail Mary* or Angelical Salutation, "Hail Mary, full of grace, the Lord is with thee"; the shorter formulation, also in Greek and Latin, for the *Name of Jesus* is "Lord Jesus Christ".

169: For *Hesychasts*, see editor's note for Ch. 1, p. 3; the *"Russian Pilgrim"* is the anonymous author of the nineteenth century Russian spiritual classic *The Way of a Pilgrim.*

170: For *Saint Bernard* of Clairvaux, see editor's note for Ch. 2, p. 29, Note 22.

171: The author's *"Outline of the Christic Message"* is Chapter 1 of the present volume.

Spiritus autem ubi vult spirat is Latin for "the wind bloweth where it listeth" (John 3:8).

"Beauty is the splendor of the true" is an axiom which the author attributes to Plato (see editor's note for Ch. 6, p. 66).

172: The author teaches that *for Christians holiness is the door to esoterism* in the following passage: "In Islam there is, so to speak, no sanctity apart from esoterism; in Christianity there is no esoterism apart from sanctity"; and he adds in a note: "There is nothing absolute in these formulations, which in each case mark a predominance rather than an exclusiveness of mode; however, they show up sharply certain fundamental differences between the two traditions in question" (*Spiritual Perspectives and Human Facts*, trans. P. N. Townsend [Pates Manor, Bedfont, Middlesex: Perennial Books, 1987], p. 87).

Saint Mary Magdalene ministered to Christ in Galilee (Luke 8:2) and was granted an appearance of him after his resurrection (Matt. 28:1-9, John 20:11-18); according to tradition, *Saint Mary of Egypt* (fifth century) lived for forty-seven years in the desert, where she was visited by a priest, Zosimus, from whom she received communion shortly before her death. *Cabalists* are Jewish esoterists and mystics.

173: *Vishnuite*, or Vaishnavite, refers to a form of Hindu *bhakti* characterized by devotion to the God Vishnu, whereas *Shivaite*, or Shaivite, Hinduism is a path of *jnâna* connected with the God Shiva.

174: For the *filioque*, see editor's note for Ch. 4, p. 40.

175: For *Ramanujan Vishnuism*, see editor's note for Ch. 13, p. 151.

176-77: The Greek letters I H S—that is, *iota, êta,* and *sigma*—are an abbreviation for ΙΗΣΟΥΣ, or *IÊSOUS,* the Name of Jesus; elsewhere the author writes in this regard, "The cipher of the Greek Letters I H S, signifying *Iesous,* but interpreted in Latin as *In Hoc Signo* ['By this sign (you shall conquer)'] or as *Jesus Hominum Salvator* ['Jesus is the Savior of men'] and often written in Gothic letters, can be analyzed in its primitive form into three elements—a vertical straight line, two vertical lines linked together, and a curved line—and thus contains a symbolism at once metaphysical, cosmological, and mystical; there is in it a remarkable analogy, not only with the name *Allâh* written in Arabic, which also comprises the three lines of which we have just spoken (in the form of the *alif,* the two *lams,* and the *hâ*), but also with the Sanskrit monosyllable *Aum,* which is composed of three *mâtrâs* (A U M), indicating a 'rolling up' and thereby a return to the Center. All of these symbols mark, in a certain sense, the passage from 'coagulation' to 'solution'" (*Stations of Wisdom* [Bloomington, Indiana: World Wisdom, 1995], pp. 131-32n).

177: The *Curé d'Ars* was Saint Jean-Baptiste Marie Vianney (1786-1859), a parish priest and much sought-after confessor from the French village of Ars, who was widely known for his gift of reading souls.

Ahmad *al-Alawi* (1869-1934), a famous Algerian Sufi *shaykh,* was Schuon's spiritual master.

"There is no lustral water like unto Knowledge" is a traditional Hindu teaching often quoted by the author, based upon the *Bhagavad Gîtâ,* 4:38.

178: The house of the *Blessed Virgin Mary,* where she is said to have lived in her later years under the care of Saint John (*cf.* John 19:27), is located in the city of *Ephesus.*

180: The Latin words of the *Ave,* the "Hail Mary", are: *Ave Maria gratia plena, Dominus tecum: benedicta tu in mulieribus, et benedictus fructus ventris tui, Jesus* (see Ch. 14, pp. 155-57 and editor's note for p. 155).

183: For *Saint Bernardino of Siena,* see editor's note for Ch. 1, p. 3, Note 3.

"My yoke is easy, and my burden is light" (Matt. 11:30).

184: *"The kingdom of God is within you"* (Luke 17:21).

"*The wind bloweth where it listeth*" (John 3:8).

"*There is no right superior to that of Truth*" is a traditional Hindu maxim attributed to the Maharajas of Benares.

185-86: The "Joyful Mysteries"—beginning with *the Annunciation*—the "*Sorrowful Mysteries*", and the "*Glorious Mysteries*" are three sets of meditations, each focused on five events in the life of Christ or the Blessed Virgin, which compose the fifteen decades of the Roman Catholic Rosary (see editor's note for Ch. 14, p. 160).

SOURCES

The selections in this anthology have been translated from the following French editions of Schuon's work. Bibliographical information is also provided for previous English translations.

1. "Outline of the Christic Message": published as "Schéma du message christique" in *Racines de la condition humaine* (Paris: La Table Ronde, 1990), Part II, *Perspectives fondamentales*, pp. 117-25; English editions: "Outline of the Christian Message", *Roots of the Human Condition* (Bloomington, Indiana: World Wisdom Books, 1991, 2002), Part Two, "Fundamental Perspectives", pp. 74-80.

2. "The Particular Nature and Universality of the Christian Tradition": published as "Nature particulière et universalité de la tradition chrétienne" in *De l'Unité transcendante des religions* (Paris: Éditions du Seuil, 1979), Chapter VIII, pp. 150-78; English editions: "Universality and Particular Nature of the Christian Tradition", *The Transcendent Unity of Religions*, trans. Peter Townsend (London: Faber and Faber, 1953), Chapter VIII, pp. 144-69; (Wheaton, Illinois: The Theosophical Publishing House, 1984, 1993), Chapter 8, pp.126-48.

3. "'Our Father Who Art in Heaven'": published as "Notre Père qui êtes aux cieux" in *Avoir un centre* (Paris: Éditions Maison-Neuve, 1988), pp. 111-17; English edition: "'Our Father Who Art in Heaven'", *To Have a Center* (Bloomington, Indiana: World Wisdom Books, 1990), Part Three: "Spiritual Perspectives", pp. 121-29.

4. "Some Observations": published as "Quelques aperçus" in *Sentiers de gnose* (Paris: La Place Royale, 1987), Part III, *Christianisme*, pp. 143-62; English edition: "Some Thoughts on Its Nature", *Gnosis: Divine Wisdom*, trans. G. E. H. Palmer (Bedfont, Middlesex: Perennial Books, 1959, 1990), "The Christian Tradition", Chapter 10, pp. 105-117.

5. "Delineations of Original Sin": published as "Sur les traces du péché originel" in *Le jeu des masques* (Lausanne: Éditions L'Âge

d'Homme, 1992), pp. 79-85; English edition: "Delineations of Original Sin", *The Play of Masks* (Bloomington, Indiana: World Wisdom Books, 1992), pp. 55-60.

6. "The Dialogue between Hellenists and Christians": published as "Dialogue entre Hellénistes et Chrétiens" in *Regards sur les mondes anciens* (Paris: Les Éditions Traditionnelles, 1980), pp. 71-87; English editions: "Dialogue between Hellenists and Christians", *Light on the Ancient Worlds*, trans. Lord Northbourne (London: Perennial Books, 1965; Bloomington, Indiana: World Wisdom Books, 1984), Chapter III, pp. 58-71.

7. "The Complexity of Dogmatism": published as "Complexité du dogmatisme" in *Approches du phénomène religieux* (Paris: Le Courrier du Livre, 1984), Part II, *Christianisme*, pp. 61-67; English edition: "The Complexity of Dogmatism", *In the Face of the Absolute* (Bloomington, Indiana: World Wisdom Books, 1989, 1994), Part Two, "Christianity", pp. 109-114.

8. "Christian Divergences": published as "Divergences chrétiennes" in *Approches du phénomène religieux* (Paris: Le Courrier du Livre, 1984), Part II, *Christianisme*, pp. 68-89; English edition: "Christian Divergences", *In the Face of the Absolute* (Bloomington, Indiana: World Wisdom Books, 1989, 1994), Part Two, "Christianity", pp. 115-36.

9. "Keys to the Bible": published as "Clefs de la Bible" in *Regards sur les mondes anciens* (Paris: Les Éditions Traditionnelles, 1980), pp. 167-72; English editions: "Keys to the Bible", *The Sword of Gnosis: Metaphysics, Cosmology, Tradition, Symbolism*, ed. Jacob Needleman (London: Penguin, 1974; Boston: Routledge and Kegan Paul, 1986), "Symbolic Truth", pp. 354-58.

10. "Evidence and Mystery": published as "Evidence et mystère" in *Logique et transcendance* (Paris: Les Éditions Traditionnelles, 1972), pp. 97-127; English editions: "Evidence and Mystery", *Logic and Transcendence*, trans. Peter N. Townsend (New York: Harper and Row, 1975; London: Perennial Books, 1984), Chapter 6, pp. 85-113.

11. "An Enigma of the Gospel": published as "Une énigme de l'E-vangile" in *La transfiguration de l'homme* (Paris: Éditions Maisonneuve Larose, 1995), pp. 75-79; English edition: "An Enigma of the Gospel", *The Transfiguration of Man* (Bloomington, Indiana: World Wisdom Books, 1995), Part Two: "Man, Truth, and the Path", pp. 75-78.

12. "The Seat of Wisdom": published as "Le siège de la Sapience" in *Approches du phénomène religieux* (Paris: Le Courrier du Livre, 1984), Part II, *Christianisme*, pp. 90-97; English edition: "Sedes Sapientiae", *In the Face of the Absolute* (Bloomington, Indiana: World Wisdom Books, 1989, 1994), Part Two, "Christianity", pp. 137-44.

13. "The Mystery of the Two Natures": published as "Le mystère des deux natures" in *Forme et substance dans les religions* (Paris: Dervy-Livres, 1975), pp. 133-41; English editions: "The Mystery of the Two Natures", *Christianity/Islam: Essays on Esoteric Ecumenicism*, trans. Gustavo Polit (Bloomington, Indiana: World Wisdom Books, 1985), Part One, "Christianity", pp. 55-66; "The Mystery of the Two Natures", *Form and Substance in the Religions*, trans. Mark Perry and Jean-Pierre LaFouge (Bloomington, Indiana: World Wisdom, 2002), Chapter 12, pp. 141-150.

14. "Christic and Virginal Mysteries": published as "Mystères christiques et virginaux" in *Sentiers de gnose* (Paris: La Place Royale, 1987), Part III, *Christianisme*, pp. 163-70; English edition: "Mysteries of Christ and the Virgin", *Gnosis: Divine Wisdom*, trans. G. E. H. Palmer (Bedfont, Middlesex: Perennial Books, 1959, 1990), "The Christian Tradition", Chapter 11, pp. 118-123.

15. "The Cross": published as "De la croix" in *Sentiers de gnose* (Paris: La Place Royale, 1987), Part III, *Christianisme*, pp. 171-76; English edition: "Of the Cross", *Gnosis: Divine Wisdom*, trans. G. E. H. Palmer (Bedfont, Middlesex: Perennial Books, 1959, 1990), "The Christian Tradition", Chapter 12, pp. 124-28.

GLOSSARY
OF FOREIGN TERMS AND PHRASES

'Abd (Arabic): "servant" or "slave"; as used in Islam, the servant or worshiper of God in His aspect of *Rabb* or "Lord".

Ad alterum (Latin): literally, "toward another"; defined in relationship to something else, in contrast to *ad se*.

Ad se (Latin): literally, "toward itself"; defined solely by or with respect to itself, in contrast to *ad alterum*.

Advaita (Sanskrit): "non-dualist" interpretation of the *Vedânta*; Hindu doctrine according to which the seeming multiplicity of things is regarded as the product of ignorance, the only true reality being *Brahma*, the One, the Absolute, the Infinite, which is the unchanging ground of appearance.

Ahimsâ (Sanskrit): "non-violence", a fundamental tenet of Hindu ethics, also emphasized in Buddhism and Jainism.

Alter (Latin): the "other", in contrast to the *ego* or individual self.

Anamnesis (Greek): literally, a "lifting up of the mind"; recollection or remembrance, as in the Platonic doctrine that all knowledge is a recalling of truths latent in the soul.

Ânanda (Sanskrit): "bliss, beatitude, joy"; one of the three essential aspects of *Apara-Brahma*, together with *sat*, "being", and *chit*, "consciousness".

Apara-Brahma (Sanskrit): the "non-supreme" or penultimate *Brahma*, also called *Brahma saguna*; in Schuon's teaching, the "relative Absolute".

Ascesis (Greek): "exercise, practice, training", as of an athlete; a regimen of self-denial, especially one involving fasting, prostrations, and other bodily disciplines.

Âtmâ or *Âtman* (Sanskrit): the real or true "Self", underlying the ego and its manifestations; in the perspective of *Advaita Vedânta*, identical with *Brahma*.

Aum or *Om* (Sanskrit): the most sacred syllable in Hinduism, containing all origination and dissolution; regarded as the "seed" of all *mantras*, its three

225

*mâtrâ*s or letters are taken to be symbolical of the *Trimûrti*, while the silence at its conclusion is seen as expressing the attainment of *Brahma*.

Avatâra (Sanskrit): the earthly "descent", incarnation, or manifestation of God, especially of Vishnu in the Hindu tradition.

Ave Maria (Latin): "Hail, Mary"; traditional prayer to the Blessed Virgin, also known as the Angelic Salutation, based on the words of the Archangel Gabriel and Saint Elizabeth in Luke 1:28 and Luke 1:42.

Avidyâ (Sanskrit): "ignorance" of the truth; spiritual delusion, unawareness of *Brahma*.

Bâlya (Sanskrit): "childhood", spiritual childlikeness; used as an expression of humility.

Barakah (Arabic): "blessing", grace; in Islam, a spiritual influence or energy emanating originally from God, but often attached to sacred objects and spiritual persons.

Bhakta (Sanskrit): a follower of the spiritual path of *bhakti*; a person whose relationship with God is based primarily on adoration and love.

Bhakti, bhakti-mârga (Sanskrit): the spiritual "path" (*mârga*) of "love" (*bhakti*) and devotion.

Bodhisattva (Sanskrit, Pali): literally, "enlightenment-being"; in *Mahâyâna* Buddhism, one who postpones his own final enlightenment and entry into *Nirvâna* in order to aid all other sentient beings in their quest for Buddhahood.

Brahmâ (Sanskrit): God in the aspect of Creator, the first divine "person" of the *Trimûrti*; to be distinguished from *Brahma*, the Supreme Reality.

Brahma or *Brahman* (Sanskrit): the Supreme Reality, the Absolute.

Brahma nirguna (Sanskrit): *Brahma* considered as transcending all "qualities", attributes, or predicates; God as He is in Himself; also called *Para-Brahma*.

Brahma saguna (Sanskrit): *Brahma* "qualified" by attributes and predicates; God insofar as He can be known by man; also called *Apara-Brahma*.

Brâhmana (Sanskrit): "Brahmin"; a member of the highest of the four Hindu castes; a priest or spiritual teacher.

Buddhânusmriti (Sanskrit): "remembrance or mindfulness of the Buddha", based upon the repeated invocation of his Name; central to the Pure Land school of Buddhism; known in Chinese as *nien-fo* and in Japanese as *nembutsu*.

Buddhi (Sanskrit): "Intellect"; the highest faculty of knowledge, to be contrasted with *manas*, that is, mind or reason; see *ratio*.

Chit (Sanskrit): "consciousness"; one of the three essential aspects of *Apara-Brahma*, together with *sat*, "being", and *ânanda*, "bliss, beatitude, joy".

Christe eleison (Greek): "Christ, have mercy"; used antiphonally with the words *Kyrie eleison*, "Lord, have mercy", in the Roman rite.

Creatio ex nihilo (Latin): "creation out of nothing"; the doctrine that God Himself is the sufficient cause of the universe, needing nothing else; often set in contrast to emanationist cosmogonies.

Darshana (Sanskrit): a spiritual "perspective", point of view, or school of thought; also the "viewing" of a holy person, object, or place, together with the resulting blessing or merit.

Dharma (Sanskrit): in Hinduism, the underlying "law" or "order" of the cosmos as expressed in sacred rites and in actions appropriate to various social relationships and human vocations; in Buddhism, the practice and realization of Truth.

Dhikr (Arabic): "remembrance" of God, based upon the repeated invocation of His Name; central to Sufi practice, where the remembrance often consists of the single word *Allâh*.

Dhyâni-Bodhisattva and *Dhyâni-Buddha* (Sanskrit): Bodhisattva and Buddha "of meditation"; a Bodhisattva or Buddha, such as Amitabha (Amida in Japanese), who appears to the eye of contemplative vision, but is not accessible in a historical form.

Ex cathedra (Latin): literally, "from the throne"; in Roman Catholicism, authoritative teaching issued by the pope and regarded as infallible.

Ex divinis (Latin): literally, "from divine things"; coming forth from the Divine, or from the divine Principle; the plural form is used insofar as the Principle comprises both *Para-Brahma*, Beyond-Being or the Absolute, and *Apara-Brahma*, Being or the relative Absolute.

Ex divino (Latin): "from God"; used in connection with the doctrine of creation *ex nihilo*: God creates "out of nothing" except Himself, the universe thus proceeding "from God".

Ex nihilo (Latin): "out of nothing"; see *creatio ex nihilo*.

Ex opere operato (Latin): literally, "from the work performed"; Christian teaching that divine grace is mediated through the sacraments by virtue of

227

the corresponding rites themselves and independently of the merits or intentions of those by whom the rites are performed; in contrast to *ex opere operantis*, "from the work of the one working".

Fanâ (Arabic): "extinction, annihilation, evanescence"; in Sufism, the spiritual station or degree of realization in which all individual attributes and limitations are extinguished in union with God.

Faqr (Arabic): "indigence, spiritual poverty"; the virtue cultivated by the Sufi *faqîr*, the "poor one", whose self-effacement testifies to complete dependence on God and a desire to be filled by Him alone.

Filioque (Latin): "and (from) the Son"; a term added to the Nicene Creed by the Western Church to express the "double procession" of the Holy Spirit from the Father "and the Son"; rejected by the Eastern Orthodox Church.

Gnosis (Greek): "knowledge"; spiritual insight, principial comprehension, divine wisdom.

Hadîth (Arabic, plural *ahâdîth*): "saying, narrative"; an account of the words or deeds of the Prophet Muhammad, transmitted through a traditional chain of known intermediaries.

Haqîqah (Arabic): "truth, reality"; in Sufism, the inward essence of a thing, corresponding to an archetypal Truth in God.

Hic et nunc (Latin): "here and now".

Hypostases (Greek): literally, "substances" (singular, *hypostasis*); in Eastern Christian theology, a technical term for the three "Persons" of the Trinity; the Father, the Son, and the Holy Spirit are distinct *hypostases* sharing a single *ousia*, or essence.

In divinis (Latin): literally, "in or among divine things"; within the divine Principle; the plural form is used insofar as the Principle comprises both *Para-Brahma*, Beyond-Being or the Absolute, and *Apara-Brahma*, Being or the relative Absolute.

Intellectus agens (Latin): "agent Intellect"; in Aristotelian and scholastic epistemology, the faculty of the mind responsible for abstracting intelligible forms from the data of sense.

Intellectus possibilis (Latin): "possible or potential Intellect"; in Aristotelian and scholastic epistemology, the faculty of the mind actuated by intelligible forms and thus prompted to an act of understanding.

Îshvara (Sanskrit): literally, "possessing power", hence master; God understood as a personal being, as Creator and Lord; manifest in the *Trimûrti* as *Brahmâ, Vishnu,* and *Shiva.*

Jagat (Sanskrit): "world"; the existing or manifested universe.

Japa (Sanskrit): "repetition" of a *mantra* or sacred formula, often containing one of the Names of God; see *buddhânusmriti, dhikr.*

Jejunium (Latin): "fasting, abstinence from food".

Jiriki (Japanese): literally, "power of the self"; a Buddhist term for spiritual methods that emphasize one's own efforts in reaching the goal of liberation or salvation, as for example in Zen; in contrast to *tariki.*

Jîvanmukta (Sanskrit): one who is "liberated" while still in this "life"; a person who has attained to a state of spiritual perfection or self-realization before death; in contrast to *videha-mukta,* one who is liberated at the moment of death.

Jnâna, jnâna-mârga (Sanskrit): the spiritual "path" (*mârga*) of "knowledge" (*jnâna*) and intellection.

Jnânin (Sanskrit): a follower of the path of *jnâna;* a person whose relationship with God is based primarily on sapiential knowledge or *gnosis.*

Jôdo (Japanese): "pure land"; the untainted, transcendent realm created by the Buddha Amida (Amitabha in Sanskrit), into which his devotees aspire to be born in their next life.

Jôdo-Shinshû (Japanese): "true pure land school"; a sect of Japanese Pure Land Buddhism founded by Shinran, based on faith in the power of the Buddha Amida and characterized by use of the *nembutsu.*

Khalîfah (Arabic): literally, "successor"; a representative or vicar, often used in reference to the successors of the Prophet Muhammad; in Sufism, every man is in principle a *khalîfah* of God.

Kshatriya (Sanskrit): a member of the second highest of the four Hindu castes; a warrior or prince.

Latria (Latinized form of the Greek *latreia*): literally, "servitude, service"; the worshipful obedience owed only to God; to be distinguished from *dulia,* the respect shown to saints, and *hyperdulia,* the reverence paid to the Blessed Virgin.

Lîlâ (Sanskrit): "play, sport"; in Hinduism, the created universe is said to be the result of divine play or playfulness, a product of God's delight and spontaneity.

Logos (Greek): "word, reason"; in Christian theology, the divine, uncreated Word of God (*cf.* John 1:1); the transcendent Principle of creation and revelation.

Mahâpralaya (Sanskrit): in Hinduism, the "great" or final "dissolving" of the universe.

Mani (Sanskrit): "jewel", often in the shape of a tear-drop; in Eastern traditions, understood to be powerful in removing evil and the causes of sorrow; see *Om mani padme hum.*

Mantra (Sanskrit): literally, "instrument of thought"; a word or phrase of divine origin, often including a Name of God, repeated by those initiated into its proper use as a means of salvation or liberation; see *japa.*

Materia prima (Latin): "first or prime matter"; in Platonic cosmology, the undifferentiated and primordial substance serving as a "receptacle" for the shaping force of divine forms or ideas; universal potentiality.

Mâtrâ (Sanskrit): literally, "measure, element"; an element or particle of sound in the *mantra* AUM.

Mâyâ (Sanskrit): "artifice, illusion"; in *Advaita Vedânta*, the beguiling concealment of *Brahma* in the form or under the appearance of a lower reality.

Mâyâ in divinis (Sanskrit and Latin): literally, "illusion within or among divine things"; an expression of the metaphysical teaching that relativity, and thus a certain degree of illusion, can be found even within the divine Principle, beginning with the personal God or "relative Absolute"; only *Brahma*, the Absolute as such, is fully real.

Namu-Amida-Bu or *Namu-Amida-Butsu* (Japanese): literally, "praise to Amida Buddha"; common formulation of the *nembutsu* in Pure Land Buddhism.

Nembutsu (Japanese): "remembrance or mindfulness of the Buddha", based upon the repeated invocation of his Name; same as *buddhânusmriti* in Sanskrit and *nien-fo* in Chinese.

Nien-fo (Chinese): same as *Buddhânusmriti* in Sanskrit and *nembutsu* in Japanese.

Nirvâna (Sanskrit): literally, "blowing out, extinction"; in Indian traditions, especially Buddhism, the extinction of the fires of passion and the resulting, supremely blissful state of liberation from egoism and attachment; compare with the Sufi idea of *fanâ*.

Om mani padme hum (Sanskrit): literally, "O Thou jewel in the lotus, hail"; a formula of Tibetan Buddhism having numerous levels of meaning; the "masculine" jewel may be interpreted as either the Bodhisattva Avalokiteshvara (Chenrezig in Tibet) or Buddhahood as such, and the "feminine" lotus may be seen as either his counterpart, Tara, or the pure and humble soul in a state of spiritual readiness.

Oratio (Latin): literally, "language, speech"; in Christian usage, words addressed to God; prayer.

Padme (Sanskrit): "lotus"; in Buddhism, an image of non-attachment and primordial openness to enlightenment, serving symbolically as the throne of the Buddhas; see *Om mani padme hum*.

Para-Brahma (Sanskrit): the "supreme" or ultimate *Brahma*, also called *Brahma nirguna*; the Absolute as such.

Paramâtmâ or *Paramâtman* (Sanskrit): the "supreme Self".

Pneuma (Greek): "wind, breath, spirit"; in Christian theology, either the third Person of the Trinity or the highest of the three parts or aspects of the human self (*cf.* 1 Thess. 5:23); see *rûh*.

Prakriti (Sanskrit): literally, "making first" (see *materia prima*); the fundamental, "feminine" substance or material cause of all things; see *Purusha*.

Prapatti (Sanskrit): "seeking refuge"; pious resignation and devotion to God.

Pro domo (Latin): literally, "for (one's own) home or house"; serving the interests of a given perspective or for the benefit of a given group.

Purusha (Sanskrit): literally, "man"; the informing or shaping principle of creation; the "masculine" demiurge or fashioner of the universe; see *Prakriti*.

Quod absit (Latin): literally, "which is absent from, opposed to, or inconsistent with"; a phrase commonly used by the medieval scholastics to call attention to an idea that is absurdly inconsistent with accepted principles.

Rabb (Arabic): "Lord"; in Islam, God in His aspect of Sovereign or Ruler; the divine complement of man as *'abd*.

Rahmân, Rahîm (Arabic): "clement", "merciful"; found in Islam in the invocatory formula *bismi 'Llâhi 'r-Rahmâni 'r-Rahîm*: "In the Name of God, the Clement, the Merciful", *Rahmân* being the compassion of God insofar as it envelops all things, and *Rahîm* being the beneficence of God insofar as it is directed toward men of good will.

Ratio (Latin): literally, "calculation"; the faculty of discursive thinking, to be distinguished from *intellectus*, "Intellect".

Religio (Latin): "religion", often in reference to its exoteric dimension.

Rosa Mystica (Latin): "Mystical Rose"; traditional epithet of the Blessed Virgin Mary, as found in the Litany of Loreto.

Rûh (Arabic): "Spirit"; in Sufism, either the uncreated Spirit of God or the spirit of man; see *pneuma*.

Samsâra (Sanskrit): literally, "wandering"; in Hinduism and Buddhism, transmigration or the cycle of birth, death, and rebirth; also the world of apparent flux and change.

Sânkhya or *sâmkhya* (Sanskrit): literally, "enumeration, calculation"; Hindu cosmological teaching in which nature is understood to result from the union of *Purusha* and *Prakriti*; one of the six orthodox *darshana*s, or perspectives, of classical Hinduism.

Sannyâsa or *samnyâsa* (Sanskrit): "renunciation"; in Hindu tradition, the formal breaking of all ties to family, caste, and property at the outset of the final stage of life.

Sannyâsin (Sanskrit): "renunciate"; in Hindu tradition, one who has renounced all formal ties to social life.

Sat (Sanskrit): "being"; one of the three essential aspects of *Apara-Brahma*, together with *chit*, "consciousness", and *ânanda*, "bliss, beatitude, joy".

Sat-Chit-Ânanda or *saccidânanda* (Sanskrit): "being-consciousness-bliss"; the three essential aspects of *Apara-Brahma*, that is, *Brahma* insofar as it can be grasped in human experience.

Sedes Sapientiae (Latin): "Throne of Wisdom"; traditional epithet of the Blessed Virgin Mary, who is the "seat" upon which her incarnate Son is enthroned; compare with *padme*.

Sephiroth or *sefirot* (Hebrew): literally, "numbers"; in Jewish Cabala, the ten emanations of *Ein Sof* or divine Infinitude, each comprising a different aspect of creative energy.

Shâkya-Muni (Sanskrit): "sage of the Shakyas"; traditional title of Siddhartha Gautama, the historical Buddha.

Sharî'ah (Arabic): "path"; in Islam, the proper mode and norm of life, the path or way willed and marked out by God for man's return to Him; Muslim law or exoterism.

Shruti (Sanskrit): literally, "what is heard"; in Hindu tradition, a category of sacred writings, including the Vedas, understood to be the direct revelation of eternal Truth; in contrast to *smriti.*

Shûdra (Sanskrit): a member of the lowest of the four Hindu castes; an unskilled laborer or serf.

Shughl (Arabic): "work"; in Sufism, spiritual exercise or effort.

Shûnyamûrti (Sanskrit): "the form or manifestation of the void"; traditional epithet of the Buddha, in whom is "incarnate" *shûnyatâ*, ultimate "emptiness", that is, the final absence of all definite being or selfhood.

Smriti (Sanskrit): literally, "what is remembered"; in Hinduism, a category of sacred writings understood to be part of inspired tradition, but not directly revealed; in contrast to *shruti.*

Sophia (Greek): "wisdom"; in Jewish and Christian tradition, the Wisdom of God, often conceived as feminine (*cf.* Prov. 8).

Sophia Perennis (Greek): "Perennial Wisdom"; the eternal, non-formal Truth at the heart of all orthodox religious traditions.

Spiritus Sanctus (Latin): the "Holy Spirit"; in Christian theology, the third Person of the Trinity.

Sunnah (Arabic): "custom, way of acting"; in Islam, the norm established by the Prophet Muhammad, including his actions and sayings (see *hadîth*) and serving as a precedent and standard for the behavior of Muslims.

Sûtra (Sanskrit): literally, "thread"; a Hindu or Buddhist sacred text; in Hinduism, any short, aphoristic verse or collection of verses, often elliptical in style; in Buddhism, a collection of the discourses of the Buddha.

Tale quale (Latin): "of such a kind as, as such".

Tariki (Japanese): literally, "power of the other"; a Buddhist term for forms of spirituality that emphasize the importance of grace or celestial assistance, especially that of the Buddha Amida, as in the Pure Land schools; in contrast to *jiriki.*

Tawhîd (Arabic): "unification, union"; in Islam, the affirmation of divine unity as expressed in the words, "There is no god but God" (*lâ ilâha illâ 'Llâh*); in Sufism, the doctrine of mystical union; see *fanâ.*

Theosis (Greek): "deification", participation in the nature of God (*cf.* 2 Pet. 1:4); in Eastern Christian theology, the supreme goal of human life.

Torah (Hebrew): "instruction, teaching"; in Judaism, the law of God, as revealed to Moses on Sinai and embodied in the Pentateuch (Genesis, Exodus, Leviticus, Numbers, Deuteronomy).

Trimûrti (Sanskrit): literally, "having three forms"; in Hindu tradition, a triadic expression of the Divine, especially in the form of *Brahmâ*, the creator, *Vishnu*, the preserver, and *Shiva*, the transformer.

'Ulamâ (Arabic, singular *'alîm*): "those who know, scholars"; in Islam, those who are learned in matters of law and theology; traditional authorities for all aspects of Muslim life.

Unio mystica (Latin): "mystical union"; in Christianity, the final stage of the spiritual path.

Upâya (Sanskrit): "means, expedient, method"; in Buddhist tradition, the adaptation of spiritual teaching to a form suited to the level of one's audience.

Vacare Deo (Latin): literally, "to be empty for God"; to be at leisure for or available to God; in the Christian monastic and contemplative tradition, to set aside time from work for meditation and prayer.

Vaisheshika (Sanskrit): literally, "referring to the distinctions"; Hindu philosophy of nature, including an analysis of the various categories and objects of sensory experience; one of the six orthodox *darshana*s, or perspectives, of classical Hinduism.

Vedânta (Sanskrit): "end or culmination of the Vedas"; one of the major schools of traditional Hindu philosophy, based in part on the Upanishads, esoteric treatises found at the conclusion of the Vedic scriptures; see *advaita.*

Viveka (Sanskrit): "discrimination, distinction"; in *Sânkhya*, the direct, intuitive discrimination of *Purusha* from *Prakriti*; in *Advaita Vedânta*, the distinction between what is eternal and what is non-eternal, *Âtmâ* and *Mâyâ.*

Walî (Arabic): literally, "benefactor, protector"; used in the Koran especially of God; in Sufism a "friend" of God or saint.

Glossary of Foreign Terms and Phrases

Yahweh (Hebrew): a transliteration of the supposed pronunciation, now lost, of the sacred Name of God in the Hebrew Bible or Christian Old Testament; revealed to Moses on Sinai and often translated as "I am" or "the One who is" (*cf.* Exod. 3:14).

Yin-Yang (Chinese): in Chinese tradition, two opposite but complementary forces or qualities, from whose interpenetration the universe and all its diverse forms emerge; *yin* corresponds to the feminine, the yielding, the moon, and liquidity; *yang* corresponds to the masculine, the resisting, the sun, and solidity.

Yogin (Sanskrit): literally, "one who is yoked or joined"; a practitioner of *yoga*, especially a form of *yoga* involving ascetic techniques designed to bring the soul and body into a state of concentration or meditative focus.

For a glossary of all key foreign words used in books published by World Wisdom, including metaphysical terms in English, consult:
www.DictionaryofSpiritualTerms.org.
This on-line Dictionary of Spiritual Terms provides extensive definitions, examples and related terms in other languages.

INDEX

'abd, 34n

Abraham, 11n, 14, 73, 78, 79n

Absolute, 3, 71, 107, 112, 116, 127, 141, 170, 217; consciousness of, 5, 65, 175; creative, 109, 129n; pure, 37, 109, 126, 129; relative, 108, 129n; and contingency, relativity, 1, 2, 27, 62, 70, 105, 152-54, 169, 179; and the Father, 37, 117, 174; and the *Logos*, 66; and personal God, 70; and the Self (*Âtmâ*), 3, 125; and the Trinity, 117-18; 122n, 124, 168, 174, 176; and unity, 125

Adam, 9, 58, 72, 83, 134n, 162, 201, 211, 216

adultery, 11

Advaita Vedânta. See *Vedânta*

Agni, 210

ahimsa, 2

Ahriman, 6, 190

Ahura Mazda, 190

al-Alawi, Ahmad, 177, 219

alchemy, mystical, 51, 110, 177

Alexander VI, Pope, 212

Alexander the Great, 175

Alexandria, school of, 64, 197, 202

Allah, 11n, 34n, 79n, 219

Amida Buddha, 21-22n, 27n, 193, 207

Amidism, Amidists, 78n, 82, 83, 97, 98

Amitabha, 21n, 78n, 193, 204

anamnesis, 98

Ânanda, 37n, 115, 168

Anaximander, 203

Anaximenes of Miletus, 68n, 203

Angelical Salutation, 44-45, 155-56, 159-60, 168, 180-83, 198, 215, 218, 219

angels, 58, 58n, 112, 201

Angelus Silesius, 211

Anglicanism, Anglican Church, 77n, 91, 93, 98, 206

Angra Mainyu, 190

animals, 8, 51, 73, 78, 140

Annunciation of the Blessed Virgin, 185, 215, 220

anthropomorphism, 151

Antioch, school of, 64, 202

Apara-Brahma, 116

apeiron, 203

apologetics, 202

Aquinas, Thomas, 47n, 51, 122-23, 199, 208, 209, 210

archetypes, 6n, 151; of persons of the Trinity, 126; and religions, 81-82, 84, 89, 95, 98

Aristotelianism, 49, 152n

Aristotle, 66, 67, 68, 69, 152, 201, 202

art: abstract, 67n; Christian, 41, 93, 139n; medieval, 84n; sacred, 93n, 94, 96, 151

Ascension of Christ, 186, 215

ascesis, 33, 45

asceticism, ascetics, 29n, 85, 97, 194

al-Ashari, Abu l-Hasan, 205

Asharite school of Islam, 87, 88, 205

Assumption of the Blessed Virgin, 186, 215

Athanasian Creed, 214

Athanasius, 189, 210

atheism, 119

Athos, Mount, 29n, 194

Âtmâ: distinguished from *Mâyâ*, 5, 108n, 129, 167-70, 175, 177, 179, 184; limitlessness of, 124; and *Brahma*, 116n; and Christian esoterism, 167; and *Sat-Chit-Ânanda*, 125

Augustine, 4, 9n, 13, 20n, 41n, 48, 83, 115, 118-19, 134n, 190, 191, 197, 199, 204, 210, 211

Aum, 219

avatâra, 32, 153, 170, 184, 193, 195

Ave Maria. *See* Angelical Salutation

BIOGRAPHICAL NOTES

FRITHJOF SCHUON

Born in Basle, Switzerland in 1907, Frithjof Schuon was the twentieth century's pre-eminent spokesman for the perennialist school of comparative religious thought.

The leitmotif of Schuon's work was foreshadowed in an encounter during his youth with a marabout who had accompanied some members of his Senegalese village to Basle for the purpose of demonstrating their African culture. When Schuon talked with him, the venerable old man drew a circle with radii on the ground and explained: "God is the center; all paths lead to Him." Until his later years Schuon traveled widely, from India and the Middle East to America, experiencing traditional cultures and establishing lifelong friendships with Hindu, Buddhist, Christian, Muslim, and American Indian spiritual leaders.

A philosopher in the tradition of Plato, Shankara, and Eckhart, Schuon was a gifted artist and poet as well as the author of over twenty books on religion, metaphysics, sacred art, and the spiritual path. Describing his first book, *The Transcendent Unity of Religions*, T. S. Eliot wrote, "I have met with no more impressive work in the comparative study of Oriental and Occidental religion", and world-renowned religion scholar Huston Smith has said of Schuon that "the man is a living wonder; intellectually apropos religion, equally in depth and breadth, the paragon of our time". Schuon's books have been translated into over a dozen languages and are respected by academic and religious authorities alike.

More than a scholar and writer, Schuon was a spiritual guide for seekers from a wide variety of religions and backgrounds throughout the world. He died in 1998.

JAMES S. CUTSINGER (Ph.D., Harvard) is Professor of Theology and Religious Thought at the University of South Carolina and Secretary to the Foundation for Traditional Studies.

A widely recognized writer on the *sophia perennis* and the perennialist school, Professor Cutsinger is an Orthodox Christian and an authority on the theology and spirituality of the Christian East. His publications include *Advice to the Serious Seeker: Meditations on the Teaching of Frithjof Schuon, Reclaiming the Great Tradition: Evangelicals, Catholics, and Orthodox in Dialogue, Not of This World: A Treasury of Christian Mysticism,* and *Paths to the Heart: Sufism and the Christian East.*

The Fullness of God is the first volume in a series of new anthologies compiled from Schuon's published and unpublished writings, and introduced and annotated by Professor Cutsinger.

ANTOINE FAIVRE is Professor Emeritus of Religious Studies at the École Pratique des Hautes Études and Chair of the History of Esoteric Currents in Modern and Contemporary Europe (Sorbonne). Professor Faivre's books in English include *Access to Western Esotericism, The Golden Fleece and Alchemy, The Eternal Hermes,* and *Theosophy, Imagination, Tradition;* he is editor (with Jacob Needleman) of *Modern Esoteric Spirituality.*